IMAGES
of America

VESSELS OF CAMDEN

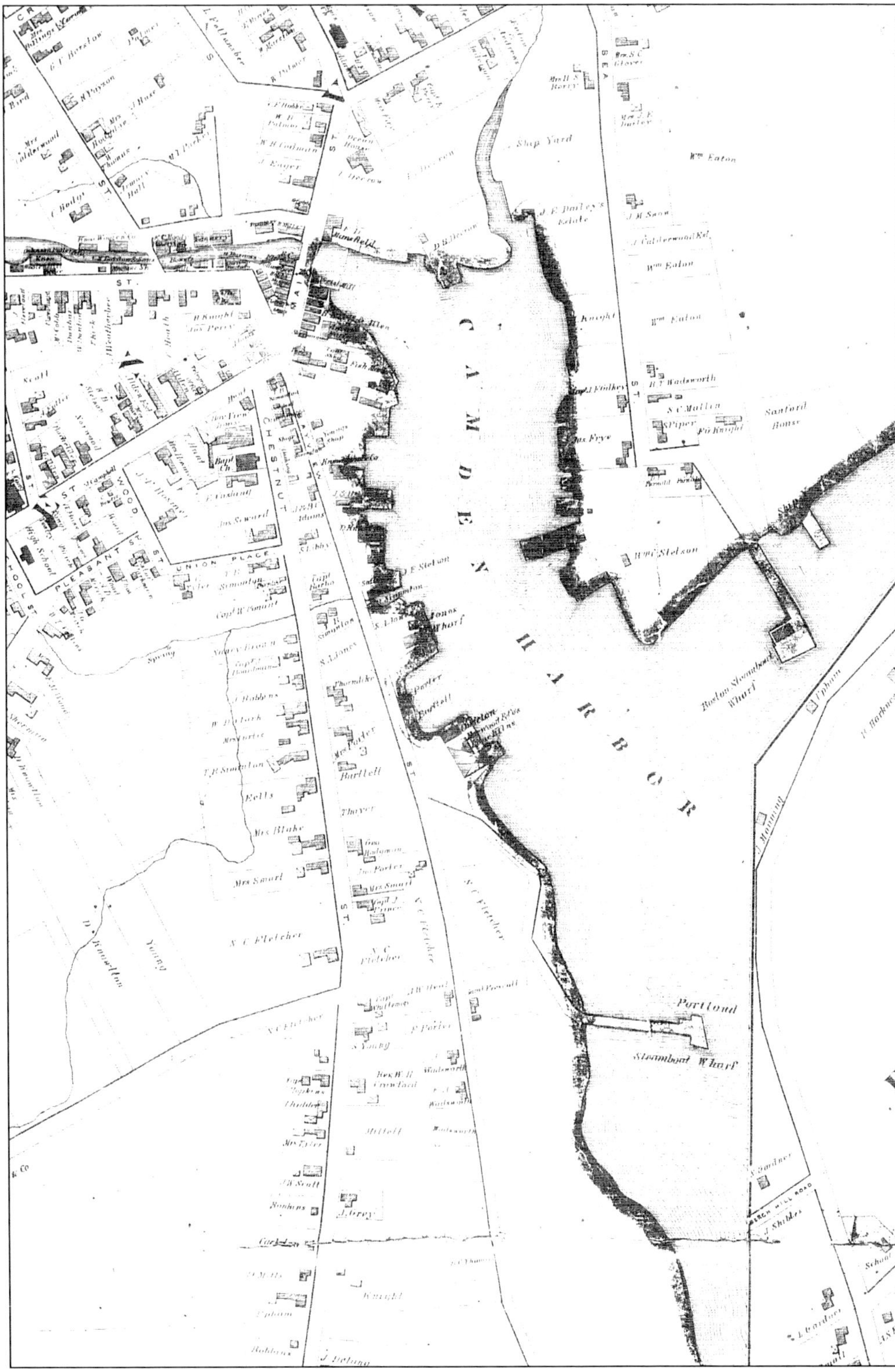

This map of 1875 shows Camden's harbor.

IMAGES
of America

VESSELS OF CAMDEN

Barbara Dyer

ARCADIA
PUBLISHING

ISBN 978-0-7385-0014-3

Published by Arcadia Publishing
Charleston, South Carolina

Printed in the United States of America

Library of Congress Catalog Card Number: 9887573

For all general information contact Arcadia Publishing at:
Telephone 843-853-2070
Fax 843-853-0044
E-mail sales@arcadiapublishing.com
For customer service and orders:
Toll-Free 1-888-313-2665

Visit us on the Internet at www.arcadiapublishing.com

CONTENTS

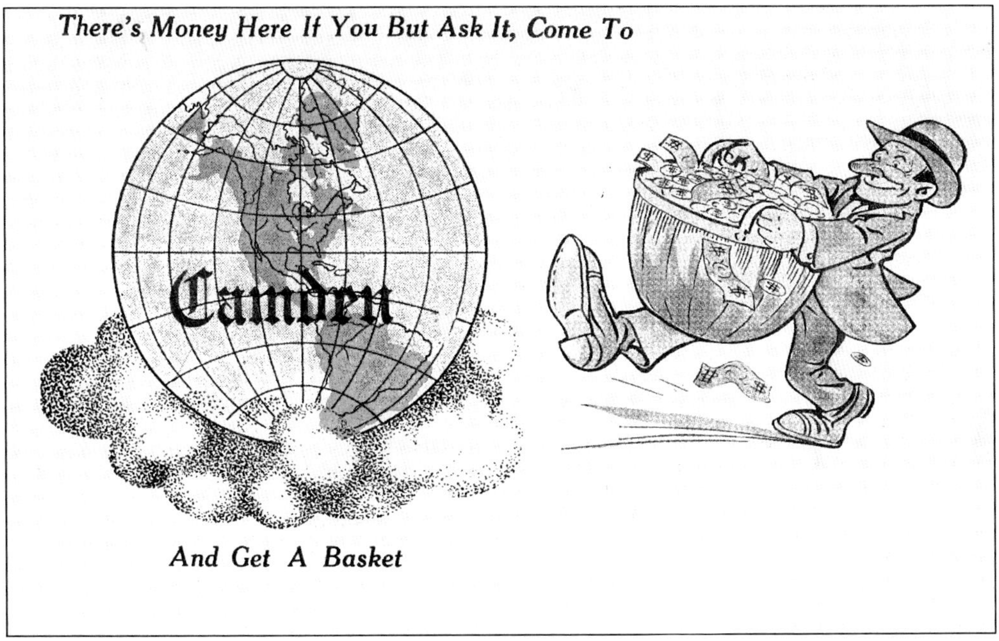
There's Money Here If You But Ask It, Come To
Camden
And Get A Basket

INTRODUCTION

Vessels are much like graceful ladies who attract attention without an introduction. However, written here is the introduction anyway, because most books are not considered complete without one.

All vessels in *Vessels of Camden* were constructed on the east side of beautiful Camden harbor. Most pictures in this book were taken by professional photographers and paid for by the company that built them. The images came into my possession because I worked for the various companies as an accountant and office manager for 44 years. My tenure taught me to learn and appreciate the art of building wooden vessels. The owners of the companies knew that I would save the history of wooden ships and those who built them, as well as any other history of Camden. It has become much more than a hobby, simply because I love the town. This is my seventh book.

There are only two places on the eastern seaboard where the mountains meet the sea. Bar Harbor, Maine, is one; Camden is fortunate enough to be the other. Camden was a working town, with its many woolen mills on the Megunticook River, its shipbuilding, and its other industries. Today Camden's three largest employers are MBNA, the Wayfarer Marine Corporation, and Tibbett's Industries. Tourists have been attracted to Camden since its incorporation in 1791. It is geared more each year to the tourist trade, and why not? It is one of the most beautiful places on earth.

My approach in writing *Vessels of Camden* was to put the photographs in chronological order, and show the wonderful craftsmanship in each one. The book's time frame is about one hundred years, from approximately 1860 to 1960. The building of wooden vessels seems to be a thing of the past. New craftsmen are not learning from the old, and fiberglass boats are easier to maintain (although I could never love one).

As you enjoy the vessels, page by page, I wish you smooth sailing!

—Barbara F. Dyer

One

Holly M. Bean Yard

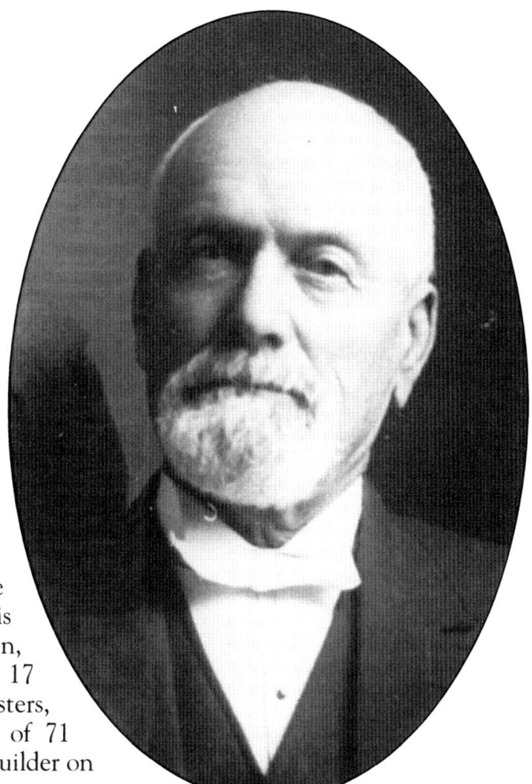

Holly M. Bean built vessels on the east side of Camden's harbor from 1875 to 1909. It is known that he built 54 vessels in Camden, including 1 brig, 1 two-master, 2 barks, 17 three-masters, 20 four-masters, 12 five-masters, and 1 six-master. He constructed a total of 71 vessels. Mr. Bean was known as the largest builder on the East Coast.

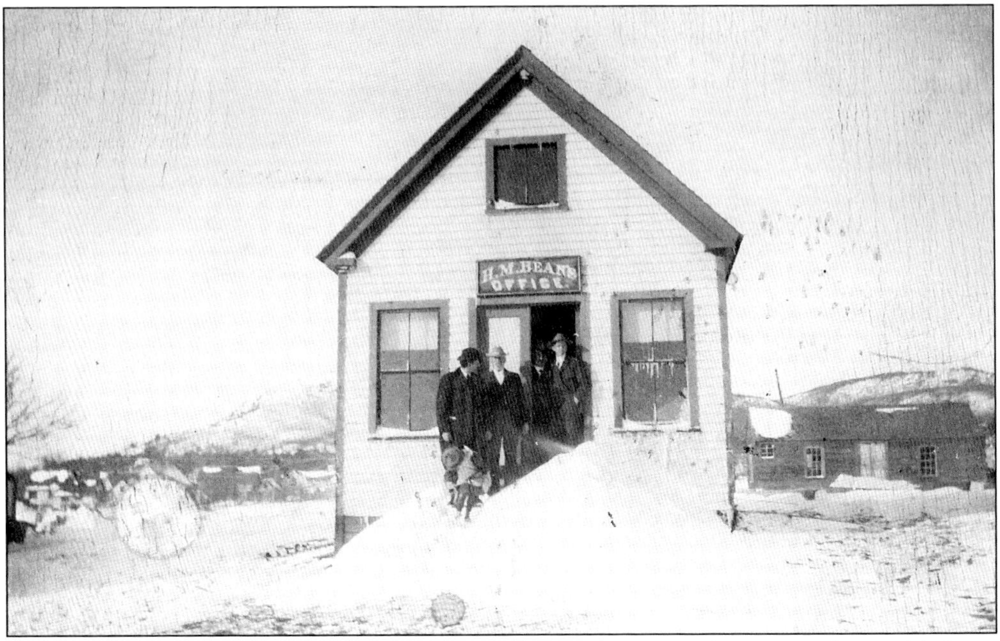

The H.M. Bean office appears to be large enough for four men, pencils, pens, and several ledgers. It was before the day of calculators, computers, printers, etc. Life was simple, but days were long. It was from sun up to sun down, and no overtime. In later years, it took larger buildings and more of them for a yard with probably the same number of workmen.

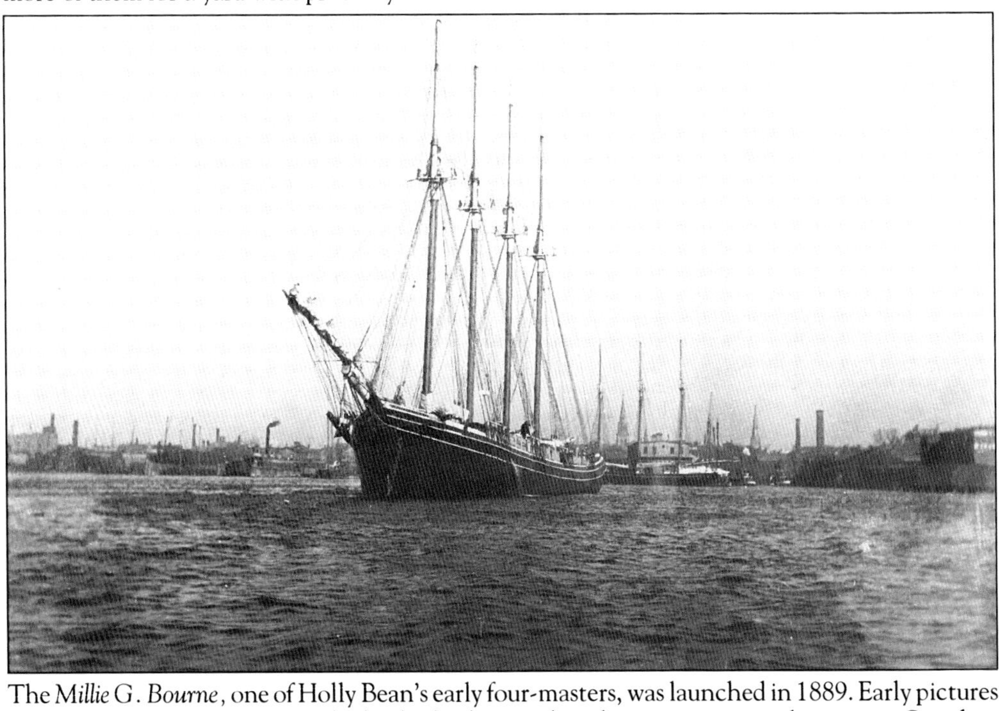
The *Millie G. Bourne*, one of Holly Bean's early four-masters, was launched in 1889. Early pictures are, of course, much harder to find. The background in the picture certainly was not Camden, Maine. It must have been taken when the vessel was docked in a port where she delivered or picked up cargo. It is a nice photograph, even without Camden in the background.

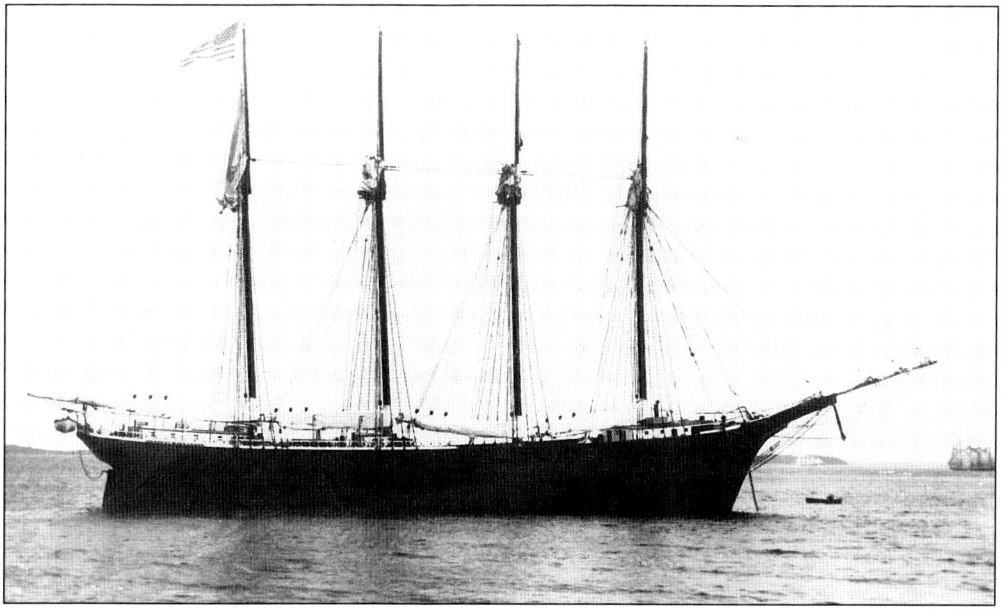

Another four-master, the *J. Holmes Birdsall*, was launched in 1894. She was 238 feet overall, with a beam (width) of 43 feet. Her homeport was Philadelphia, Pennsylvania. Four young ladies christened the vessel, but instead of the customary breaking of a bottle over the bow, they threw flowers instead. With no liquor to celebrate the launching, it was taken by some as a bad omen for the vessel.

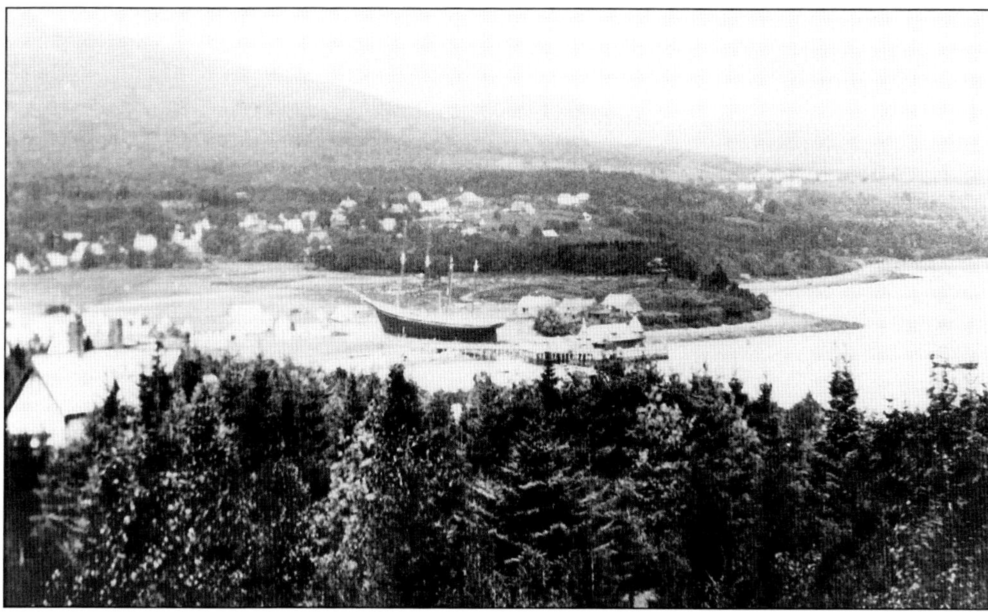

The *Alma E.A. Holmes* was launched August 29, 1896, just before noon. They laid her keel only four months before she was launched. The distant picture of the vessel was taken from Chestnut Street. It shows the mountains, the harbor, the Eastern Steamship Wharf, and Eaton Field before it was filled in with homes. The vessel met her demise on October 10, 1914, when the steamer *Belfast*, running in a thick fog, collided with her. The schooner went down off Baker's Island, Massachusetts. Fortunately, no lives were lost.

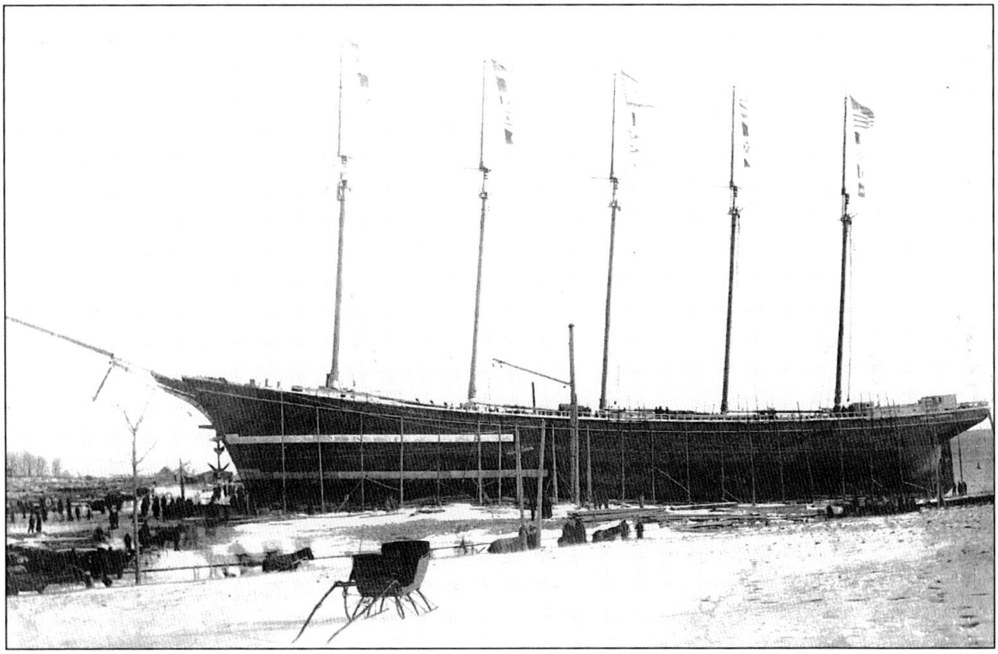

With launching flags in place, ten thousand people watched as the first five-master from the Bean Yard, the *John B. Prescott,* hit the water on January 13, 1899. She was the second five-master ever built. The cold made the launching grease hard and her weight was so immense that it took about 15 minutes for her to move ever so slowly down the ways.

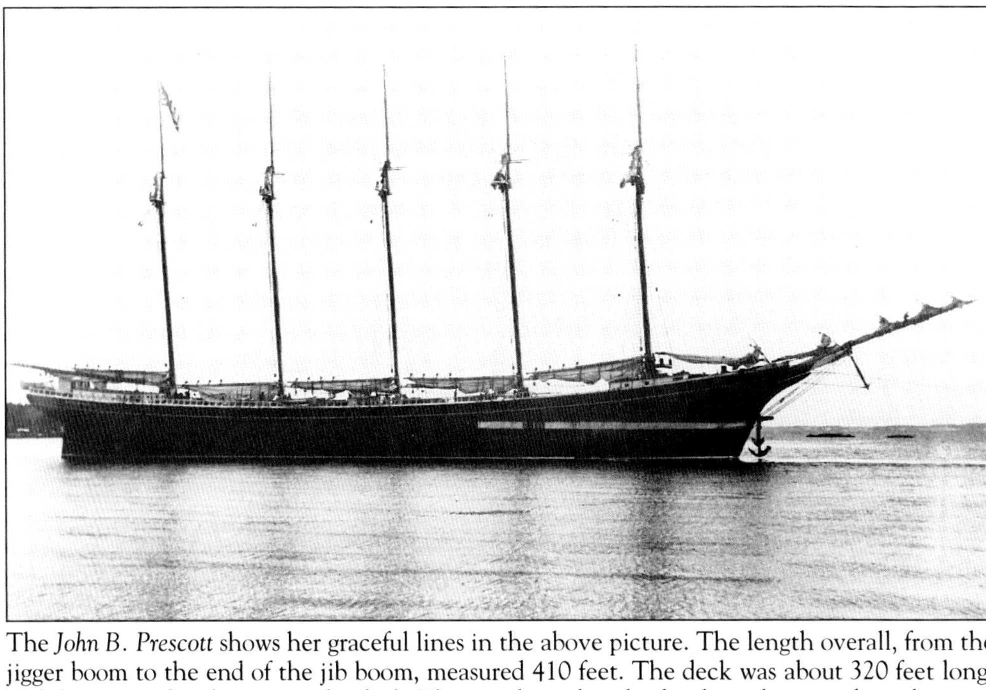

The *John B. Prescott* shows her graceful lines in the above picture. The length overall, from the jigger boom to the end of the jib boom, measured 410 feet. The deck was about 320 feet long, and there were four houses on the deck. The woods used in the finish work were ash, mahogany, cypress, and sycamore. The blocks and castings were made by the Knowlton Bros. of Camden, a firm that could make almost any fitting for a vessel.

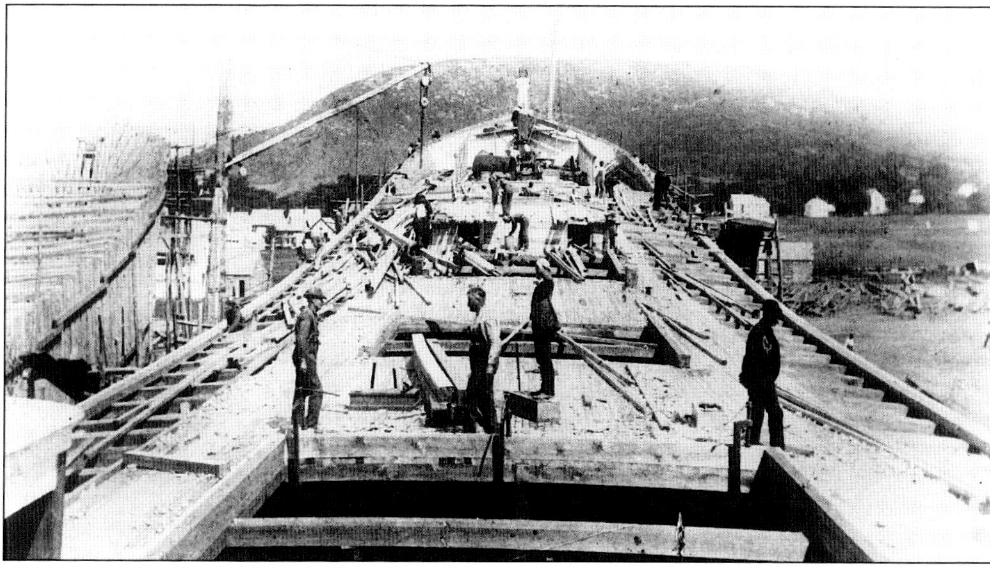

The bow of the *George W. Wells* is shown here under construction, and is pointed toward Mt. Battie. With the workmen in the picture, it gives an idea of how large this vessel was. Her beam was 48 feet and 6 inches. Her frame was of white oak throughout and all the planking and ceiling was of hard pine.

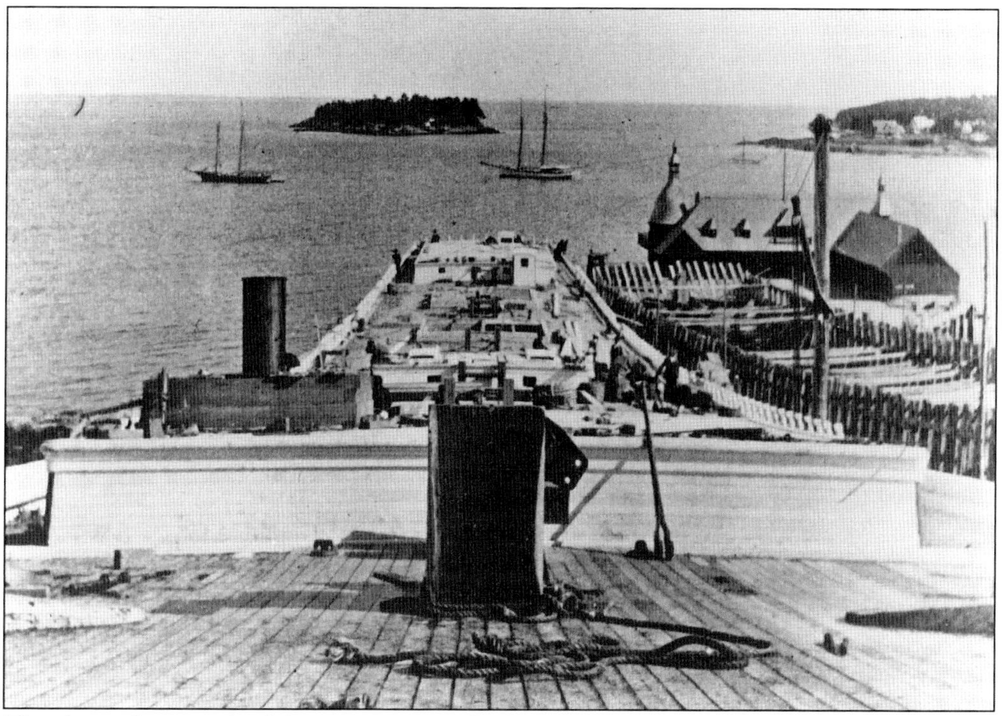

The above photograph of the *George W. Wells* shows the stern of the vessel under construction in 1899. Curtis Island is in the background and the Eastern Steamship Wharf is on the right. Twelve vessels of this size, in a line dockside, would occupy a mile. When finished she could carry twice as much coal as the first five-master ever built (the *Gov. Ames*, built in Waldoboro, Maine).

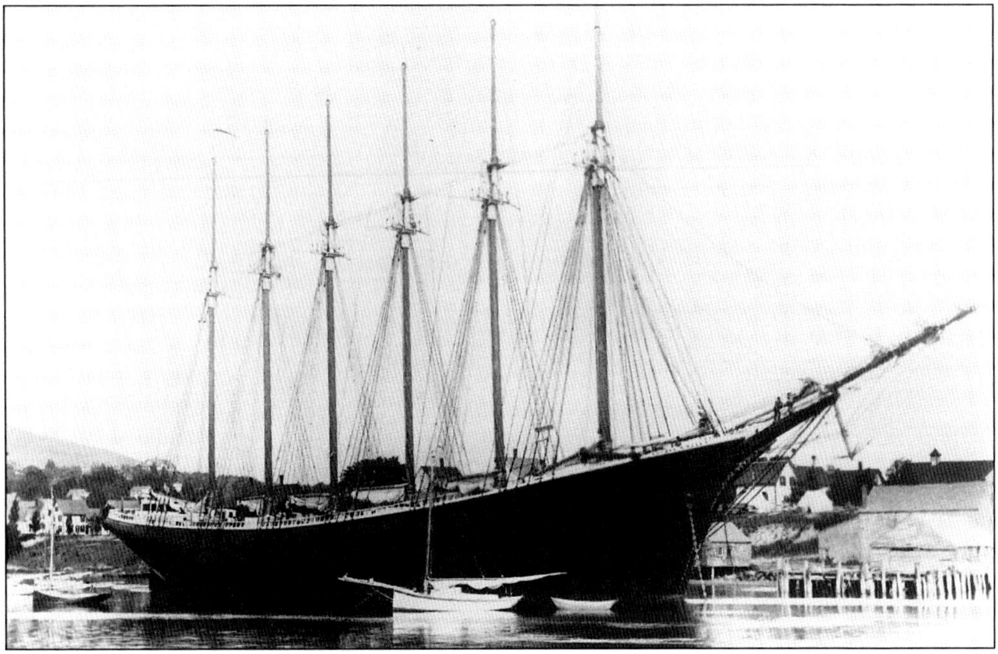

The *George W. Wells* was the first six-master ever built. It was a big day when she was launched on August 14, 1900. The vessel was 340 feet long, with two full decks. The six lower masts were of Oregon pine and measured 119 feet tall. They were named, from bow to stern, the foremast, mainmast, mizzenmast, spankermast, jiggermast, and drivermast. She carried 12,000 square yards of canvas.

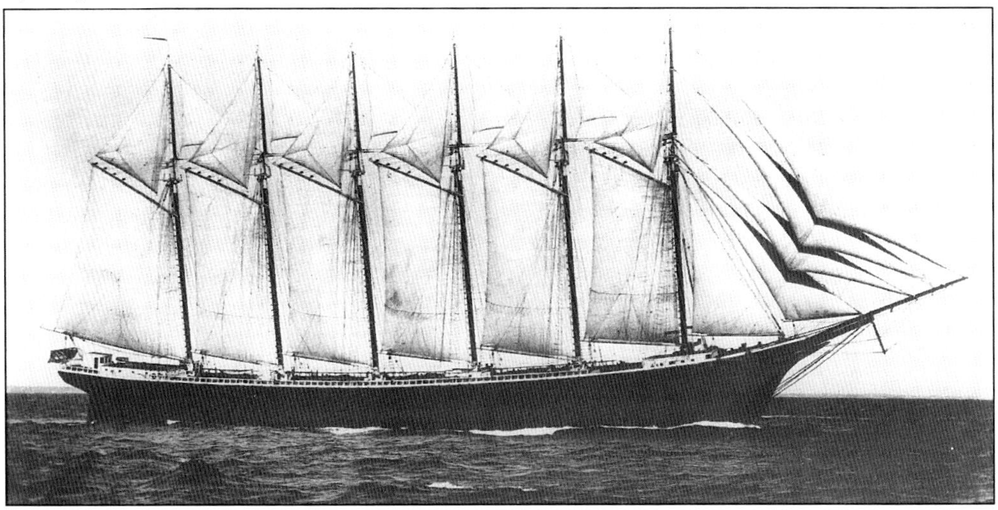

The *George W. Wells* is shown here under sail. Her first collision was when the second six-master ever built, the *Eleanor Percy* (built in Bath), met up with her. The only two six-masters in the world collided. Damage was minimal but neither captain said he was at fault. The *George W. Wells* met her demise in September of 1913, when she ran into a storm off North Carolina. The wind blew out her sails and they could not save the vessel. Everyone aboard was saved, including two women, two infants, a goat, a dog, and "Fluffy," the ship's cat. However, six-masters were not as practical as they had anticipated. They were heavy in the bow and stern, causing them to hog in the middle.

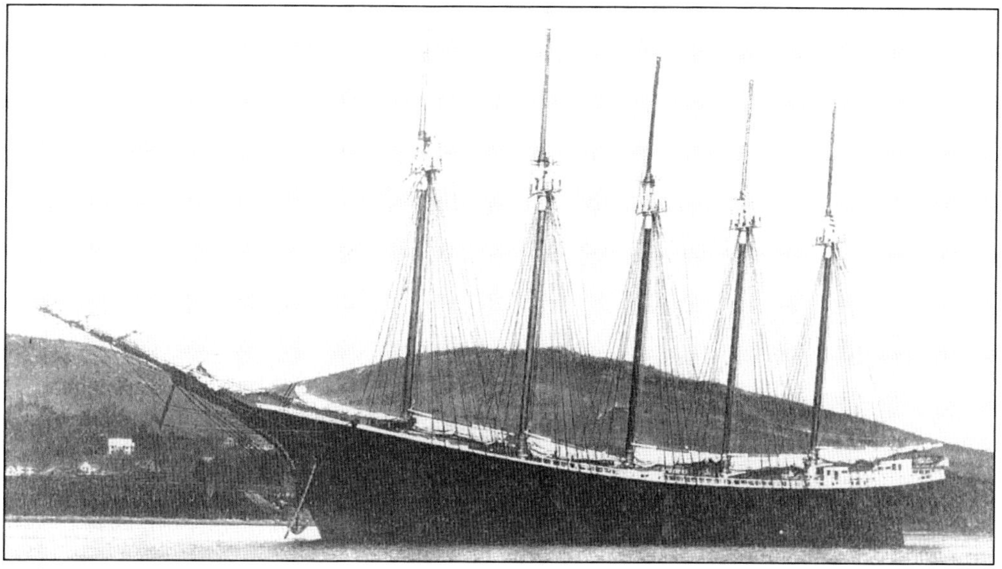

A five-master, the *Van Allens Boughton*, was launched on November 28, 1900. H.M. Bean's 66th vessel was a fair-sized schooner, but looked small compared to the *George W. Wells* and the *John B. Prescott*. She was 280 feet in length overall, with a beam of 46 feet, and she carried four anchors, two of which weighed 5,500 pounds each. In comparison, the *George W. Wells* had one anchor weighing 8,280 pounds and another weighing 7,500 pounds.

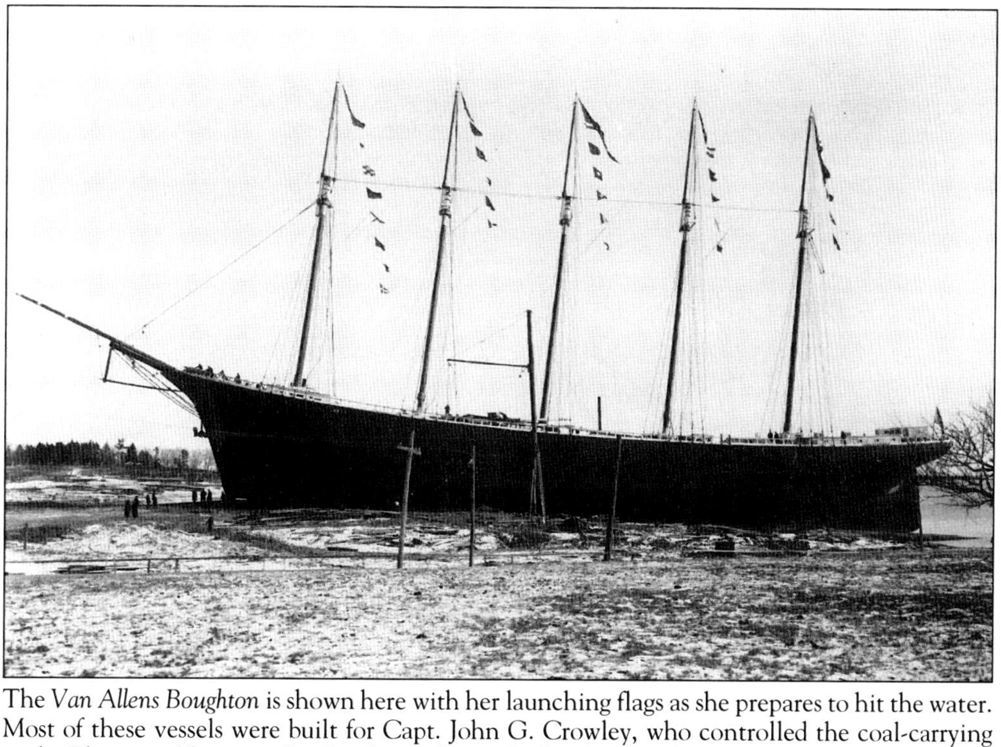

The *Van Allens Boughton* is shown here with her launching flags as she prepares to hit the water. Most of these vessels were built for Capt. John G. Crowley, who controlled the coal-carrying trade. This vessel happened to be the sixth one for his fleet, with more to come. That evening Holly M. Bean had a supper in the Masonic Hall for the workers, furnishers, owners, and their wives. It was a celebration for another great vessel built by H.M. Bean.

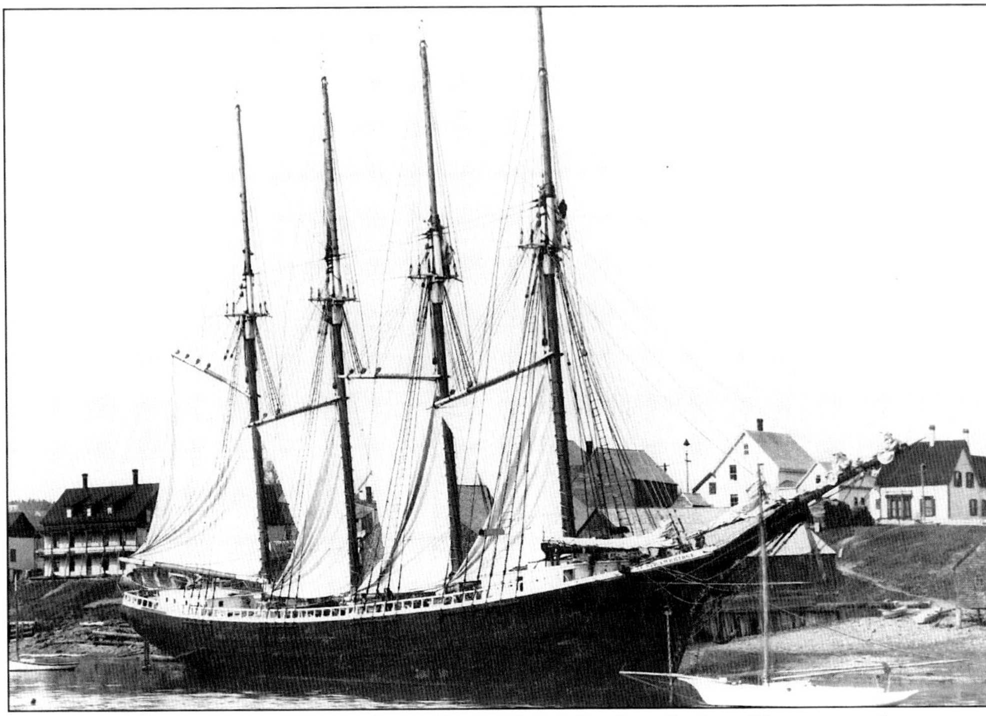

This photograph depicts drying the sails on the *J.C. Strawbridge*. She was a four-master launched April 19, 1901. The vessel was christened by six young ladies—Lucy Allen, Edith Long (granddaughter to Holly Bean), Catherine Wilbur, Alice Herrick, Marion Wadsworth and Frances Herrick. They tossed flowers and evergreen from the bow. The vessel was later abandoned February 24, 1911, off Bermuda.

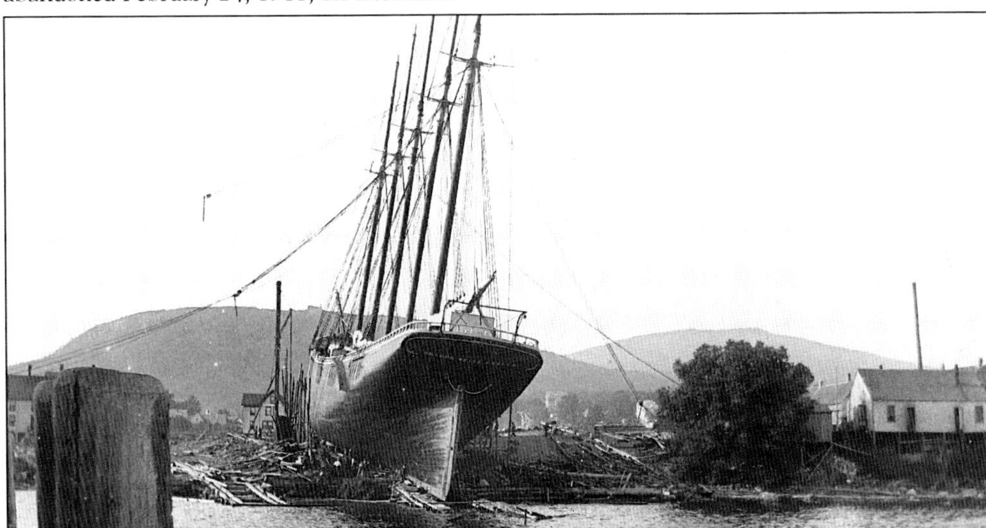

The *Arthur Seitz* was scheduled to be launched on September 4, 1901. However, she crushed her blockings and tipped to the port side, onto her bilge. Mr. Bean's granddaughter told me that he just turned his back and walked out of the yard. He was not going to watch the vessel tip over completely. The workmen placed guy wires to hold her upright. The next day they fixed the blockings and successfully launched the vessel on a high tide.

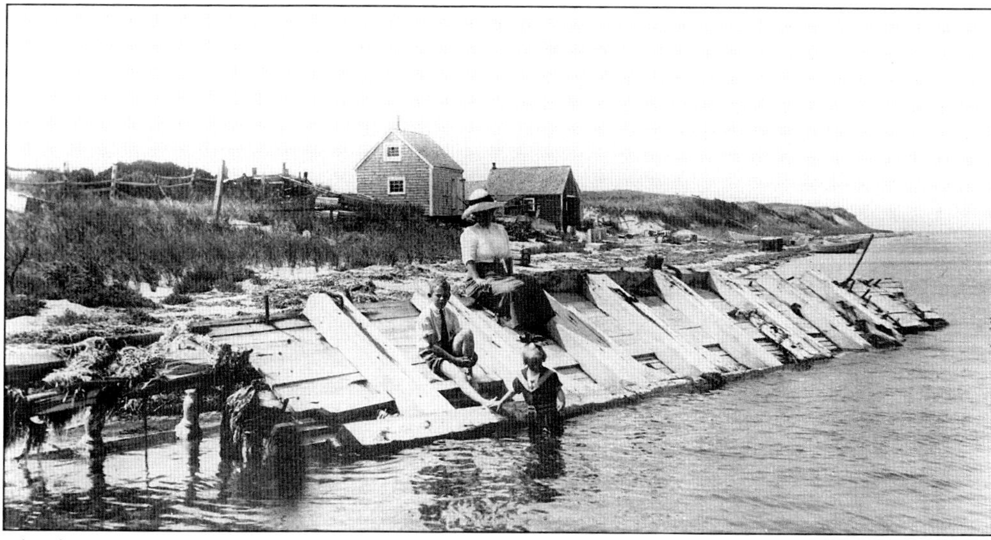

The five-masted schooner *Arthur Seitz* met her demise on May 25, 1902. She was wrecked on Skiff Island Reef in a northwest gale. The wreckage washed up near Nantucket, Massachusetts. The above photograph was taken about 1924. The lady and children sitting on what was left of the ship had no idea what a beautiful vessel she had been, nor the man-hours put into her construction.

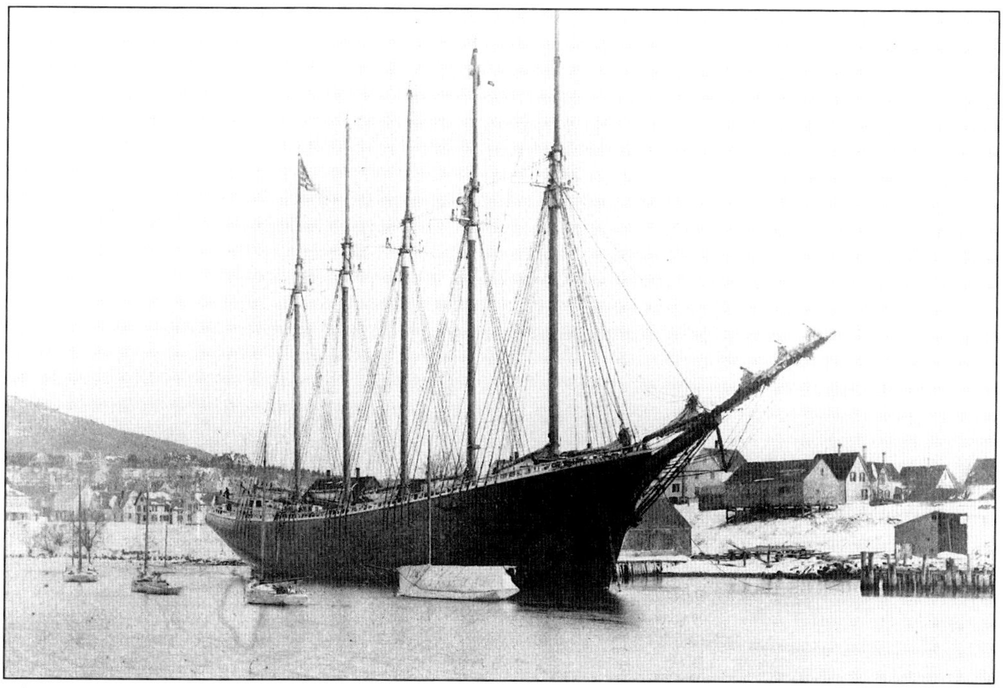

The name of a vessel was chosen by the person who had the major financial investment in her. The above is the *T. Charlton Henry*, launched from the H.M. Bean Yard on November 27, 1902. Her christening was changed from flowers to a bottle of champagne smashed over her bow. She was 400 feet long overall, with a 48-foot beam, and had three full decks. The five Oregon masts measured 120 feet in length and 30 inches in diameter. The topmasts measured 58 feet each.

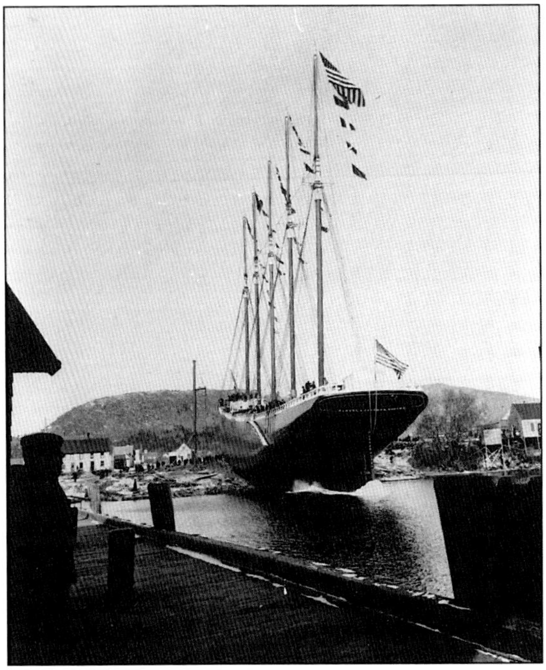

The five-master *Samuel A. Goucher* glided into the ocean on December 9, 1904. She was the heaviest framed schooner ever built on the East Coast. Her planking was yellow pine 6 inches thick to the rail. The 10-inch ceiling to the rail was the heaviest ever put in a schooner before. Her carrying capacity was 4,500 tons of coal. The vessel had three full decks. The after house contained forward and after cabins, the captain's cabin, officers' staterooms, a chart room, and a bathroom. The midship house had the kitchen, mess room, second-mate's room, steward's room, and carpenter shop. The forward house contained the forecastle, engineer's room, and engine room. The cost of the vessel was $125,000.

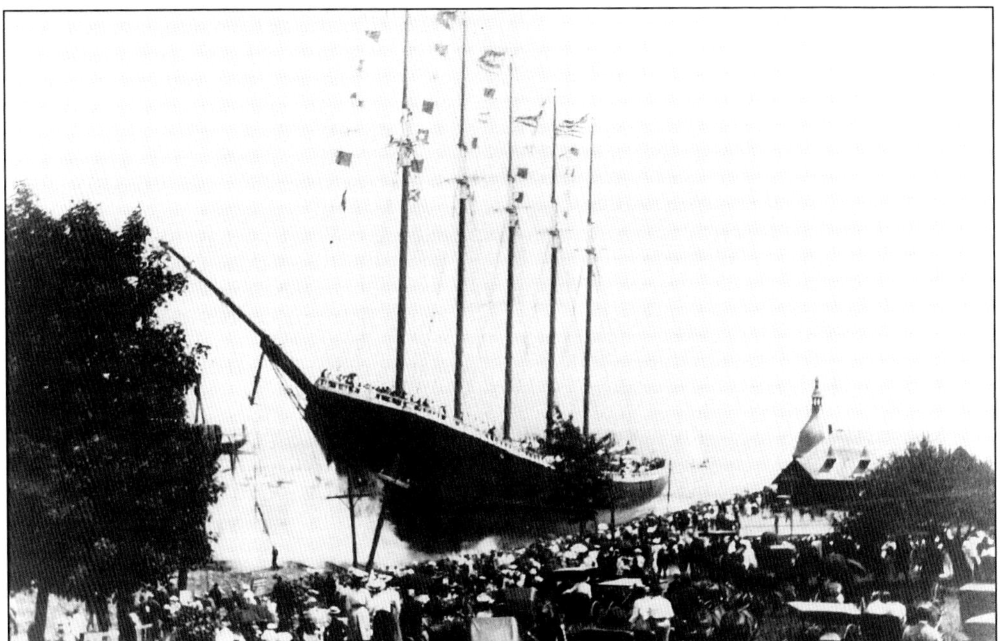

Thousands of people came to witness the launching of the *Helen J. Seitz* on October 30, 1905. This picture shows some of the people, horses and buggies, etc., on the road to the Eastern Steamship Wharf. The schooner was about as large as any five-master that had been built in the H.M. Bean Yard. Lunch was served on board, after the launching, to invited guests. That evening Captain and Mrs. Crowley entertained at their home in Rockport, Maine. Celebrations usually followed all launchings. This vessel was short lived, however, as she was stranded at Beach Haven, New Jersey, on February 9, 1907.

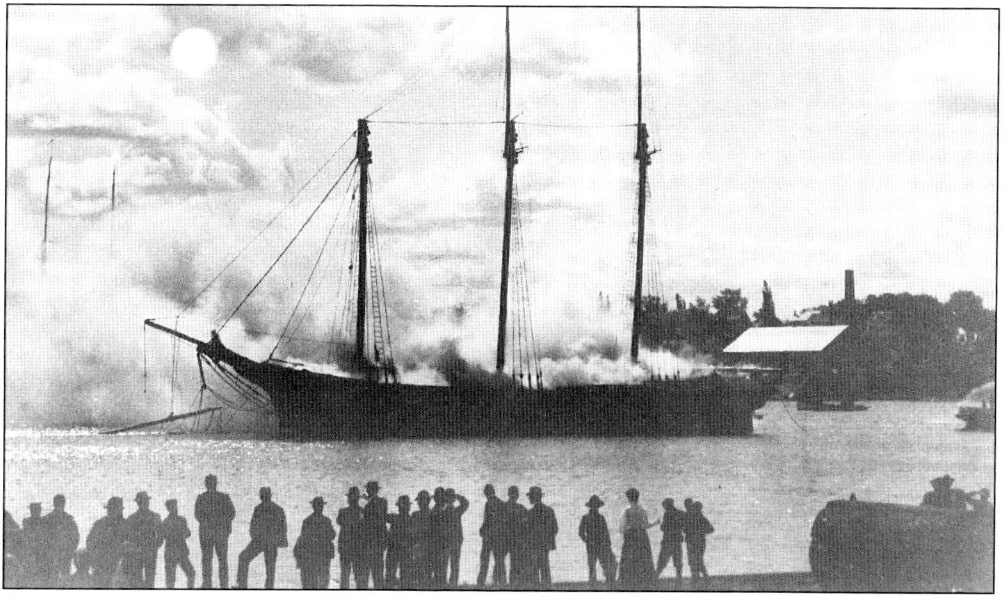

The *Annie L. Henderson* served her owners well until September 1, 1906, when she caught fire in Bangor. After they tied the vessel up, they trimmed the coal, causing her to catch on fire. Two alarms were turned in, but apparently one was wrong, because the Bangor Fire Department was confused. They tried to remove the vessel from the dock, but she was hemmed in by one boat across her bow and another across her stern. She burned herself loose and drifted across to the Brewer side all ablaze. Men chased her in boats but she made it across and started setting fires on the Brewer side. Her captain did not want to lose her because there was no insurance on the vessel. By the time they did reach her, she was a total loss. So were buildings on both the Bangor and Brewer sides.

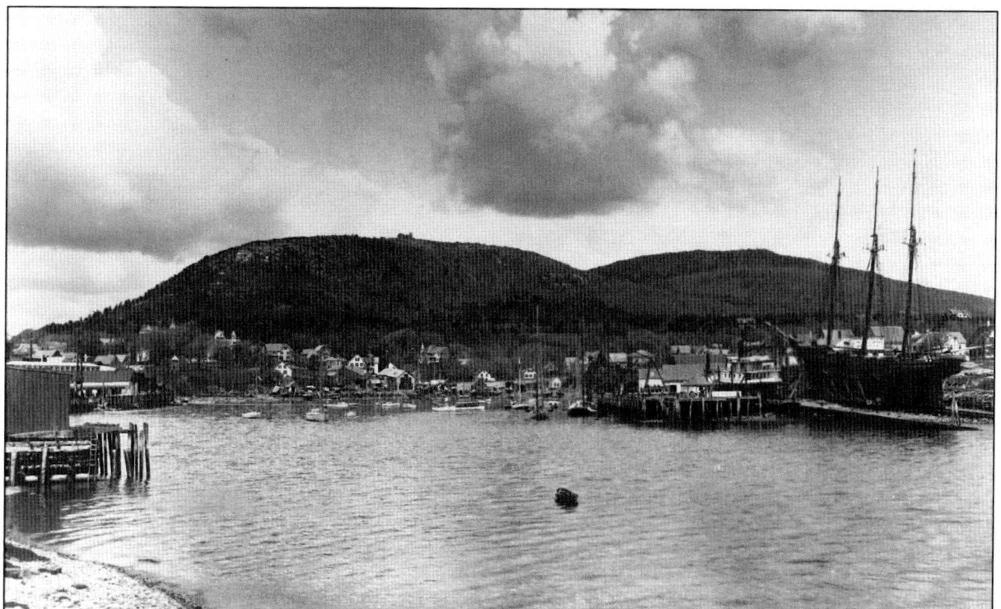

This view of Mt. Battie (with a hotel on top), Mt. Megunticook, and Camden Harbor was taken in 1905. A three-master has been hauled on the railway, probably for repairs.

PARTIAL LIST OF VESSELS BUILT BY HOLLY M. BEAN

NAME OF VESSEL	YEAR	NAME OF VESSEL	YEAR
EDITH BEAN	1877	MARJORIE	1890
R. BOWERS	1879	WILLIAM JOHNSON	1890
ROBBIE FOSTER	1880	WILLIAM SMITH	1890
ANNIE L. HENDERSON	1880	FANNY ARTHUR	1891
ALICIA A. HALL	1881	KATHERINE D. PERRY	1891
GEN. ADELBERT AMES	1881	R.& T. HARGRAVES	1891
MORRIS W. CHILD	1881	J. HOLMES BIRDSALL	1894
DORA MATHEWS	1882	MARY MANNING	1894
JOHN F. MORROW	1882	HENRY W. CRAMP	1896
WILLIAM HAYS	1882	ALMA A. E. HOLMES	1896
JONATHAN BOURNE	1883	JOHN B, PRESCOTT	1899
JOSEPH HILTON	1883	ANNA MURRAY	1899
MAY O.NEIL	1883	MALCOLM BAXTER, JR.	1900
SARAH A. FULLER	1883	GEORGE W. WELLS	1900
WILLIAM H. ALLISON	1883	VAN ALLEN BOUGHTON	1900
RACHAEL & MAUDE	1884	J. C. STRAWBRIDGE	1901
SARAH E. WARD	1884	ARTHUR SEITZ	1901
KING PHILLIP	1886	T. CHARLTON HENRY	1902
POCAHONTAS	1887	MARGARET HASKELL	1904
CORNELIUS HARGRAVES	1889	SAMUEL GOUCHER	1904
MILLIE G. BOURNE	1889	HELEN J. SEITZ	1905
ALICE HOLBROOK	1890		

Two

CAMDEN MANUFACTURERS

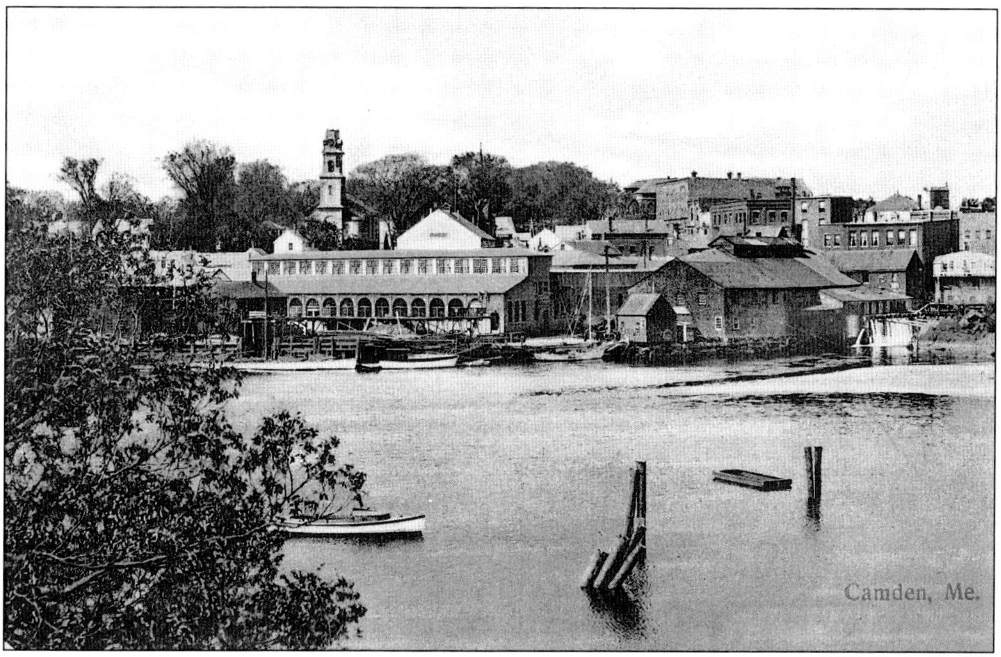

The Camden Anchor Works was located where the Camden Public Landing is today. It was established in 1866 by William and Horatio Alden. Known as the largest plant of its kind in this country, it had the capability of making anchors up to 4 tons. I quote from an old New York paper: "All stately ships that come out of Maine shipyards, look to Camden for their anchors. Sturdy smiths swing their hammers all day in the black smoky shops, where anchors are forged. Sometimes the triphammers are going all night and the blazing of the fires and the ringing of the hammers are seen and heard for miles across Penobscot Bay."

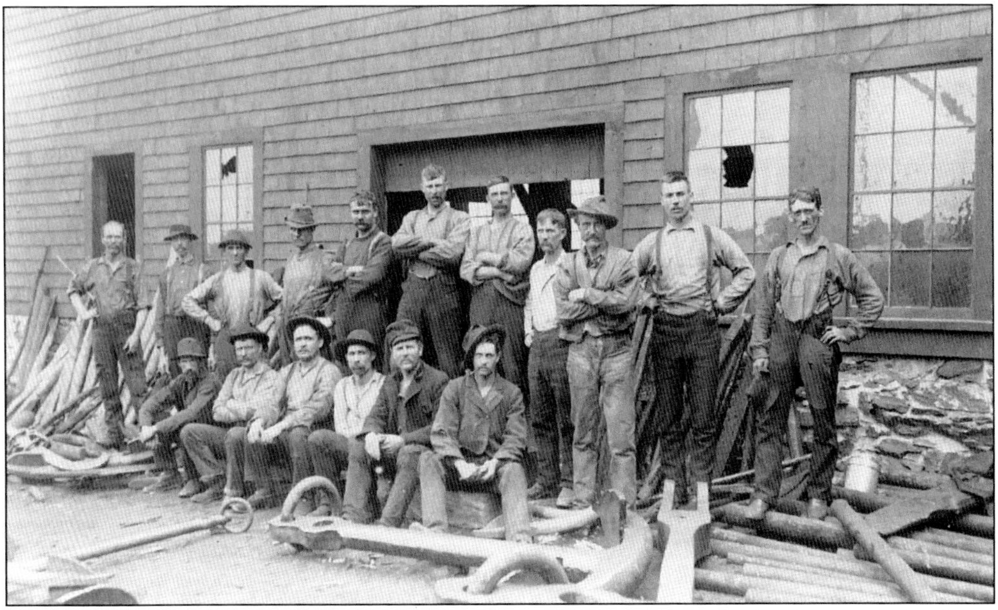

Shown here are some of the anchor factory workmen, in a photograph taken in 1888. From left to right they are as follows: (front row) Roncello Eldridge, Frank Prince, Roderick Cross, Merrill Richards, Luke Allen, and Levi Tibbetts; (back row) Samuel Ogier Jr., Orrington Cross, Samuel Dunton, Cecil Currier, Frank Day, Colin McDonald, William Raye, Samuel Dyer, Silas Heal, Tom Nash, and Ed Prince.

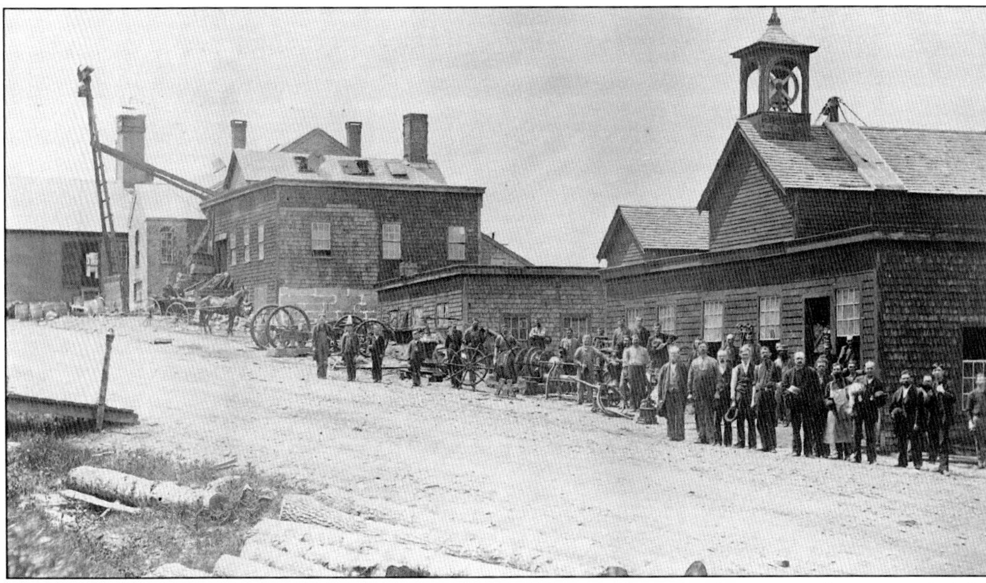

Knowlton Bros., Machine Shop and Foundry could manufacture almost anything needed for vessels. This photograph was taken on July 19, 1883. David Knowlton was an ingenious man and great inventor. He designed a machine that would make 15,000 plugs a day for vessels. Another machine he made for the block factory could make dead eyes. From his foundry came power capstans, portable cargo winches, ship's steering wheels, head pumps, and many other things for the shipbuilding industry. These items were shipped all over the country, but Knowlton's Foundry was especially convenient for local shipbuilders.

Three

ROBERT L. BEAN YARD

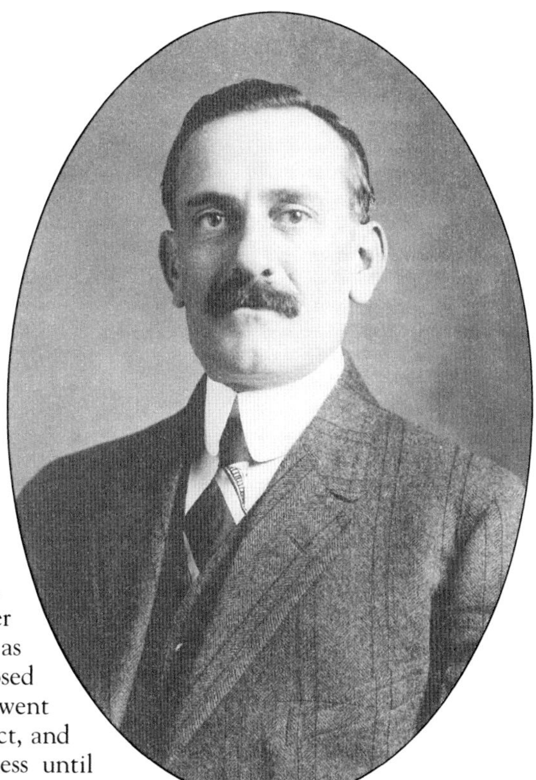

Robert L. Bean began working with his father, Holly M. Bean, in about 1899. He participated in the building of five-masters and the famous six-master *George W. Wells*. Shipbuilding was in his blood. His father retired, and about five years later Robert started up the business again, known as the R.L. Bean Yard. Within two years it closed due to lack of business. But in 1914, Robert went to New York and came back with a contract, and others followed. He continued the business until 1920.

R. L. BEAN

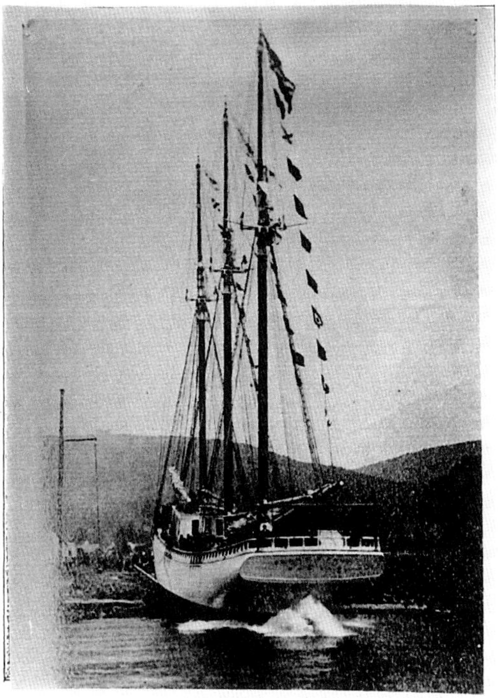

Schooner Frank M. Low, Launched from the Ship Yard of R. L. Bean, Camden, Oct. 27, 1909.
photo by Hall, Camden, Me.

Largest and one of the Best Located and Equipped Ship Yards on the Entire Coast

SHIP BUILDER

CAMDEN, MAINE, U. S. A.

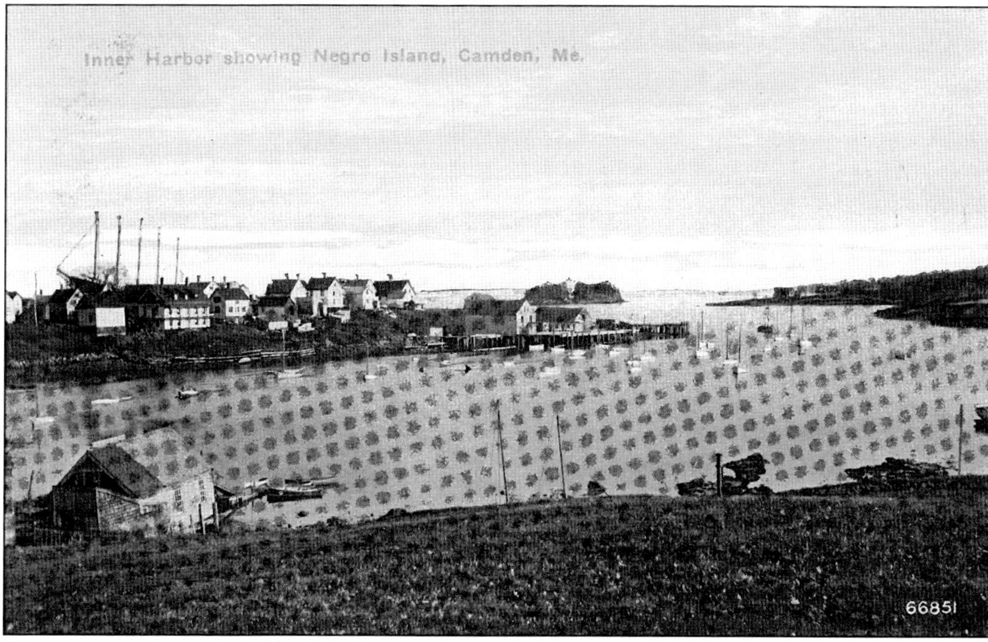

This picture of Camden's harbor shows a five-master on the way in the Bean Yard. The harbor had a few small boats but was not the busy, crowded harbor of today. Harbor Park, in the foreground, had not yet been landscaped by the Olmstead firm. The buildings on the east side of the harbor were small and few, as compared to today.

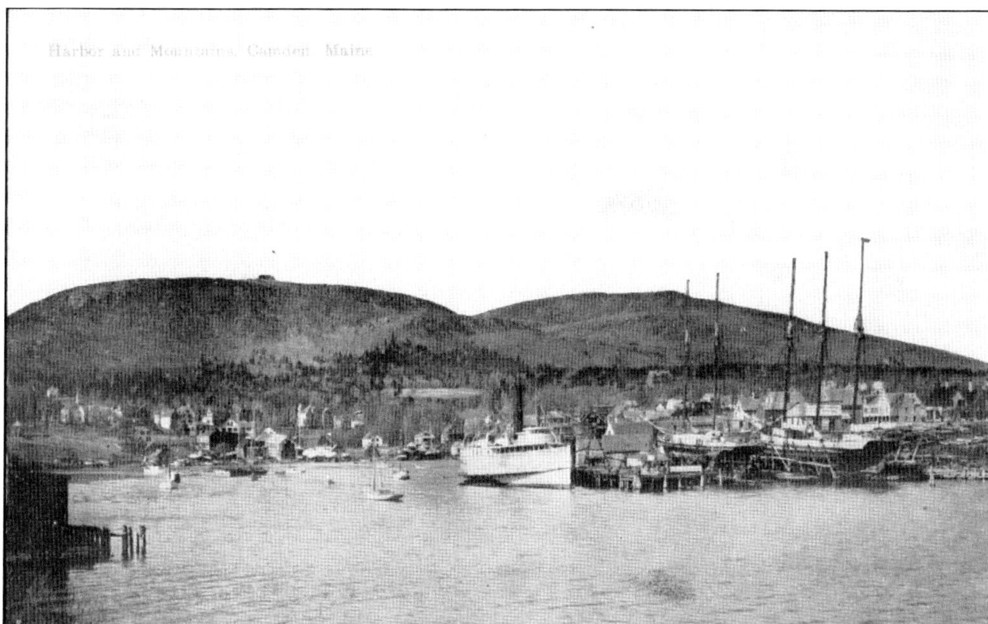
Another picture of Camden's harbor, in the early 1900s, shows both Mt. Battie (with its hotel) and Mt. Megunticook. At the dock is a steamboat. Shown on the ways for repair are one two-master and one three-master. Such vessels were going out of style about that time. Interest was growing to build the vessels bigger and better, with four or five masts.

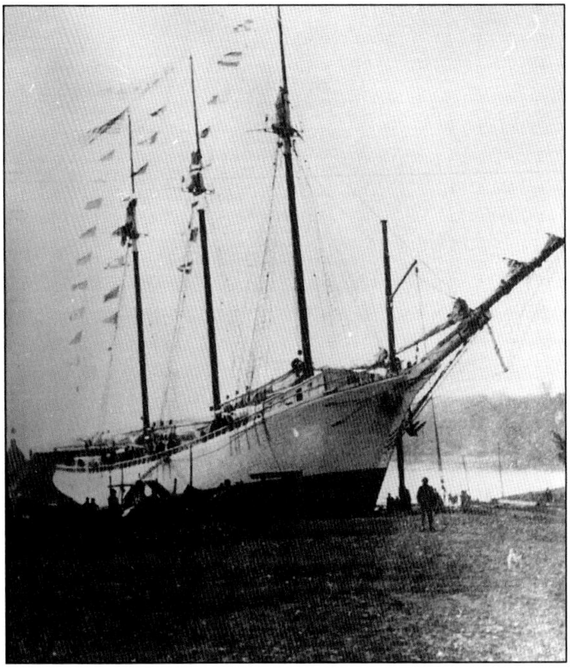

A three-master, the *Frank E. Swan*, was one of the first vessels that Robert L. Bean constructed in his new yard. The site of his yard was a bare field. He had no machinery, tools, or buildings, but what he did have was the courage and determination to construct vessels. His first master builder was C.A. Robinson, followed by W.G. McAuley for the last nine. Bean employed about one hundred men, with a payroll of $9,000 a month.

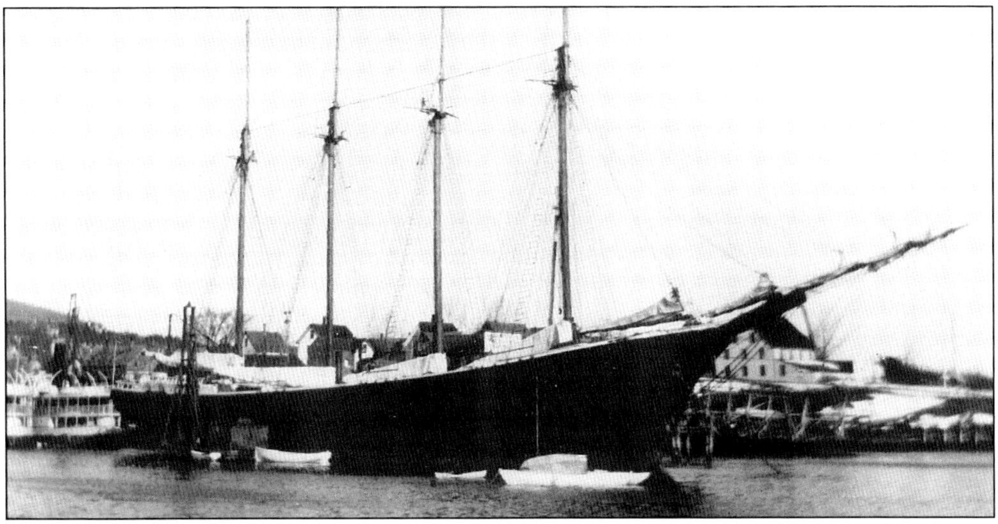

On December 23, 1916, the *Percy R. Pyne II* glided down the ways, all 233 feet of her. It was the first launching in seven years, during a bitter cold day with a northwest gale. But two things were missing at this launching—one, no colors were flying (that was most unusual), and two, the vessel was not christened. As the vessel was completely rigged, the workmen towed her to the outfitting dock. Within a few days, a 360-horsepower Bollender engine arrived, along with men to install it. It was the largest auxiliary power schooner on the coast. Later a crew of ten arrived from Germany, and it was said that she became a commerce raider. The contract was made with a company in New York, but it was sold immediately to the German government. A painting of the vessel called *The Skeleton* was done by George Bellows. Another hangs in the Camden Public Library, *Building The Ship* by Leon Kroll. The reason for the two paintings was not because it was a "special" vessel, but because both well-known artists happened to be working on the Maine coast during that time.

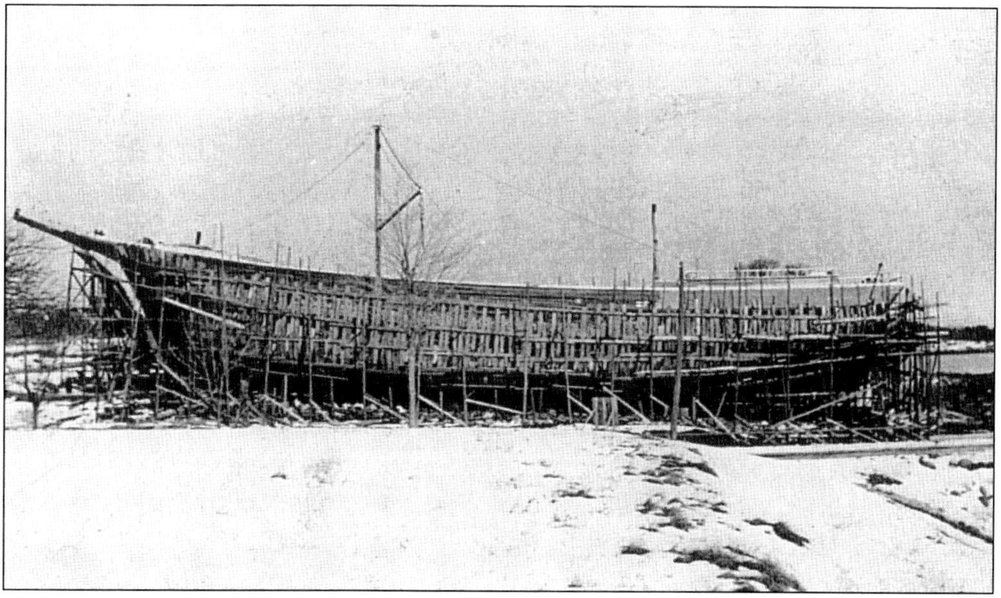

The above picture is of a vessel under construction, the *Charlotte A. Maxwell*. She was launched on April 19, 1917. Bad weather prevented the launching for two days. Even then it was held back about one-half hour because the tide was not quite high enough. The four-master could carry 1,000 tons of coal and had already been chartered to deliver coal to Brazil for $15 per ton. Capt. E.H. Tinker, who lived in Camden, commanded the vessel, and his wife accompanied him on his voyages. While that vessel was being launched, a third schooner was already framed, and would be launched within a few months.

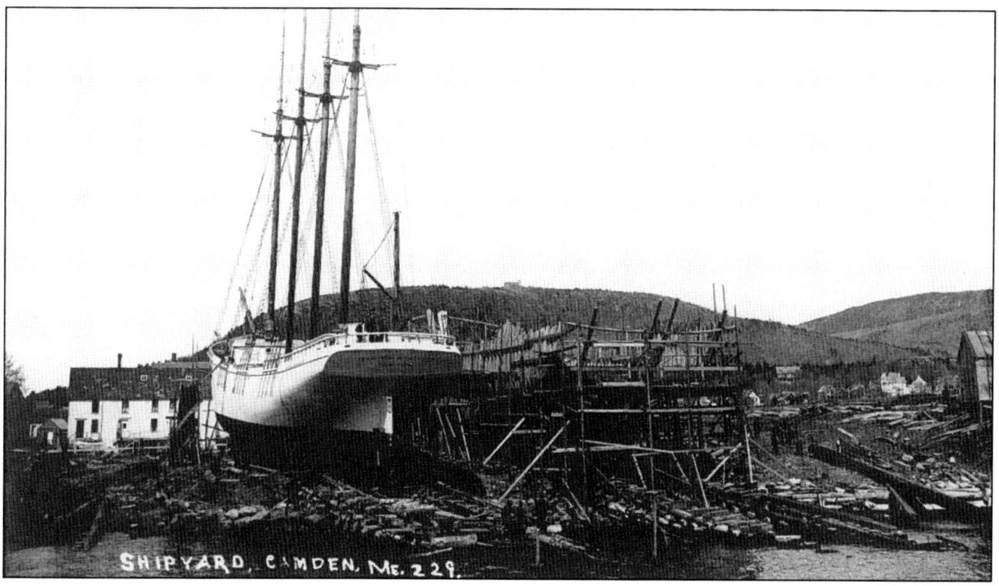

The above picture of the *Charlotte A. Maxwell* shows her on the ways, but not quite ready, to be launched. Other vessels under construction can be seen on her right. The R.L. Bean Yard kept busy with more than one vessel going at a time, so launchings would be within months of each other. With money coming in, the crew could be kept busy all the time.

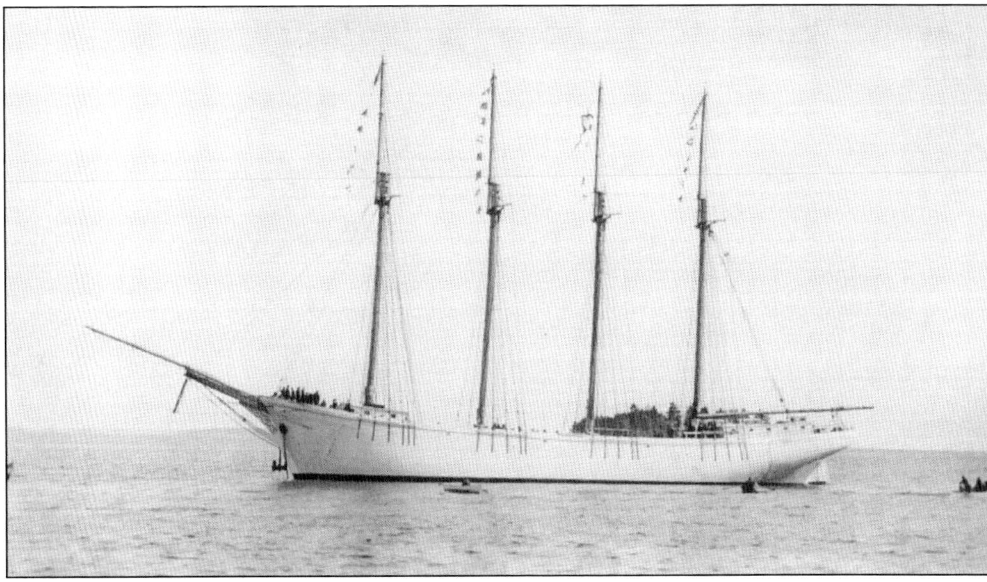

Another view of the *Charlotte A. Maxwell*, after the launch, shows her in the water being towed to the outfitting dock. Her measurements were 160 feet on the keel, with a 36-foot beam. The depth of the hole was about 14 feet. The cabin had modern conveniences, including a hot-water heater. In order for a wife to travel on the voyages, she wanted all the comforts she could get. But even at that, sailing could be rough and dangerous. It was not always a pleasure without risk.

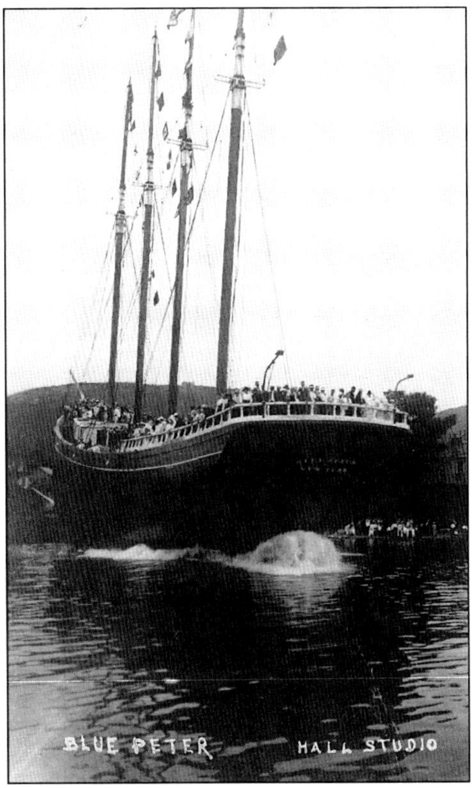

This shot of the *Blue Peter* shows her hitting the water, after the launch. It is a clear view of the crowd that launched aboard, as well as the people on the shore watching. There was something very exciting about a launching. Some people had followed the construction from the time the keel was laid until the vessel was finished. As the vessels were built outdoors, and people were always around watching their progress. They felt a part of the birth of a new vessel. The *Blue Peter* was built for the English government.

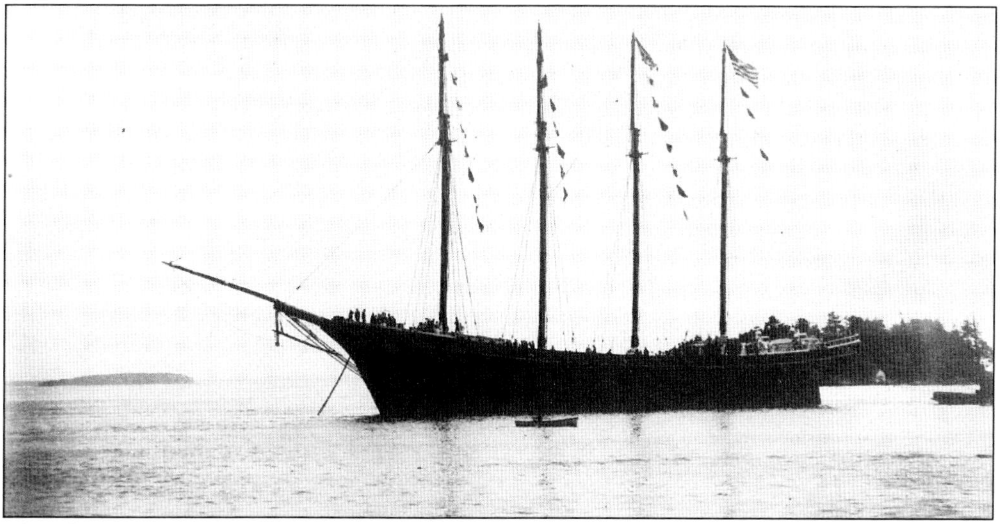

The *Blue Peter* was another four-master. Her keel was 30 feet longer than the previous vessel. She was launched on August 4, 1917, in perfect weather. The Camden Band added to the festivities and many of the summer residents were launched aboard. Her length overall was 230 feet with a 40-foot beam. She had two full decks, with a poop deck extending 12 feet forward of the after house. The windlass, blocks, and castings were made in town by the Knowlton Bros. Foundry. The tenders were made by A.G. Young of Camden, and the vessel was furnished by the F.L. Curtis store in town. About 75 invited guests enjoyed lunch in the cabin after the launching.

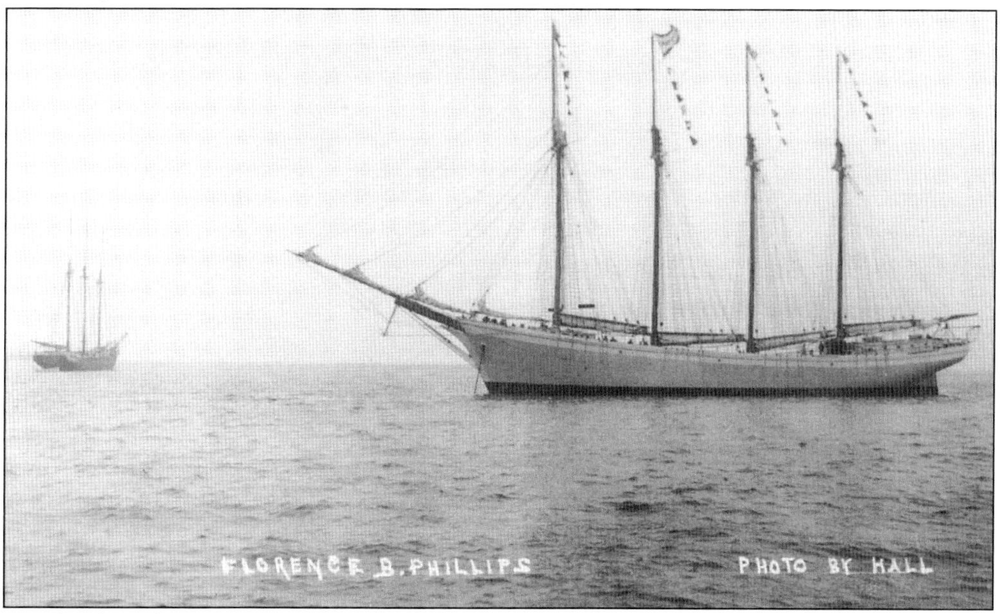

In a drizzle of fine snow, the *Florence B. Phillips* was launched on November 28, 1917. She was photographed in the outer harbor soon after the launching. A three-master was also out there looking on. The *Florence B. Philips* was built for Capt. J.B. Philips of Sag Harbor, and cost about $76,000. His daughter Elizabeth christened it with red, white, and blue flowers. A gasoline engine furnished power for hoisting the sails and anchor. An auxiliary engine aft furnished power for cargo work.

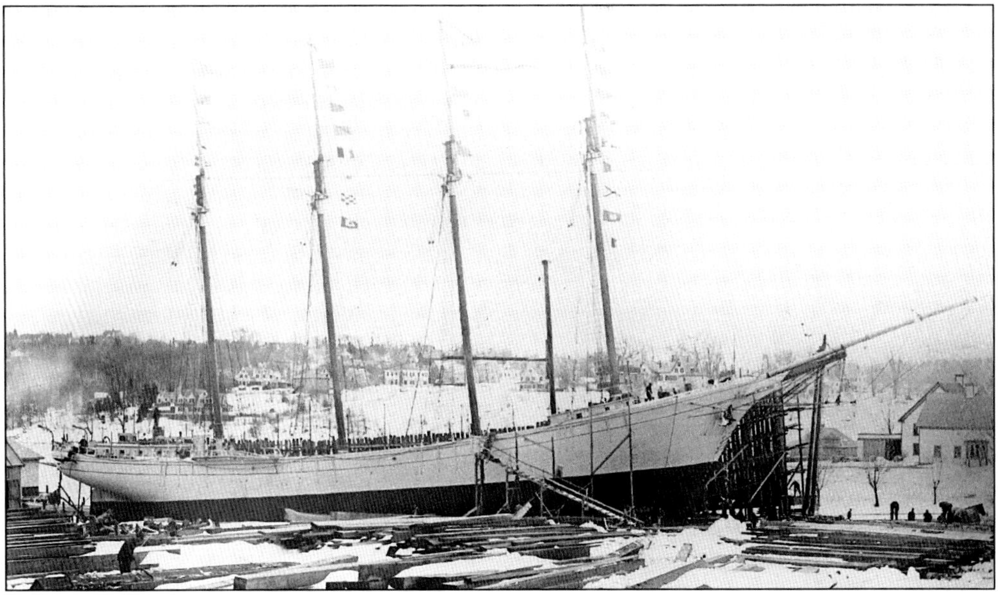

There was snow on the ground while they were building the *Laura A. Barnes*. She was the fifth four-master built in the R.L. Bean Yard in 20 months. A sixth one was already framed and a frame was ready to be put in place on the seventh vessel. The *Laura A. Barnes* was launched on March 15, 1918. She carried about the same tonnage as the *Charlotte A. Maxwell* and the *Florence N. Philips*.

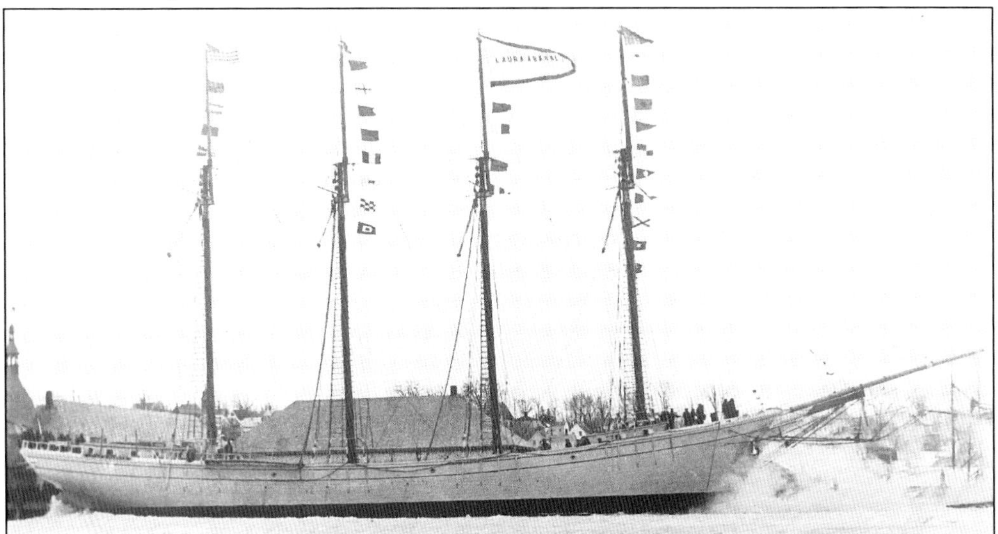

This photograph shows the *Laura A. Barnes* launched with flags flying; one flag included the name of the vessel. She was 179.5 in length and had a 37-foot beam. Her homeport was Marblehead, Massachusetts. All the vessels had official numbers and signal letters; her number was 216001 and her signal letters were L.J.R.F. Most of the captains lived in town while their vessel was being built, so they could oversee what would become their home for months at a time. The *Laura A. Barnes* had a hardwood bottom and spruce top. The lower masts were of Oregon pine and were 90 feet in length, while the topmasts were 45 feet long. Her total cost was $85,000.

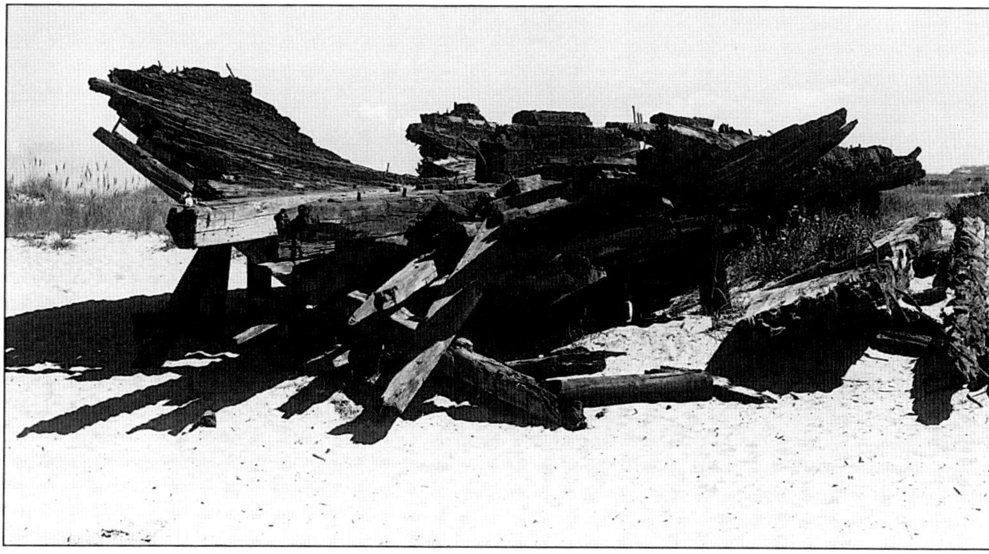

The *Laura A. Barnes* met her fate on the outer banks of North Carolina, as did numerous other vessels. A few years ago just a few ribs were left of her and a plaque was placed on the timbers, with a picture of her and information about the vessel. It is always sad to see a vessel that had been hand-crafted end up as a pile of driftwood.

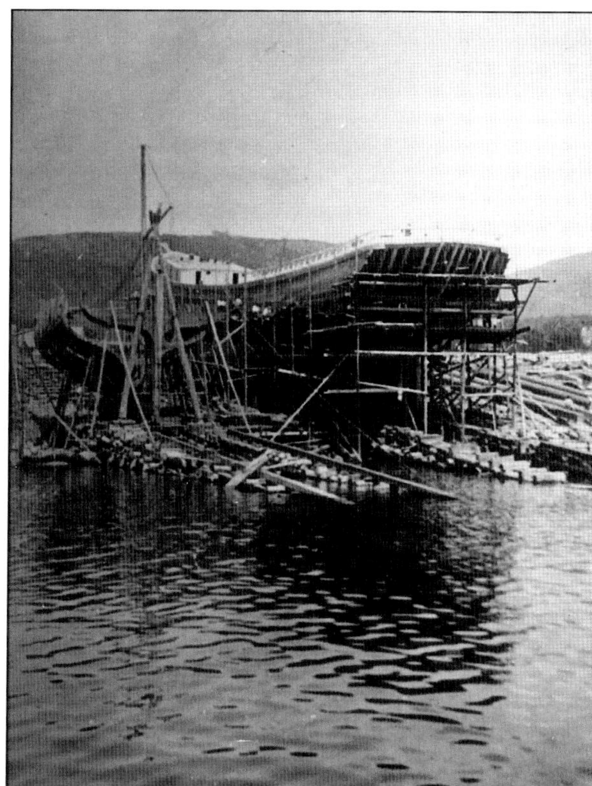

The president of the Fidelity Trust Co. of Boston named the next four-master, the *Edna M. McKnight*, after his daughter. The vessel was christened by his daughter with red roses. Her keel was 197 feet, her beam was 41 feet, and she could carry about 2,000 tons of coal. She was built to be very strong, so no expense was spared, and she cost approximately $200,000. At launching time she was already chartered to take coal to South America.

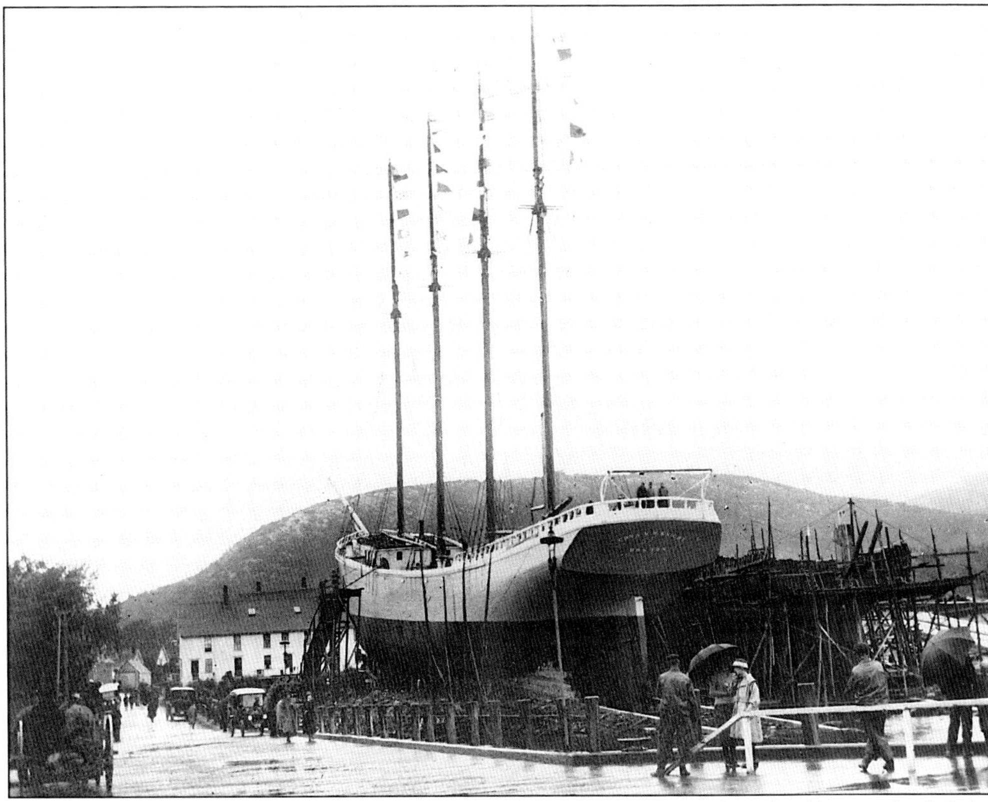

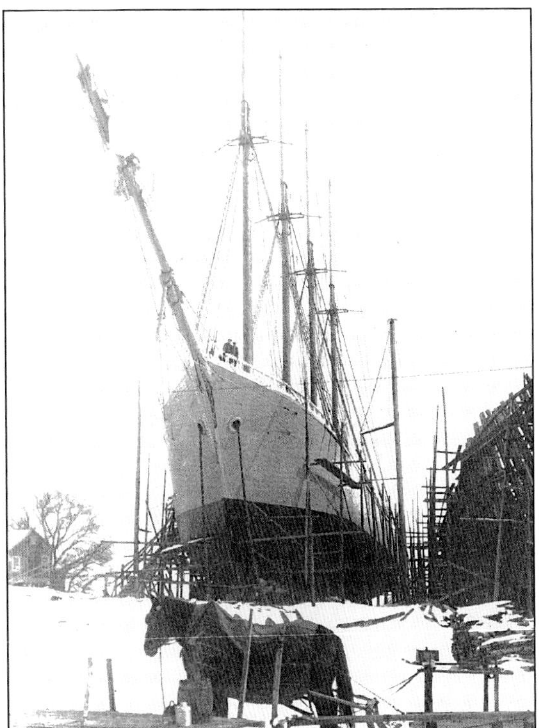

When a launching had been scheduled, it was necessary to make it happen. As you can see by the picture of the vessel *Edna M. McKnight*, it was a rainy day, but people lined up on the way to the Eastern Steamship Wharf anyway. They came with their umbrellas, some in horse-drawn buggies, some in a newer mode of transportation—cars. The date was September of 1918. Her length overall was 209.4 feet. Bath Iron Works furnished her engine, and the Knowlton Bros. made all of her castings, blocks, and windlass.

What an interesting photograph this is of the nearly completed schooner *Charles A. Dean*. The workhorse hauling a sled looks small compared to the four-master, with her 180-foot keel and 41-foot beam. The vessel had two houses. In the forward house were the engine room, galley, and forecastle. The after cabin was finished in oak, with hardwood floors.

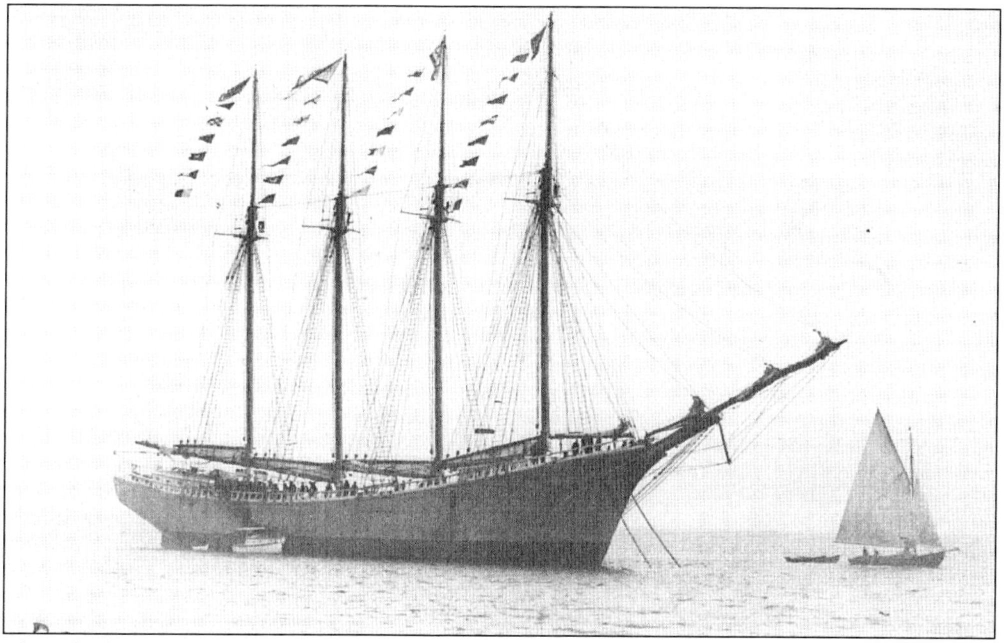

The *Charles A. Dean*, shown here in the outer harbor after launching, appears to be anchored. Captain Quinlan of Baltimore would command the vessel. He had his daughter christen it. The Oregon masts were 100 feet tall, plus the four topmasts. Many Camden firms furnished it—the plumbing was done by A.H. Parsons, the hardware by J.C. Curtis, the furniture by F.L. Curtis, the crockery by Carleton, Pascal & Co., and the small boats by A.G. Young.

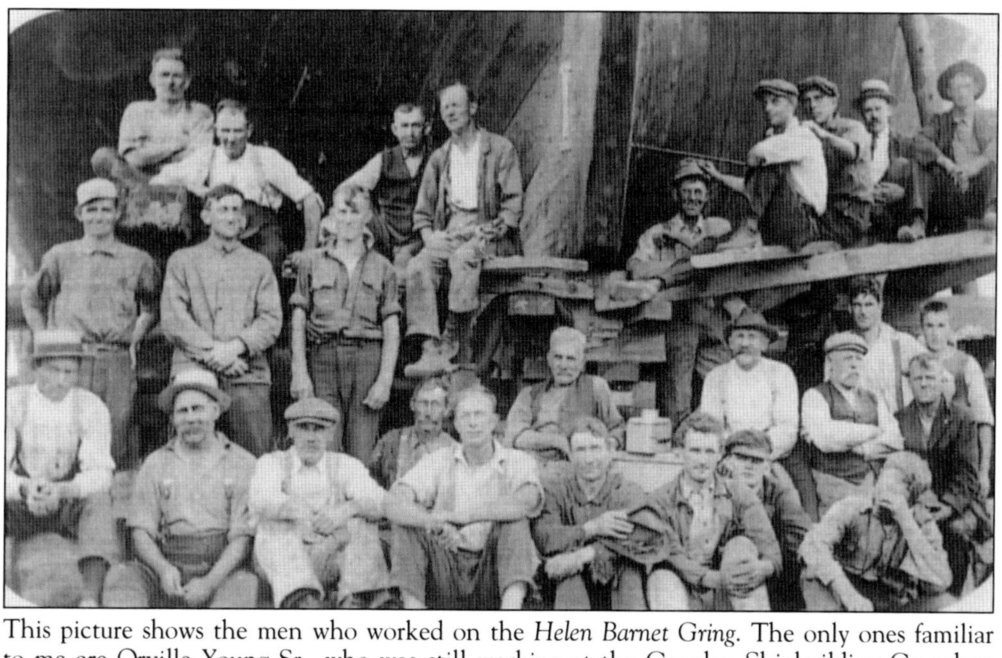

This picture shows the men who worked on the *Helen Barnet Gring*. The only ones familiar to me are Orville Young Sr., who was still working at the Camden Shipbuilding Co. when I worked there, and Vernley Gray. They look like a rugged group of workmen, both young and old.

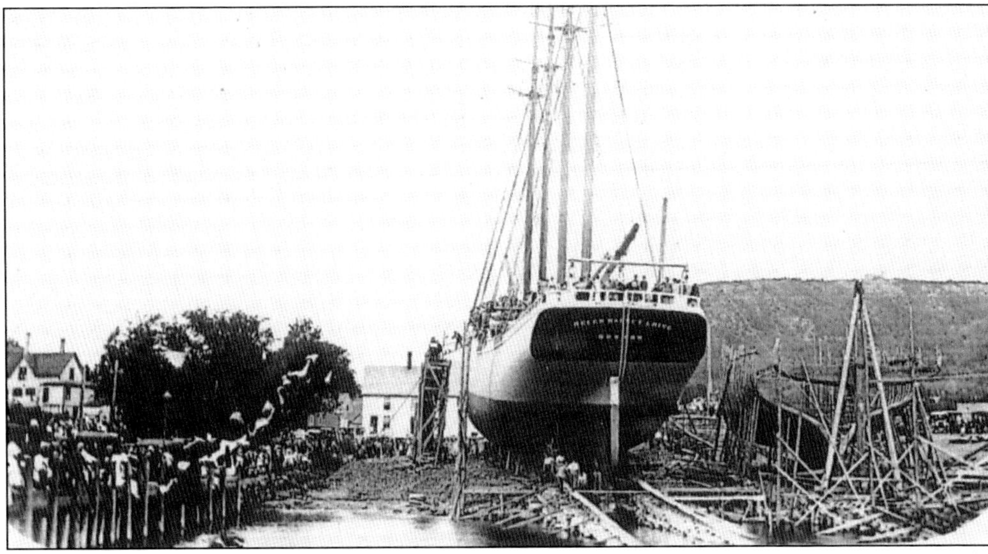

The *Helen Barnet Gring*, on July 19, 1919, became the eighth four-master to be launched in the Robert L. Bean Yard. Besides the launching party of 35 people, who came from Boston, a large crowd was launched on board. Again the Camden Band entertained with their music. It was christened by the woman for whom it was named. She scattered beautiful roses over the bow while two white doves were released. After the vessel came to anchor, the people on board were brought ashore in motorboats. Their launching party was held at the Whitehall Inn. The vessel was owned chiefly by four individuals, but Cromwell & Thurlow managed it. According to the description, it was built in a thorough and substantial manner. From the time the *Helen Barnet Gring* was launched until she met her demise on October 12, 1940, she made many voyages. There were trips to Portugal, Barbados, Venezuela, Cuba, Nova Scotia, England, and many ports in the United States. In the end, she struck a reef on Cayo Verde, Cuba, that opened a large hole in her. She became a total loss.

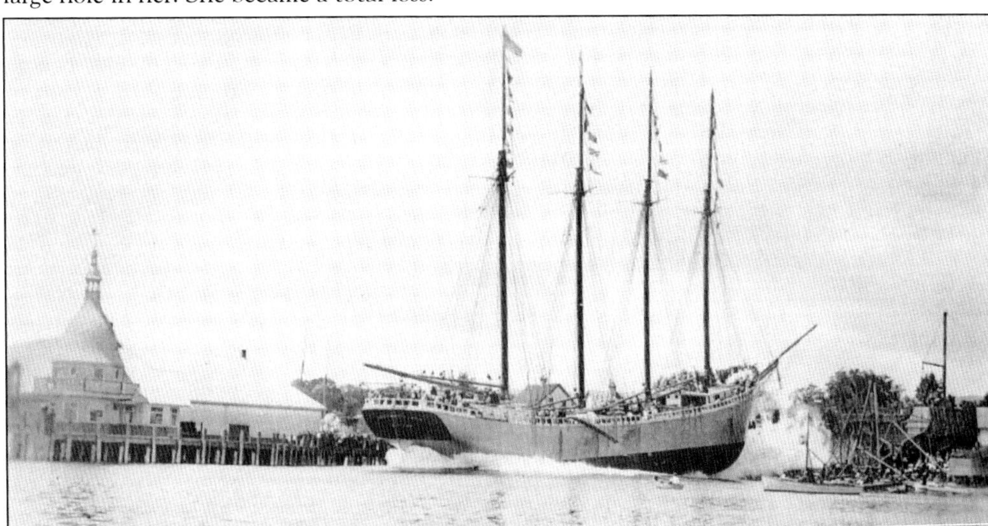

The *Helen Barnet Gring* is shown here being launched down the ways beside the Eastern Steamship Wharf. She made waves and all her launching flags were flying. It was another exciting day at the Bean Yard.

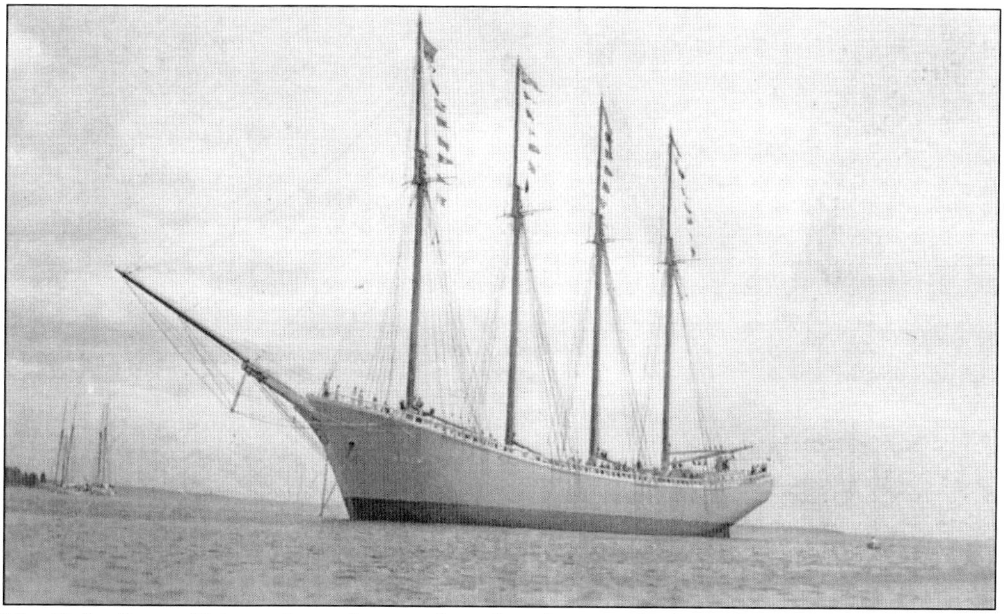

The *Helen Barnet Gring* is shown here anchored in the outer harbor, allowing one to appreciate her beauty and the size. The length of her keel was 190 feet and her beam was 41 feet. She could carry 2,000 tons and her cost was about $200,000. She was square fastened with 1.25-inch-thick iron bolted between every frame. The outboard planking had three streaks of garboard 8 inches thick, and the balance of the planking was 5 inches thick to the rail. It was a vessel built to last and it did.

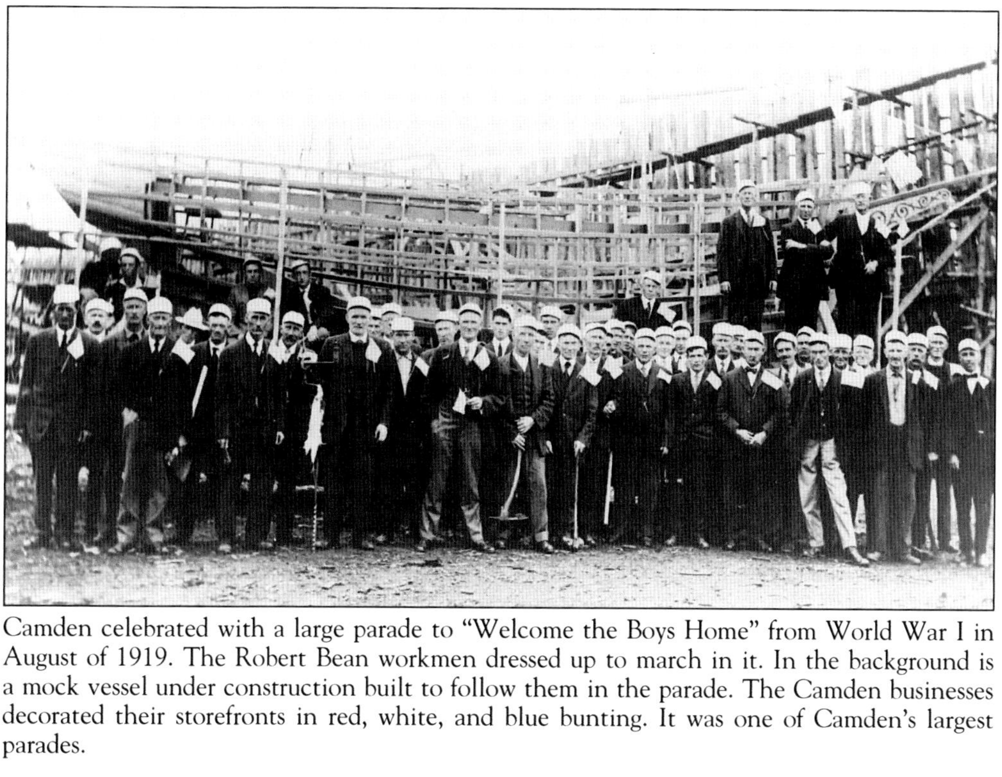

Camden celebrated with a large parade to "Welcome the Boys Home" from World War I in August of 1919. The Robert Bean workmen dressed up to march in it. In the background is a mock vessel under construction built to follow them in the parade. The Camden businesses decorated their storefronts in red, white, and blue bunting. It was one of Camden's largest parades.

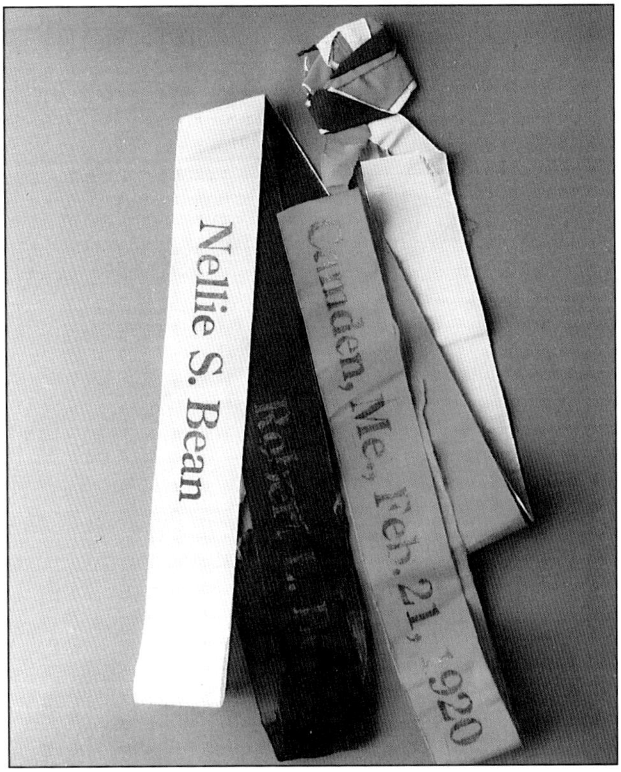

The *Robert L. Bean*, named for the owner of the yard, was launched on February 21, 1920. Nellie Bean, Robert's wife, had the honor of christening. The christening ribbon (shown here) has been saved for 70 years. The white ribbon reads "Nellie S. Bean"; the blue ribbon bears the name of the vessel, *Robert L. Bean*; and the red ribbon shows the date of the launching, "Camden, Me., February 21, 1920."

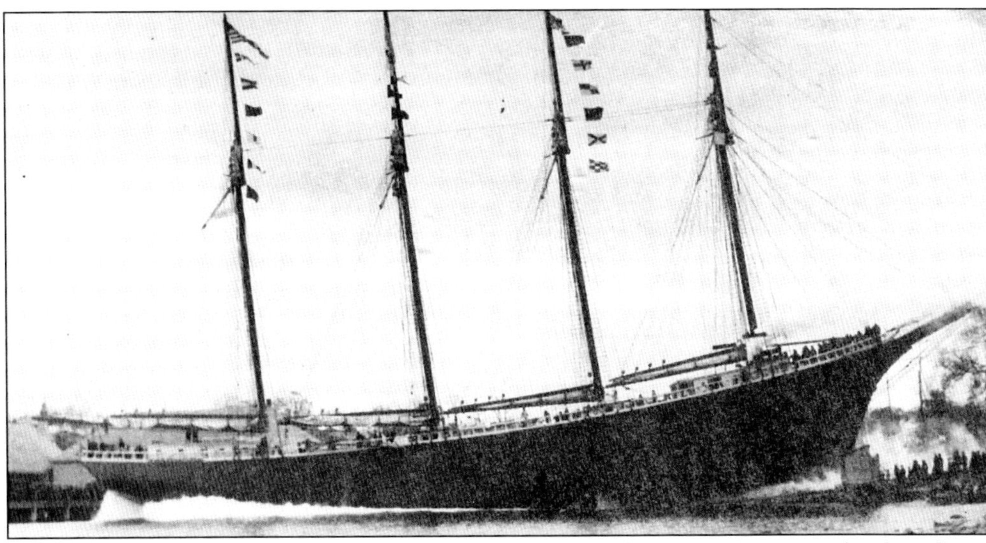

The ninth schooner, the *Robert L. Bean*, hit the water at about 11:45 a.m. on the date shown on the launching ribbon. The owner of the yard was part owner of the vessel, along with some summer residents. It hailed from Thomaston because Dunn & Elliot, of that town, were the managing owners. Mr. and Mrs. Bean entertained a small group of friends at Bowden's after the launching. The event was witnessed by a very small crowd because of the weather. The trolleys had not gotten through and people did not want to stand around in the deep snow. The length of the vessel's keel was 209 feet and the beam was 41 feet. She was commanded by Capt. Augustine Anderson of Providence, Rhode Island.

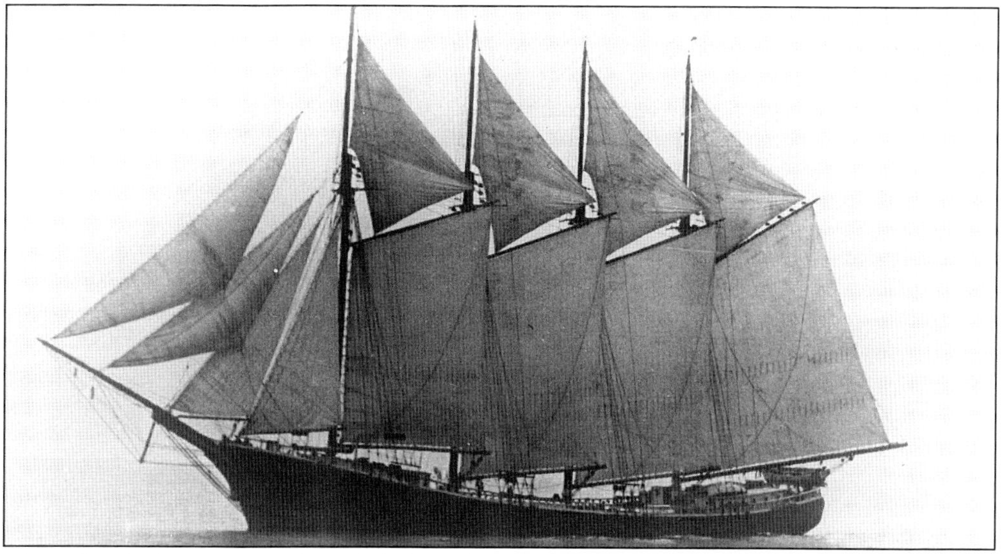

The *Robert L. Bean* was a sight to behold under sail. Her length overall was 216 feet. There was an underlying note of sadness in the newspaper account of the vessel, and later we found out why, after the launching of the next vessel. A year-and-a-half before the yard closed, Mr. Bean was told that wooden shipbuilding days were over. He held firm to his belief that wind and water were the cheapest method of transportation. Within two years after World War I, it was not possible to sell a four-master for $500. The last vessels he built sold for $225,000. He ran into serious financial difficulty. The era of tall ships was lost to progress.

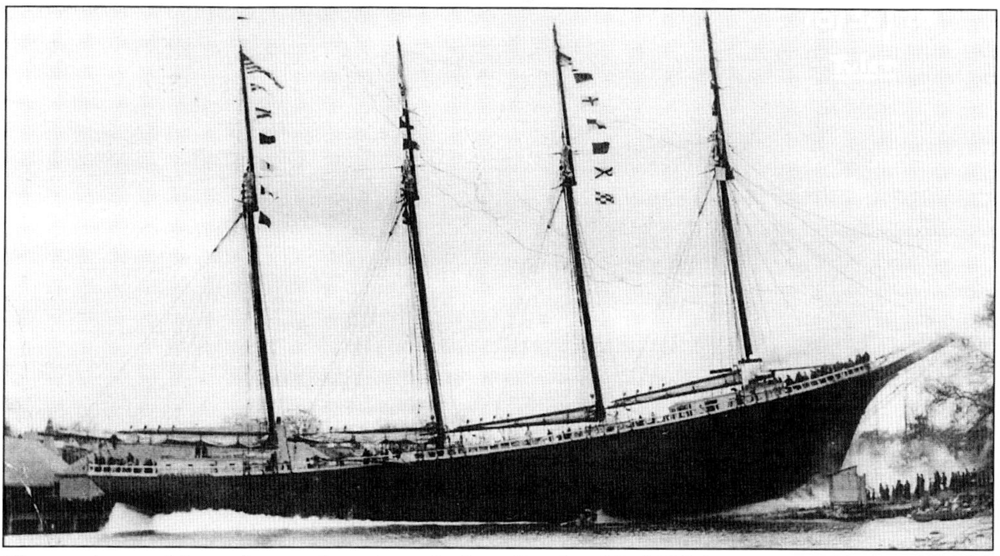

The tenth vessel from that yard was launched on October 29, 1920. It was named *T.N. Barnsdall* in honor of Mrs. Robert Law's father. Mrs. Law lived at "Roxmont," the present home of *Down East* magazine. When the vessel was launched, she was fully rigged and equipped for her trip to Norfolk, Virginia, the following week. She was built for foreign trade and expected to carry coal to South America. She measured 233 feet overall, with a beam of 41 feet, and her hull was painted black. Her four masts were 103 feet tall and the topmasts 53 feet each. She was to carry a crew of nine, with Fred Nutt of Rockport as cook. The Robert L. Bean Yard remained silent for the next 21 years, until World War II revived it.

List Of Vessels Built By Robert L. Bean

Launched	Name of Vessel	Keel	Captain
December 23, 1916	PERCY R. PYNE II	205'	(German) name unkno
April 19, 1917	CHARLOTTE A. MAXWELL	160'	Captain E. H. Tinker
August 4, 1917	BLUE PETER	190'	
November 28, 1917	FLORENCE B. PHILLIPS	165'	Captain J. B. Phillips
March 15, 1918	LAURA A. BARNES	165'	Captain Charles Barne
September, 1918	EDNA M. MCKNIGHT	197'	Captain Frank Rutledg
March 4, 1919	CHARLES A. DEAN	180'	Captain Peter Quinlan
July 29, 1919	HELEN BARNET GRING	190'	Captain James W. Ho
February 20, 1920	ROBERT L. BEAN	209'	Captain Augustine An
October 29, 1920	T. N. BARNSDALL	200'	Captain Ernest A. Joh

These vessels ranged in price from $76,000 to $225,000.

Four

Camden Shipbuilding and Marine Railways

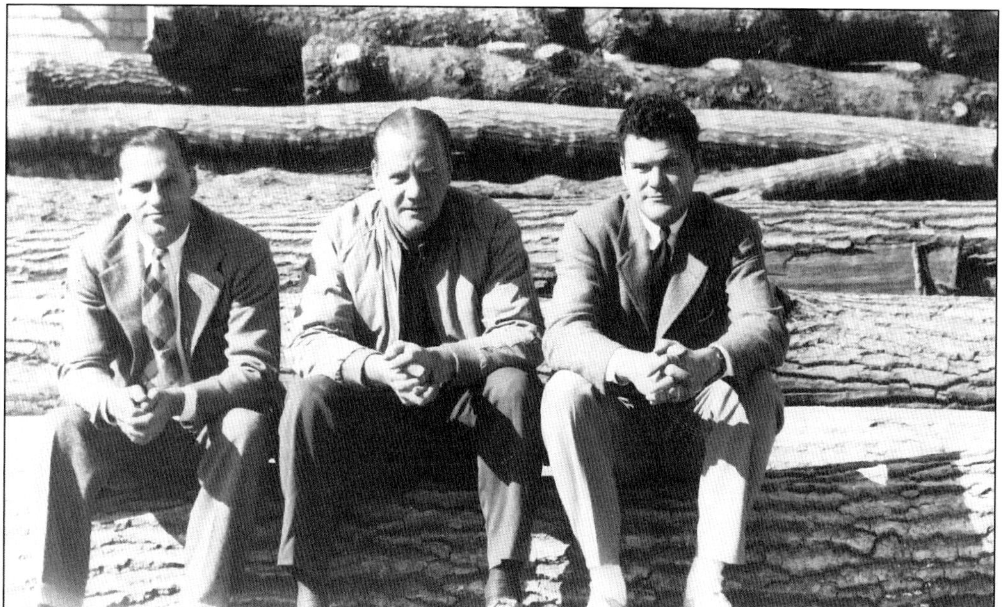

On December 16, 1940, the Camden Shipbuilding & Marine Railway Co. was formed as a corporation. It began operation on January 1, 1941. Pictured are treasurer Clinton A. Lunt, vice-president Cary W. Bok, and president Richard V.R. Lyman. All were under the age of 30. Appointed as clerk and attorney was John A. Willey; John Gamage was general superintendent; William S. Warner became assistant superintendent for hulls; and Robert T. Maccoun was assistant superintendent for machinery. Henry Bickford was hired as the personnel manager. World War II was on, and the yard was ready to roll.

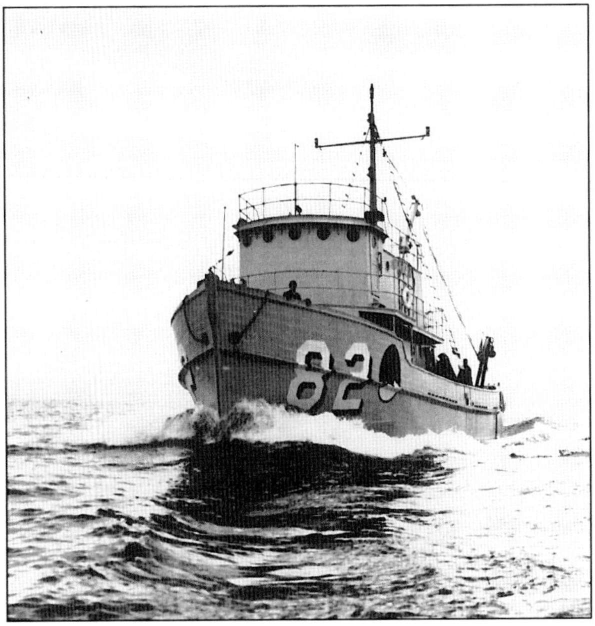

The first "try out" order from the Navy was for two minesweepers. AMc#82 was launched July 26, 1941, and named *Governor*. She was christened by Mrs. Richard Lyman and delivered on January 12, 1942. The second minesweeper was built and launched on February 22, 1942. The two minesweepers were approved as well constructed, but the Navy had no more contracts to "let out" at that time. Employment had gone from 10 to 150 and back down to 25.

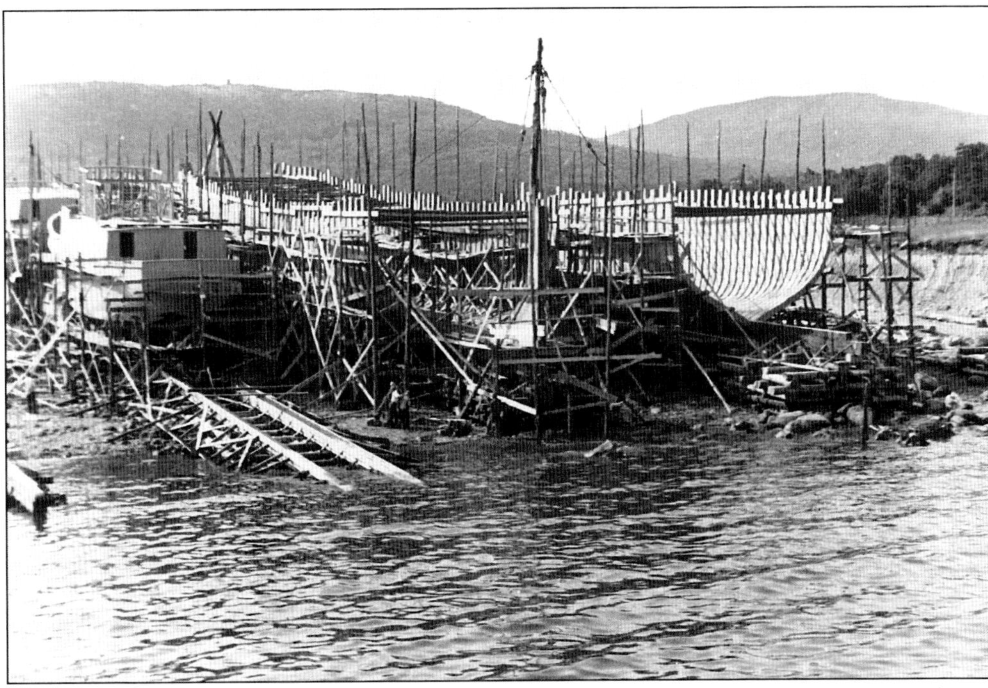

President Franklin D. Roosevelt remembered seeing tugs towing strings of barges out of New York harbor, carrying coal to Boston and points north. His concern about the availability of fuel for New England homes and industries caused him to believe that they could shift that burden from land to sea. But the Maritime Commission found that the builders of steel craft were too busy for the lowly barges. Camden was ready for any contracts and said that they would be happy to build them. Of course, no one knew how to build them, but Camden received the first contracts anyway. The picture above shows several barges under construction. Their design was based on half models built after the Civil War.

N. Nav. 410
(June 1929)

LOG BOOK

OF THE

USS Governor

TEMPORARILY ATTACHED TO THE

SEVENTH NAVAL DISTRICT

District Headquarters at MIAMI, FLORIDA

Section Headquarters at KEY WEST, FLORIDA

Beginning 1 May, 1942, and ending 30 June, 1942

4—3385

List of Persons Attached to the USS Governor *Attached to the* 7th *Naval District.*

NAME	RATING	REPORTED	DETACHED	DUTY
A.F. Page Jr.	Lt(jg)	1/29/42	5/3/42	O-in-C.
D.D. Long Jr.	Lt(jg)	5/1/42	—	O-in-C.
E.P. O'Callaghan	Ens.	1/29/42	—	Executive Off.
J.H. Cahn	Ens.	1/29/42	—	Gunnery Off.
Bonnabel, H.J.	CBM	1/29/42	—	Deck
Brooks, W.R.	CMM	1/29/42	—	Engineroom
Mancuso, S.R.	QM 2/c	1/29/42	—	Bridge
Haddon, L.M.	MM 2/c	1/29/42	—	Engineroom
Hebert, L.	MM 2/c	1/29/42	—	Engineroom
Dubre, W.P.	SC 2/c	1/29/42	—	Cook.
Hoffpauir, J.	RM 3/c	1/29/42	—	Radio
Lawler, E.J.	EM 3/c	2/23/42	—	Electrical
Toups, E.J.	F 1/c	1/29/42	—	Engineroom
Beaube, D.E.	Sea 1/c	1/29/42	—	Deck
Calloway, M.L.	Sea 1/c	1/29/42	—	Deck
Jenkins, H.T. Jr.	Sea 2/c	1/29/42	—	Deck
Gahagan, J.J.	Sea 2/c	1/29/42	—	Deck.
Galley, S.E.	Matt 3c	1/29/42	—	Officers Qtrs.

4—3385

Examined and found to be correct.

D.D. Long Jr.
Lt (jg), U.S. N.R.
Commanding.

Log of the U.S.S. GOVERNOR, AMc 82 TEMP Attached to the Section Base, Key West, 7th Naval District, Friday May 1st, 1942

Hour	Wind		Barometer		Temperature		State of the Weather by Symbols	Clouds			Condition of the Sea
	Direction	Force	Height in inches	Thermometer, attached	Air, dry bulb	Air, wet bulb		Forms of, by symbols	Moving from—	Amount covered, tenths	
A. M. 4	NE	3	3001	–	74	–	C	ci st	NE	9	—
8	ENE	3	3001	–	74	–	B/C	cu	ENE	4	3
12 M.	E	3	3001	–	73	–	B/C	ci St	E	3	4
P. M. 16	E	2	3002	–	83	–	B/C	ci St	E	3	~
20	E	2	3000	–	74	–	B/C	St	E	5	3
24	NE	2	3000	–	74	–	B/C	St	NE	4	~

REMARKS

By authority of Commander Inshore Patrol, Seventh Naval District, the use of Deck Log Book (N. Nav. 330) and Smoothe Log (N. Nav. 43) were discontinued, and, in lieu of the above, commenced using Patrol Log Book (N. Nav. 410)

0000 moored starboard side to Section Base Pier, Key West, Fla. 0732 Underway on various courses standing out northwest Channel. 0856 Smith Shoal light abeam/stbd. c/c 279° T. 1027 Dropped dan buoy at entrance to mine field channel. c/c 180° T. Commenced patrol of area west of mine field. 1115 c/c 000° T. 1205 c/c 180° T

4—3384

Examined and found to be correct.

____

______________________, U. S.
Commanding.

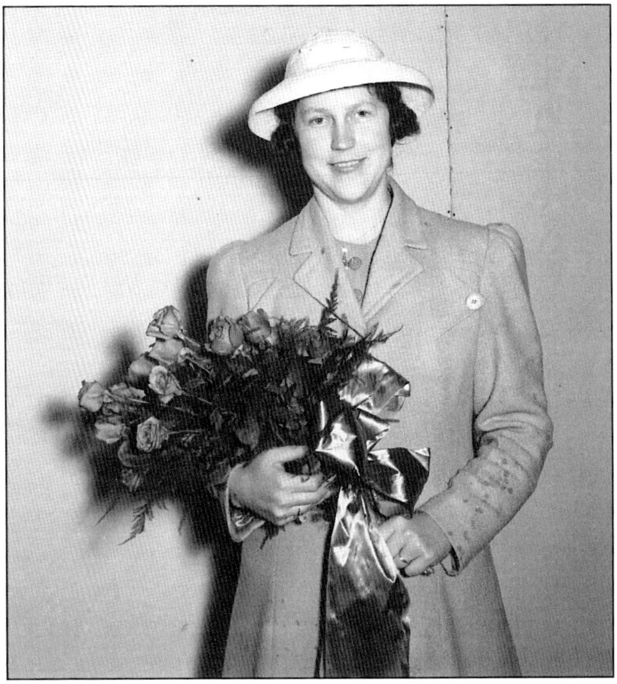

Contracts arrived for APc's, most of which were headquarter ships for LST or LCI commanders. APc#15 was sponsored by Mrs. Clinton Lunt and launched on July 18, 1942. The vessel was delivered on October 17, 1942.

William E. Peterson, the flotilla commander of APc#15, lived in Camden while his ship was being built. He liked Camden so much that he returned after the war to run the post-war shipyard. APc#15 ran into a winter gale off Cape Hateras (where so many vessels, over the years, had met their fate in storms) and the ship developed serious troubles. They made it into the Navy yard in Charleston, South Carolina. The Navy then called the master builder, the architect, and the yard president for consultation. The outcome of the conference was the decision to strengthen the design of the craft and all future APc's.

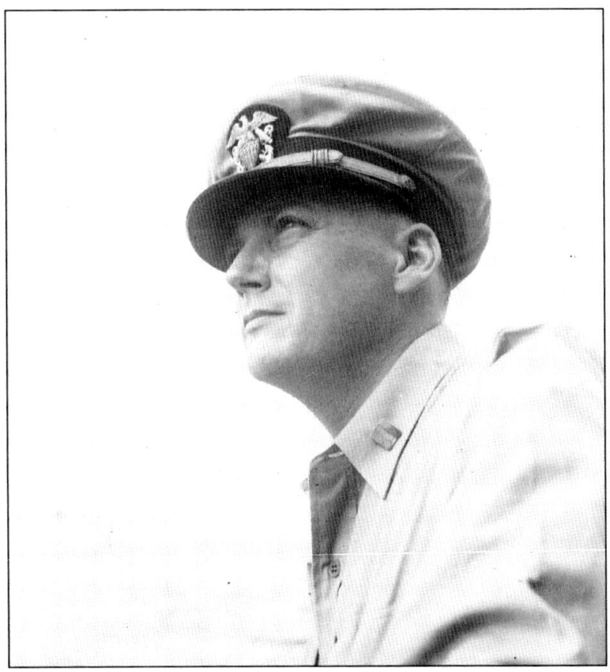

Because of the shortage of manpower, a full-page advertisement appeared in the *Camden Herald* on November 19, 1942. It stated that the shipyard "would even hire women." It went on to say, "Remember ladies before you rush to apply, these are men's jobs you are expected to fill. There will be no opportunity to exploit feminine charm. The winter days will be bitter and work will be in the open where heavy socks, boots, and mackinaws are the only acceptable clothing. If we were to be facetious, we would say noses will be red and lips will lose their allure. The shipyard wants men or women, who can do men's work." Well, they could say that 50 years ago.

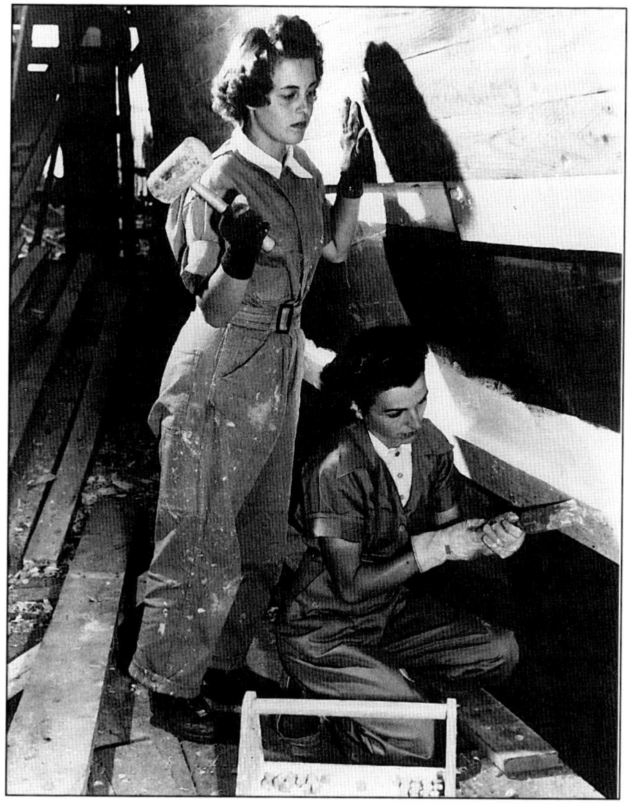

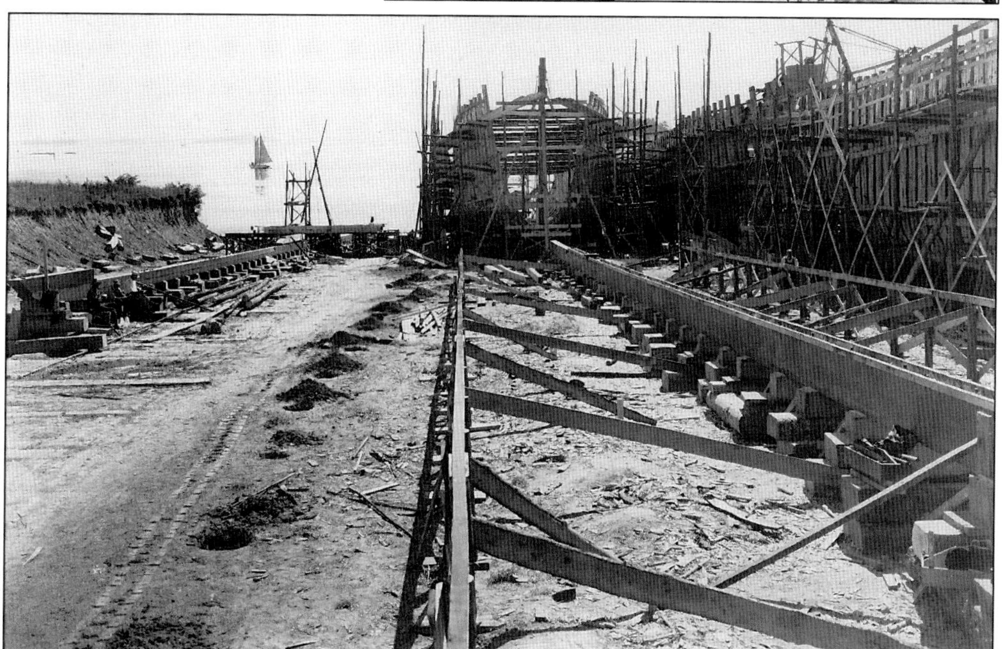

The picture above shows the launching ways, with boats under construction. It became a very busy yard for the war effort. Many vessels were built at the same time. A keel might be laid for one while another was framed or planked.

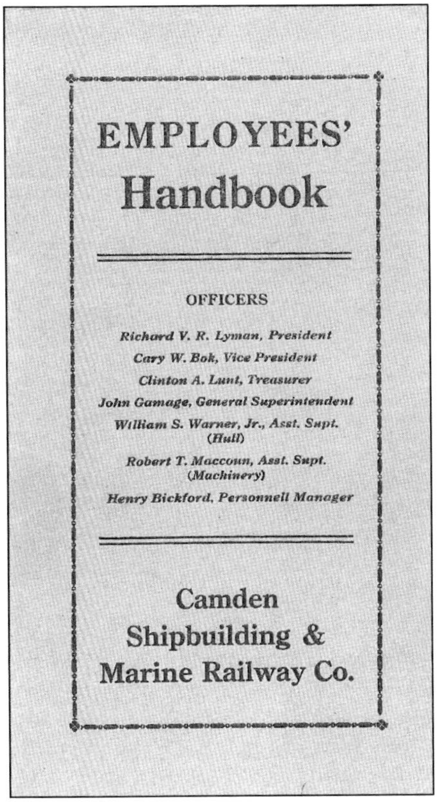

EMPLOYEES'
Handbook

OFFICERS

Richard V. R. Lyman, President
Cary W. Bok, Vice President
Clinton A. Lunt, Treasurer
John Gamage, General Superintendent
William S. Warner, Jr., Asst. Supt. (Hull)
Robert T. Maccoun, Asst. Supt. (Machinery)
Henry Bickford, Personnell Manager

Camden
Shipbuilding &
Marine Railway Co.

Each employee received the "Employees' Handbook." It told about filling out timeslips, punching timeclocks, and a few other bits of information. Each employee was required to wear their identification pin (a round metal pin with numbers on it—anyone could have picked one up and "borrowed" it to get into the yard). There were no pictures on them or any identification.

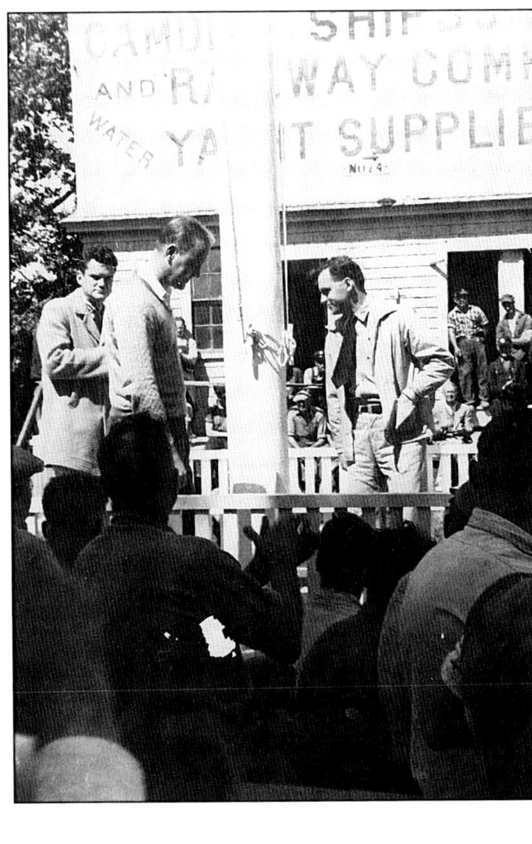

The employees presented a flagpole to the yard in 1942. This photograph shows Richard Lyman, Cary Bok, and Clinton Lunt accepting it before a crowd of on-looking workers. Patriotism ran high in those days and the workers wanted to fly the American flag where they worked.

Mrs. Franklin D. Roosevelt arrived in Camden on February 8, 1943, to christen the first coal barge built, *Pine Tree I.* As no FBI men came, I was able to photograph the "First Lady" after she had lunch at the Lyman home on Chestnut Street and was getting into a car. She moved about Camden very freely.

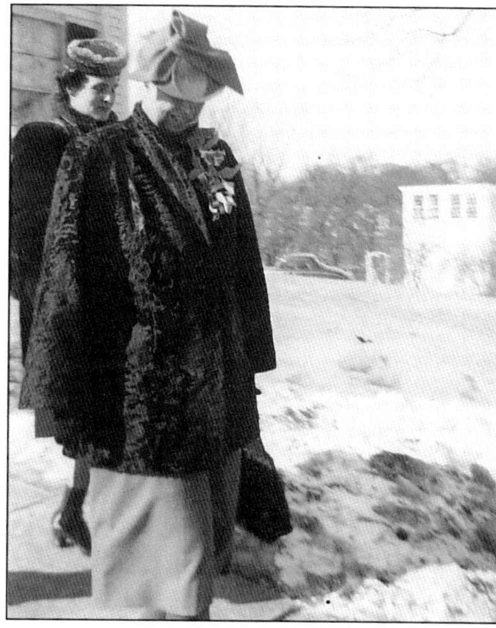

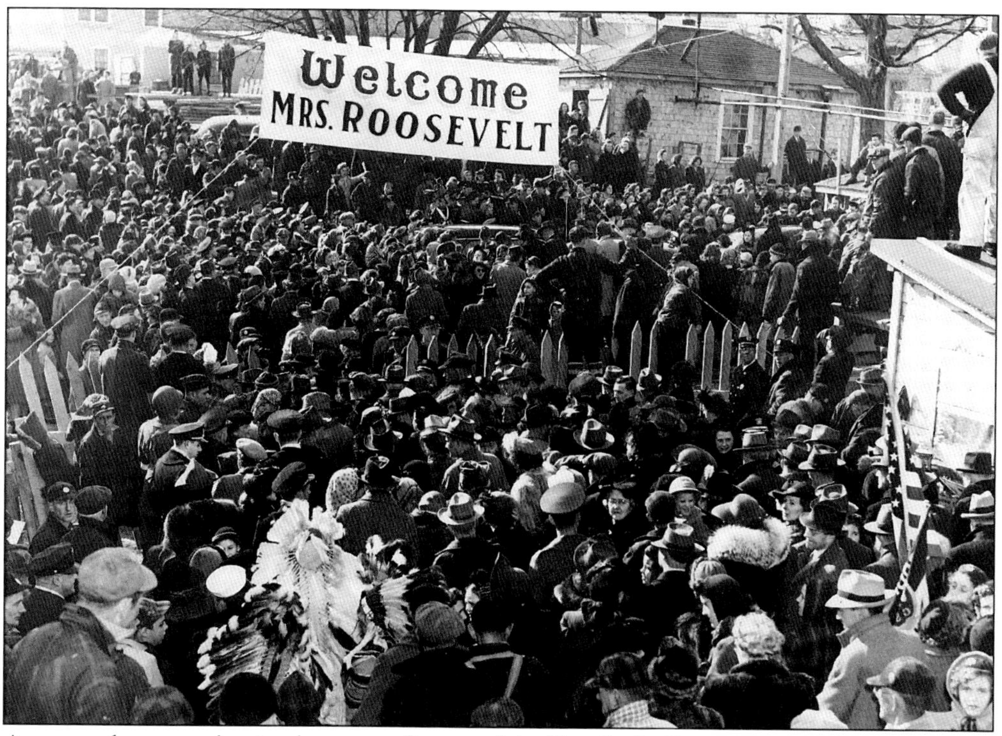

A tremendous crowd arrived to get a glimpse of the First Lady. During a time when televisions did not exist, it was much more important for people to witness news first hand. One can see that the yard was packed with people and the only security was Camden's firemen, in their dress uniforms. Camden, at that time, had only one man on the police force; his primary job was to walk the business district at night to check that store doors had been locked. Ladies and gentlemen both wore hats in the 1940s.

Camden Shipbuilding & Marine Railway Co.

requests the honor of your presence

at the launching of the "Pine Tree"

for the U. S. Maritime Commission

Eleanor Roosevelt, Sponsor

and U. S. S. APc 62

Loraine M. Price, Sponsor

February 8, 1943 1.15 p. m.

An invitation was sent out to some for the double launching that day. Loraine Price sponsored Apc#62 and Eleanor Roosevelt christened the first coal barge constructed. Sumner Sewall, the governor of Maine, and his wife also attracted much attention.

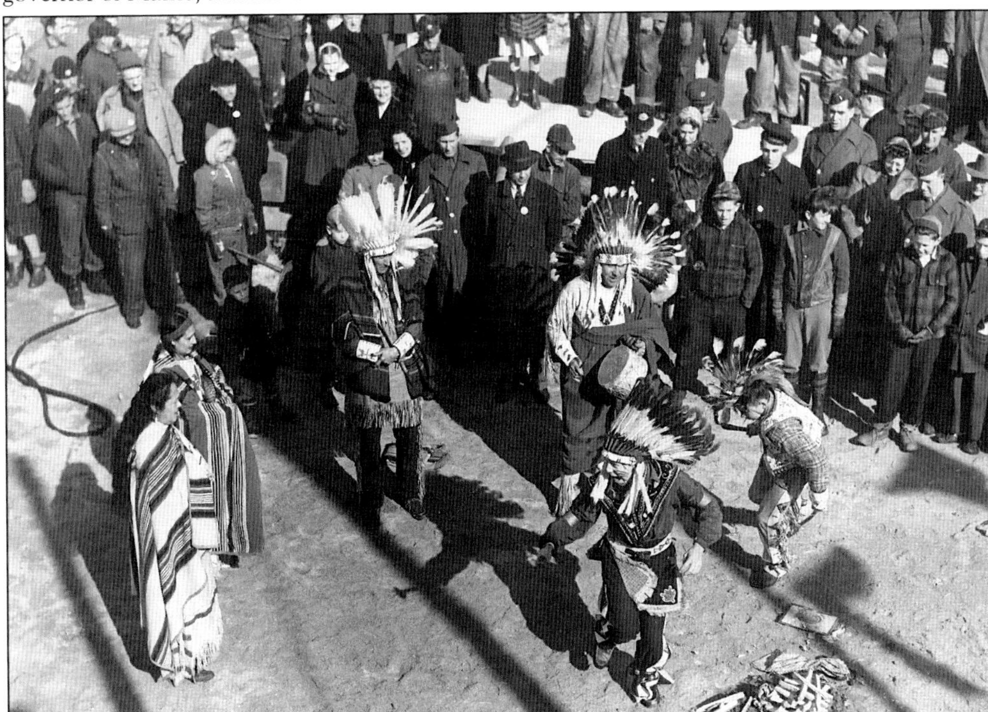

The Penobscot Nation made the tenders for the coal barges, so they attended in full dress to honor Mrs. Roosevelt. They did a ceremonial dance and proclaimed her "Princess Watawaso." Translated that meant "princess of many trails," as Eleanor was covering much territory. She was quite a First Lady.

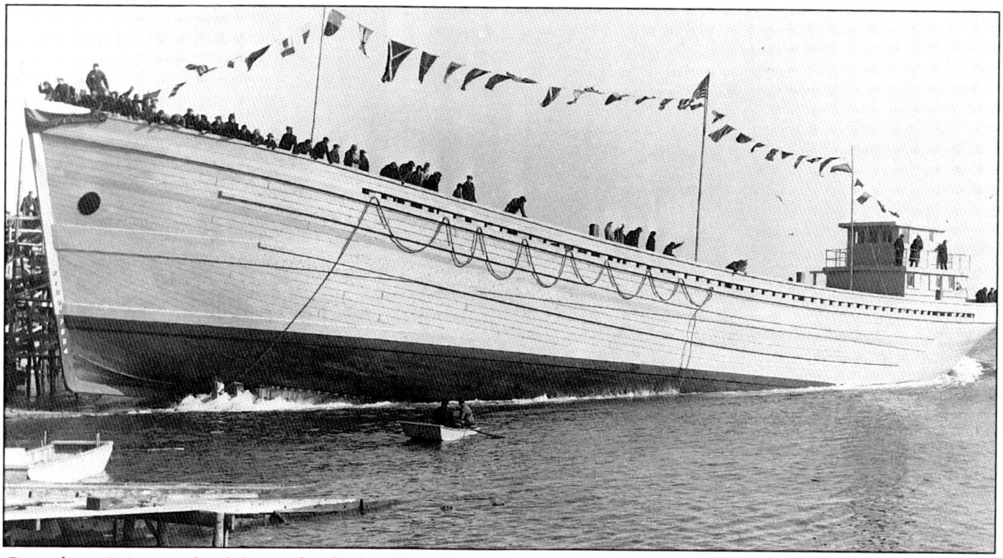

Camden, Maine, had launched the first barge MCc851, named the *Pine Tree I,* with many people aboard. She was so large and heavy that it appeared she would not come to a halt until she reached Curtis Island. She was the largest wooden vessel launched in the United States in 23 years. Not only were Camden people excited by having Eleanor Roosevelt in town, but calls came in from Associated Press, Wide World, International News Service, Fox Movietone, Hearst, and several others. Many reporters wrote their story ahead of time and confirmed it with a phone call, after it actually happened. That's how news was reported so many years ago.

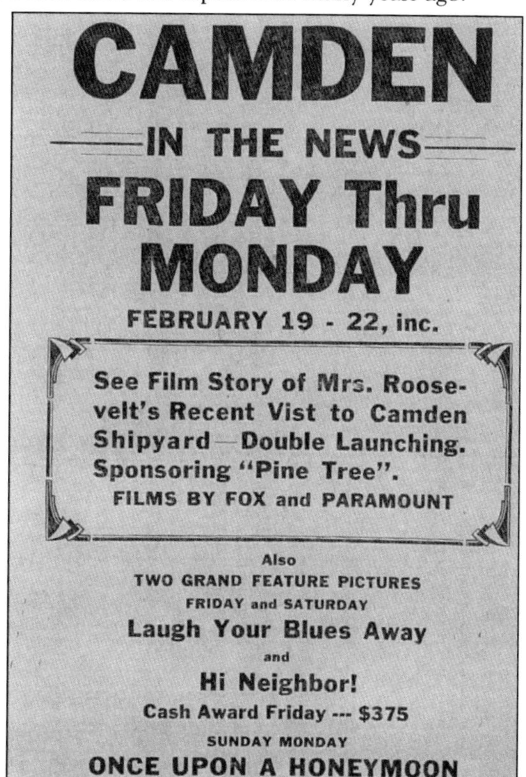

As you can see by the above advertisement, the special event made the movies in our local theater from February 19 through 22. Although most had seen the news as it happened, they loved seeing it again in the local theater. For the same price of admission, one also saw two movies and had a chance of winning a few hundred dollars given away on "money night."

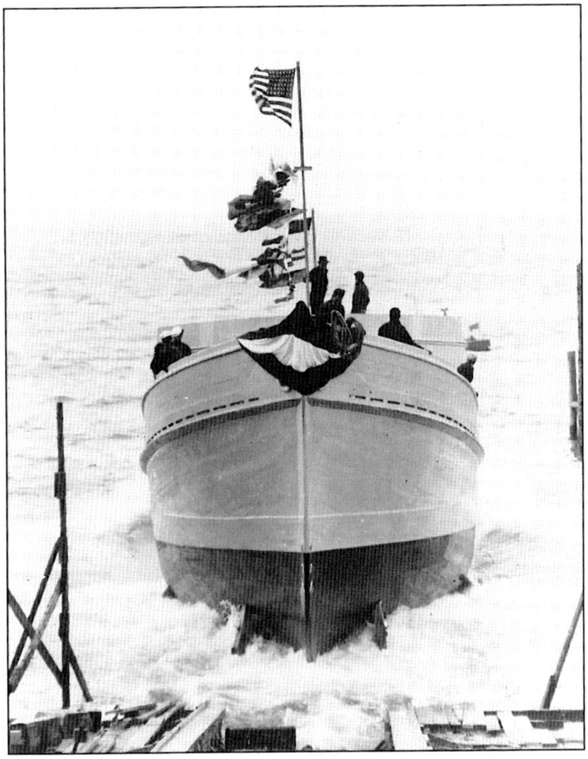

The other vessel launched the same day was APc#62. It is shown going down the ways after being christened by Loraine M. Price. Actually, the vessel was launched at 1:35 p.m. and the *Pine Tree I* followed 15 minutes later. A Methodist minister and his little daughter went to the launching, and coming back over Sea Street the little girl was crying. A reception was being held at the Officer's Club and a naval officer standing on the porch asked what the trouble was. The minister said the crowd was so large and his little girl so small, she did not see Mrs. Roosevelt. So the naval officer took her in, where she sat on Mrs. Roosevelt's lap drinking milk and eating cookies. Then they left for a service in her father's church. The little girl ran down the aisle yelling, "I just sat in the government's lap!"

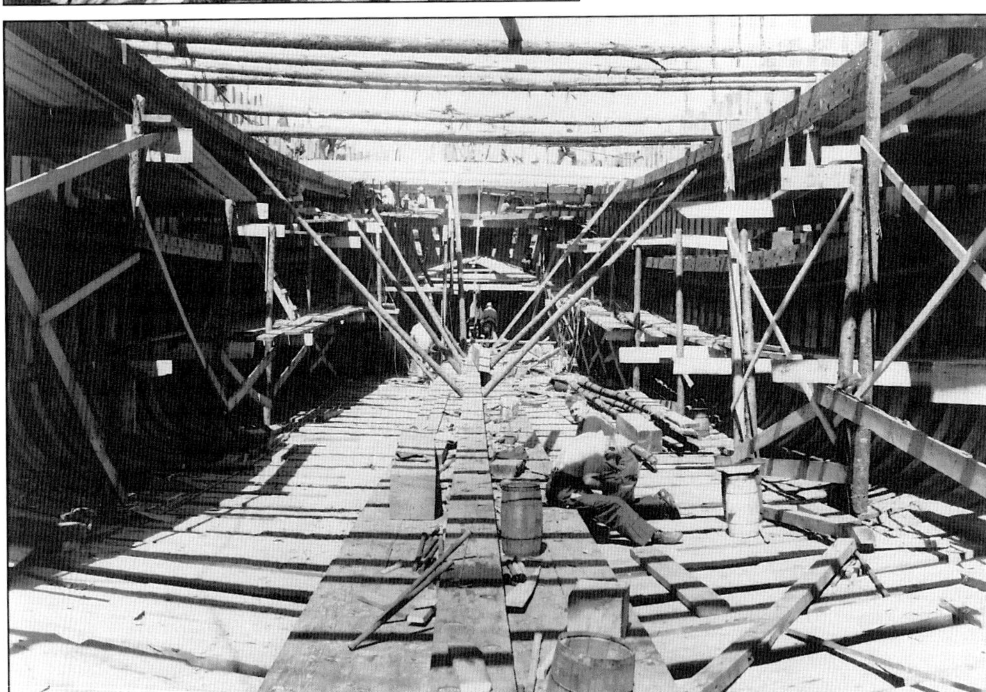

This is the inside of another barge being constructed. It gives an idea of how large the hull was. Those barges were the answer to our need in New England for fuel. The winters were extremely cold.

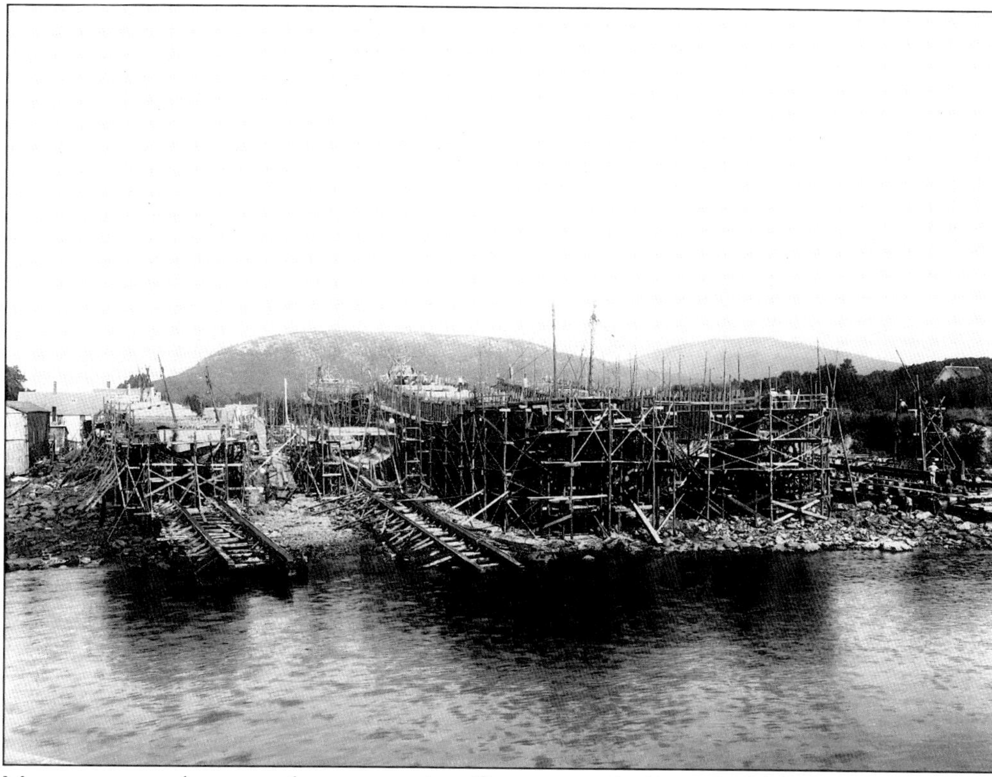

Many more vessels were under construction all at once in the Bean Yard (that name is still used today). Two of Camden's mountains can be seen in the background.

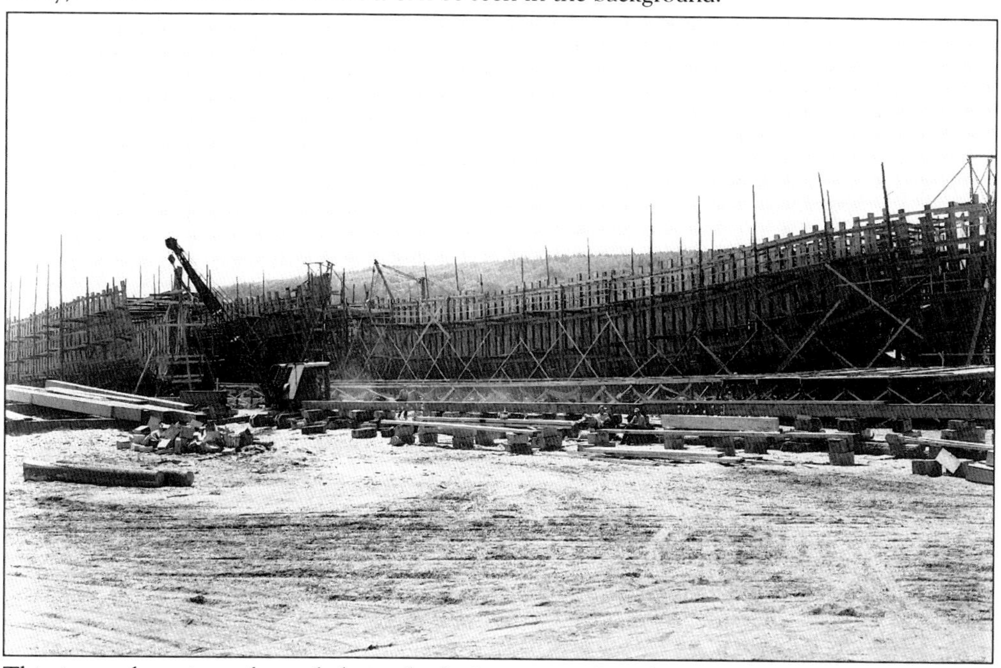

This is another view of vessels being built. It appears that there are more coal barges under construction.

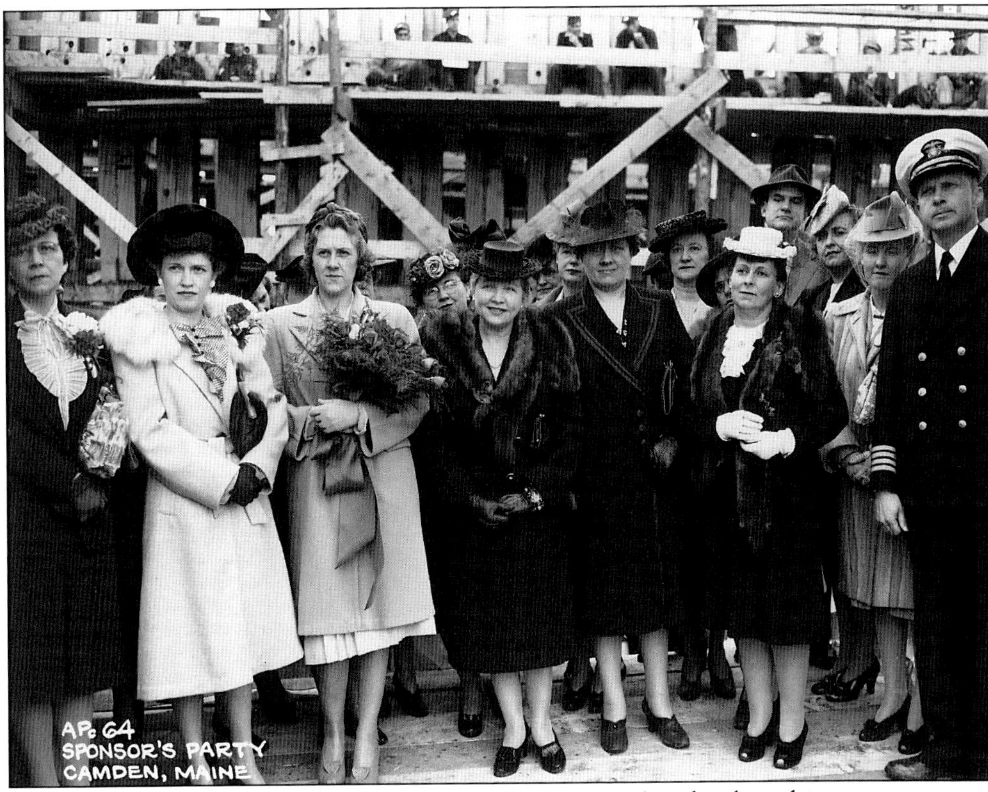

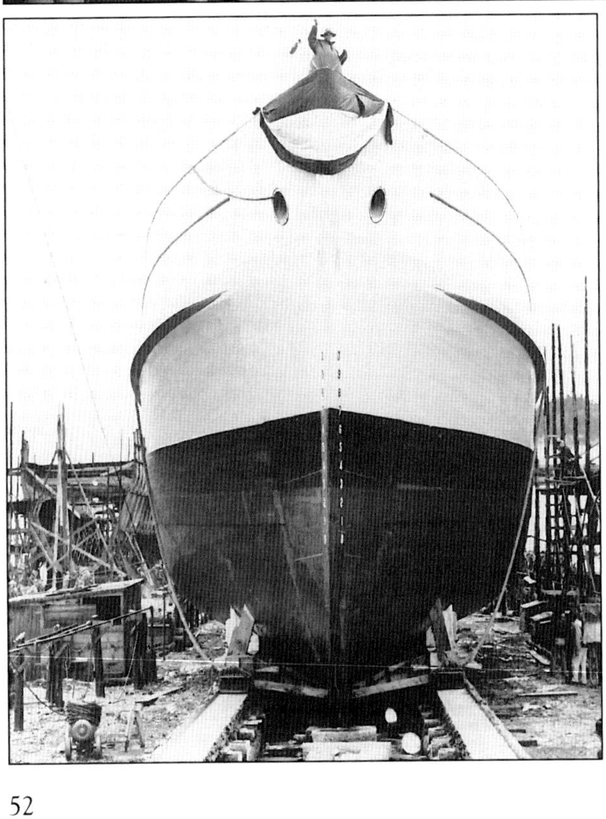

Another launching party was held on May 4, 1943, for APc#64. The four people listed from left to right are Doris Payson, Helen Pettipiece, Evelyn Mayhew, and Mrs. Sumner Sewall. All the ladies dressed in their finest. The workmen looked on from above while eating their lunch.

Pine Tree III was launched on June 5, 1943. This picture shows the coal barge starting down the ways. The vessel was sponsored by Rep. Margaret Chase Smith. It had taken the workmen an extra 15 minutes to knock out the keel blocks, as Maine oak is tough. She was the 17th craft for World War II built by the Camden Shipbuilding & Marine Railways Co. Mrs. Smith said, "Some day we will watch the last craft go out, and will watch it come back, when peace is won."

This photograph shows the barge as she hit the water at the end of the ways.

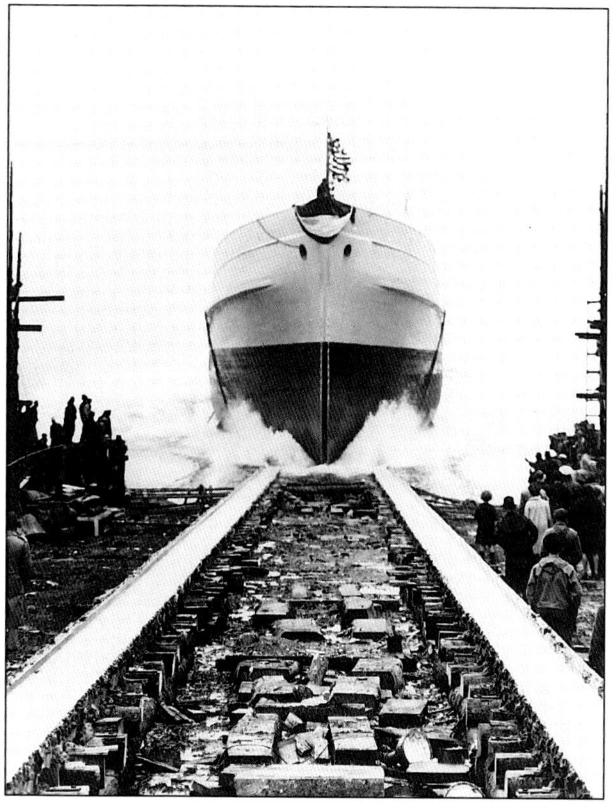

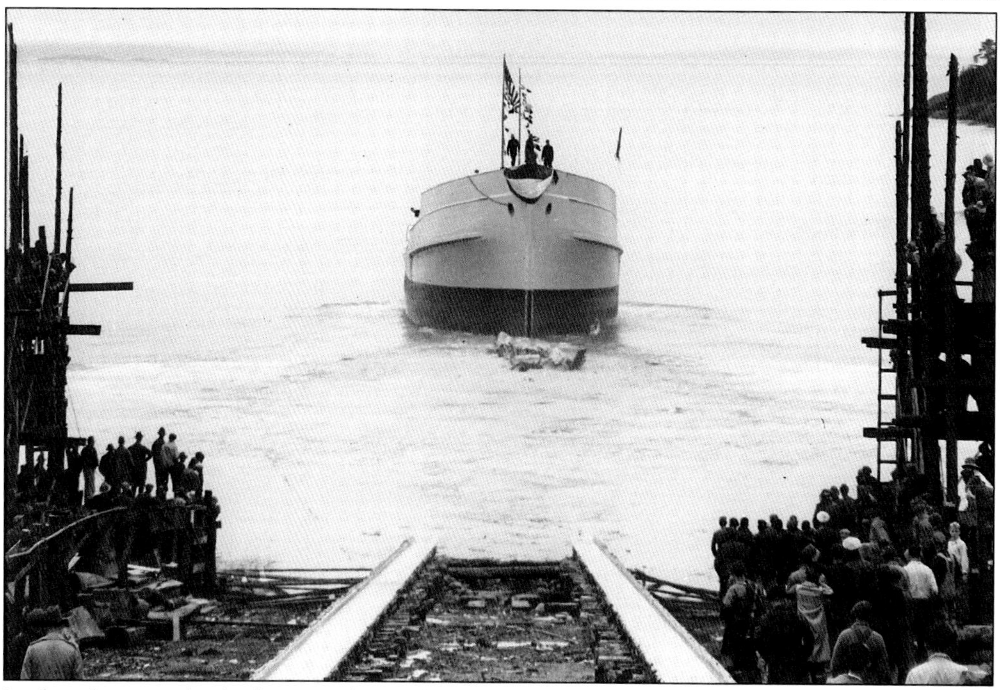

In this photograph, the barge is shown floating in the water. People were still standing around watching the successful launch.

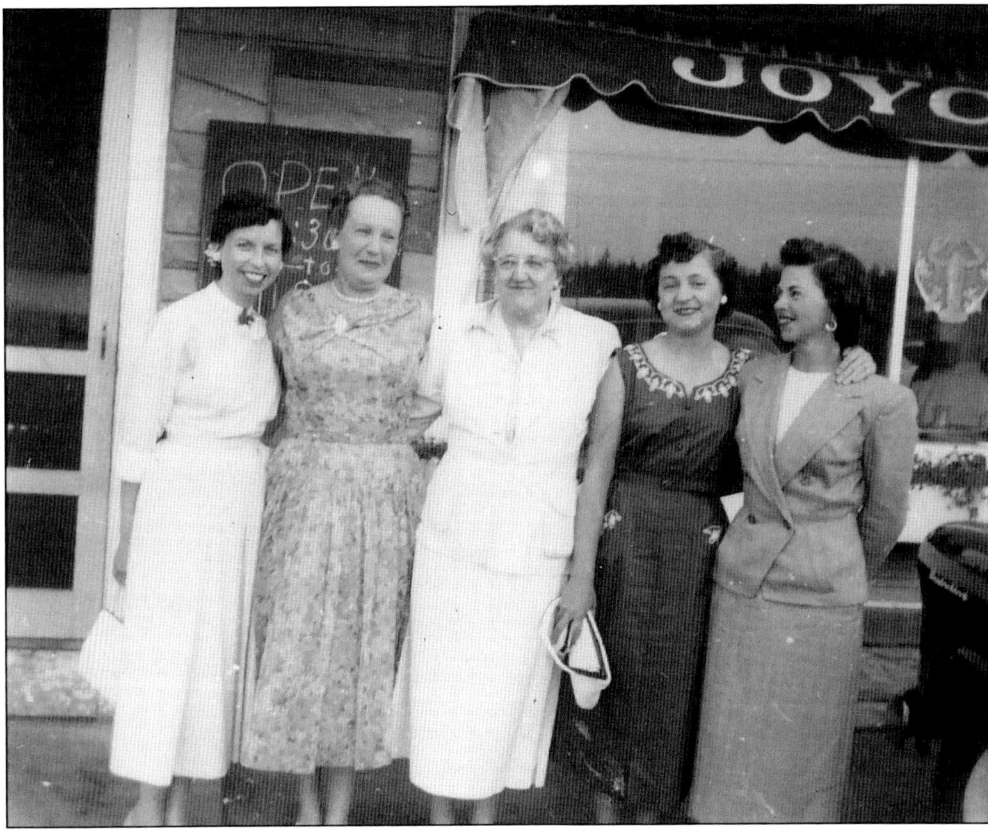

A group of office workers met for a luncheon together one Sunday. They were Dorothy MacDonald, Alberta Garland, Evelyn Thompson, Peggy Randall, and Barbara Dyer. Two are now deceased, but the other three still remain friends after 50 some years.

Camden Shipbuilding & Marine Railway Co.

requests the honor of your presence

at the launching of the

Pine Tree 4

for the U. S. Maritime Commission

Mary Louise Bok, sponsor

July 4, 1943 12.01 A. M.

This invitation shows that *Pine Tree IV* was launched at midnight on the Fourth of July. That certainly was very patriotic. A wonderful benefactor to Camden and Rockport, Mary Louise Bok, was the sponsor. She was also the mother of the yard vice-president, Cary W. Bok, and was a lady that everyone in Camden and Rockport loved.

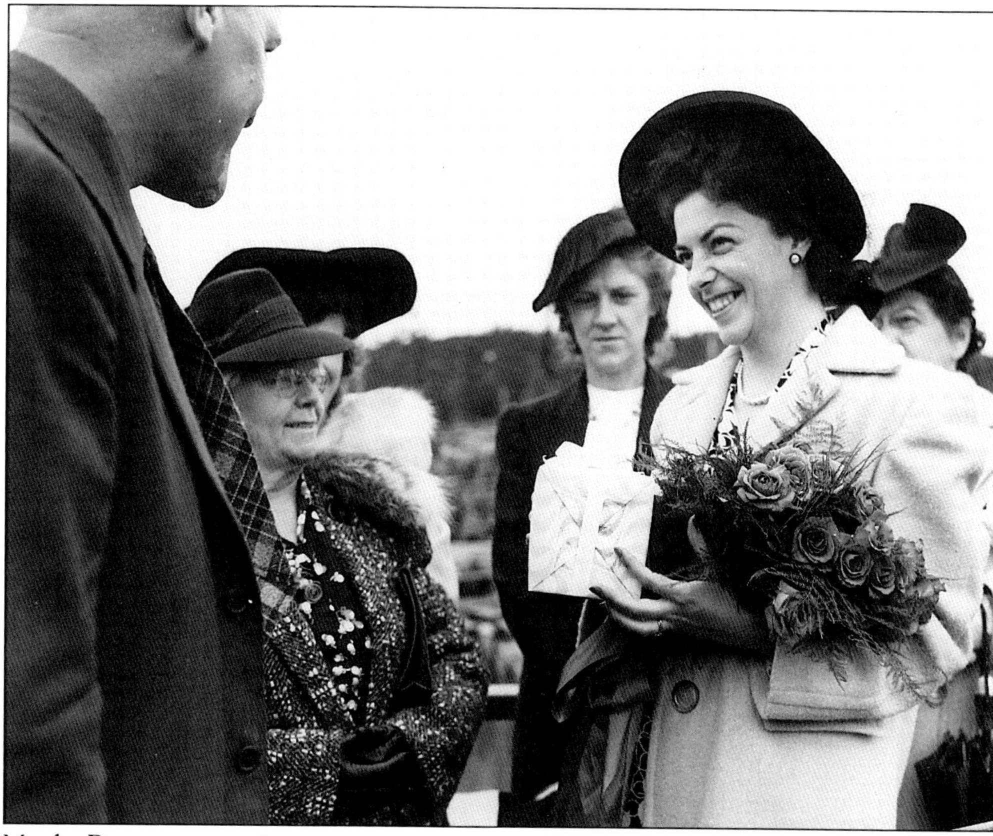

Martha Dean, an executive secretary at the yard, was chosen to sponsor the next vessel. It was ATR#19, a rescue salvage tug. The vessel, which had been built for Britain under the lend lease, was 165 feet long. Now it could be told that the hull was of oak, but the superstructure was made of steel. Much of that work had to be done at the outfitting dock, after the launching. Twelve of these vessels were built at Camden Shipbuilding from July 1943 to October 1944. The fifth to the twelfth were built for the United States Navy.

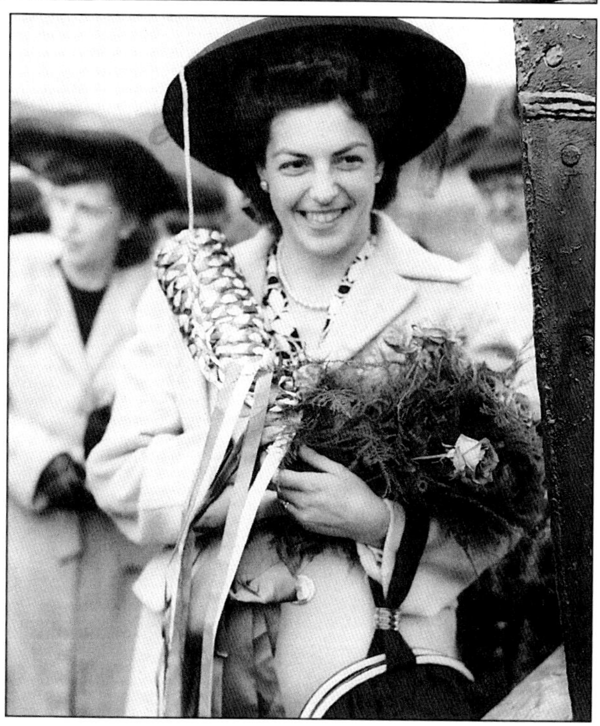

This photograph shows how pretty Martha was in her picture hat, with the launching bouquet and launching bottle scored and wrapped in braided ribbons. Of course, it was an honor and very exciting to sponsor a vessel.

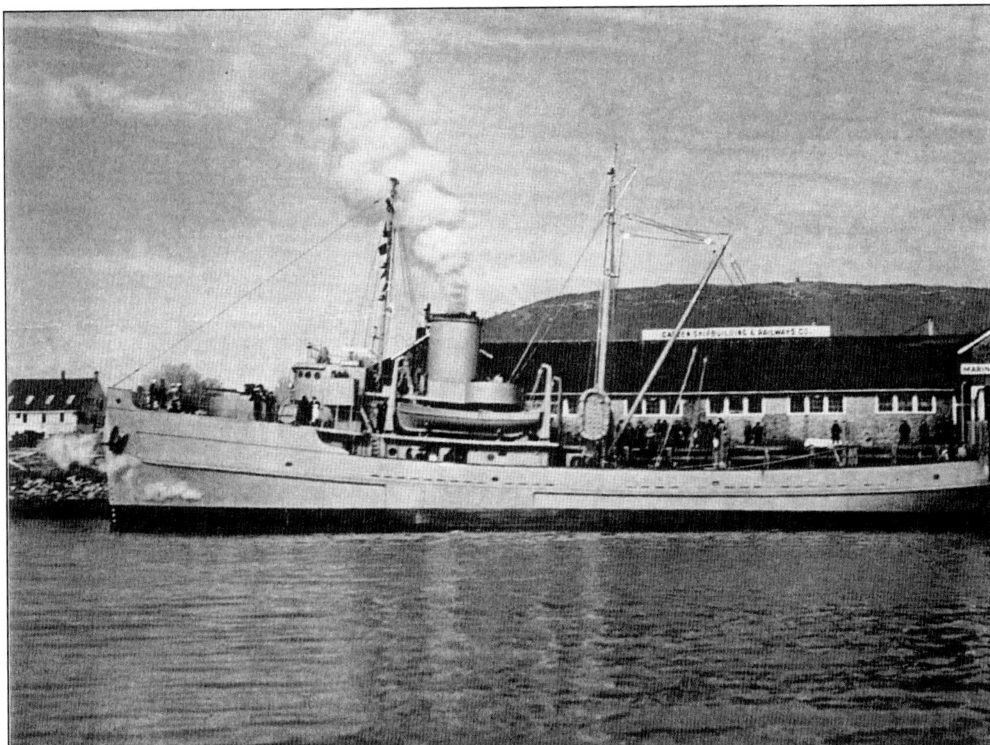

"*A handful of these ships around the coasts of England saved or salvaged over 2½ million tons of shipping in the first three years of the war.*"

Commander Lionel Greenstreet, R.N.

CAMDEN SHIPBUILDING & MARINE RAILWAY Co

CAMDEN, MAINE

"Member of Maine Boat Builders and Repairers Association"

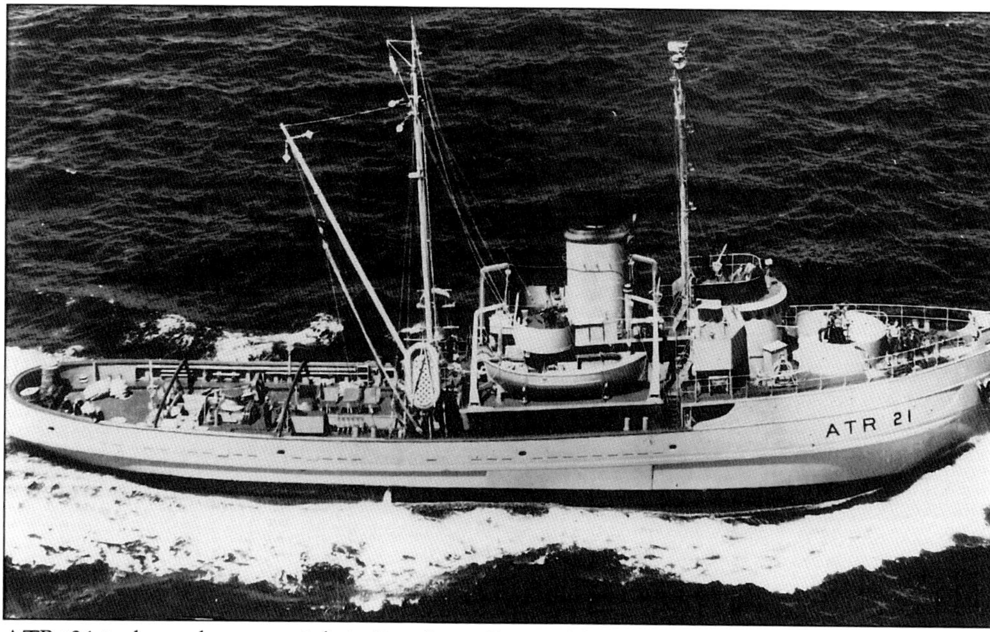

ATR#21 is shown here on trials in Penobscot Bay on May 20, 1944. This view is of the Rescue Tug broadside.

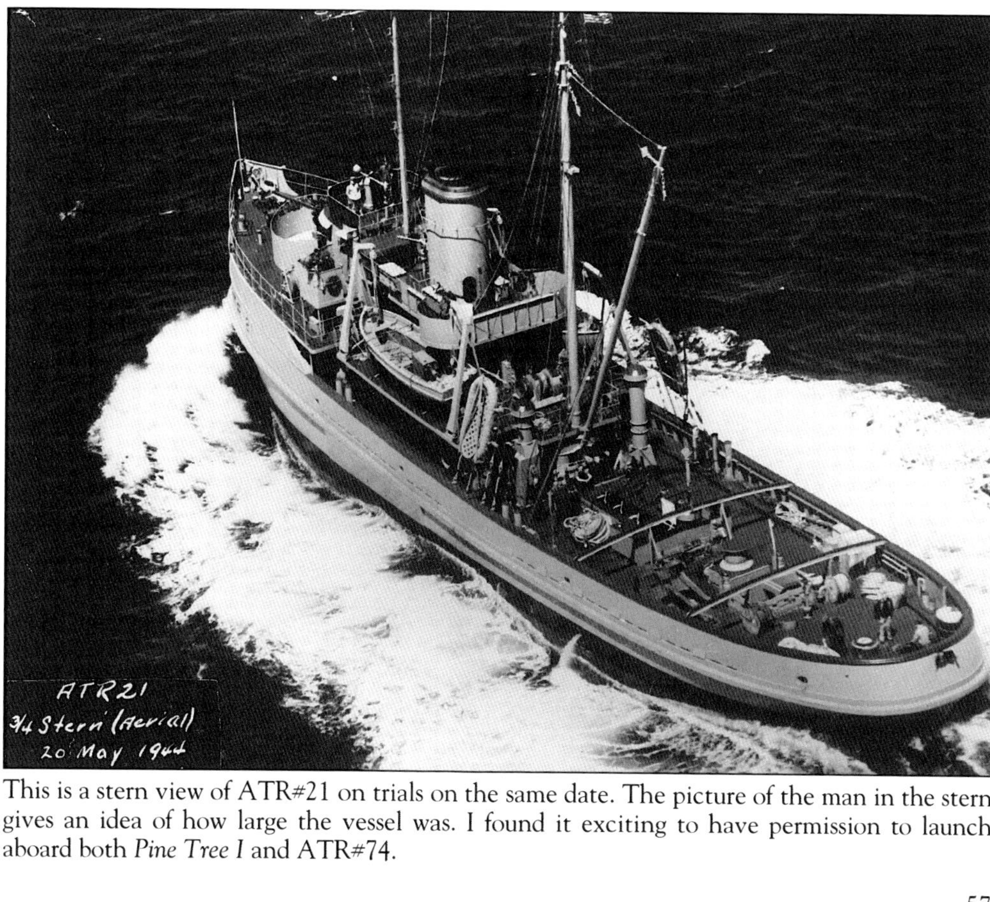

This is a stern view of ATR#21 on trials on the same date. The picture of the man in the stern gives an idea of how large the vessel was. I found it exciting to have permission to launch aboard both *Pine Tree I* and ATR#74.

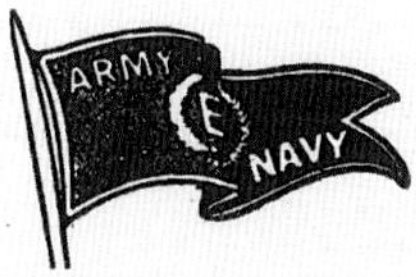

You are Cordially Invited to

Attend the Presentation

of

ARMY-NAVY "E" AWARD

to the Employees of the

Camden Shipbuilding
and Marine Railway Company
CAMDEN, MAINE

August 16, 1944 at 11:30 a. m.

An exciting occasion was when the 1,500 employees were awarded the Army-Navy E Award for excellence in production of war materials. One of the speakers was Rear Adm. W.T. Cluverius, who had been a naval cadet of the battleship *Maine* when she was sunk in Havana in 1898. He had also served on the second battleship *Maine*, and was a commanding officer in World War I. Each worker received the pin, and the yard was presented with a large "E Award" flag for its flagpole.

The program for August 14, 1944, tells all about the award ceremony. Advertisements were put in the local paper congratulating the shipyard and its workers. One advertisement was from a gift shop: "The Smiling Cow now laughs with glee, because the Shipyard got its 'E'." Another was from a local barbershop: "From these chairs we've clipped the locks And shaved the mugs of many; Due to our constant work We've earned a welcome penny. You've told us when the keels were laid, And just how Camden ships are made; So now we're happy as can be Because you got the Navy E."

PROGRAM *of* PRESENTATION

Posting of Colors
U. S. Naval Air Station
Color Guard

Introductory Remarks by Master of Ceremonies
H. S. BICKFORD
Personnel Director
Camden Shipbuilding & Marine Railway Co.

Presentation of Army-Navy "E" Award
REAR ADMIRAL W. T. CLUVERIUS
(USN Ret.)

Acceptance of Army-Navy "E" Award
O. W. MAYHEW
Purchasing Agent
Camden Shipbuilding & Marine Railway Co.

Raising of Army-Navy "E" Flag
U. S. Naval Air Station
Color Guard

Presentation of "E" Insignia
MAJOR GENERAL FULTON Q. C. GARDNER
Commanding General
Northeastern Sector
Eastern Defense Command

Acceptance of Insignia on Behalf of Employees
FRED WITHERSPOON

Final Remarks by Master of Ceremonies

(Bring this Program with You)

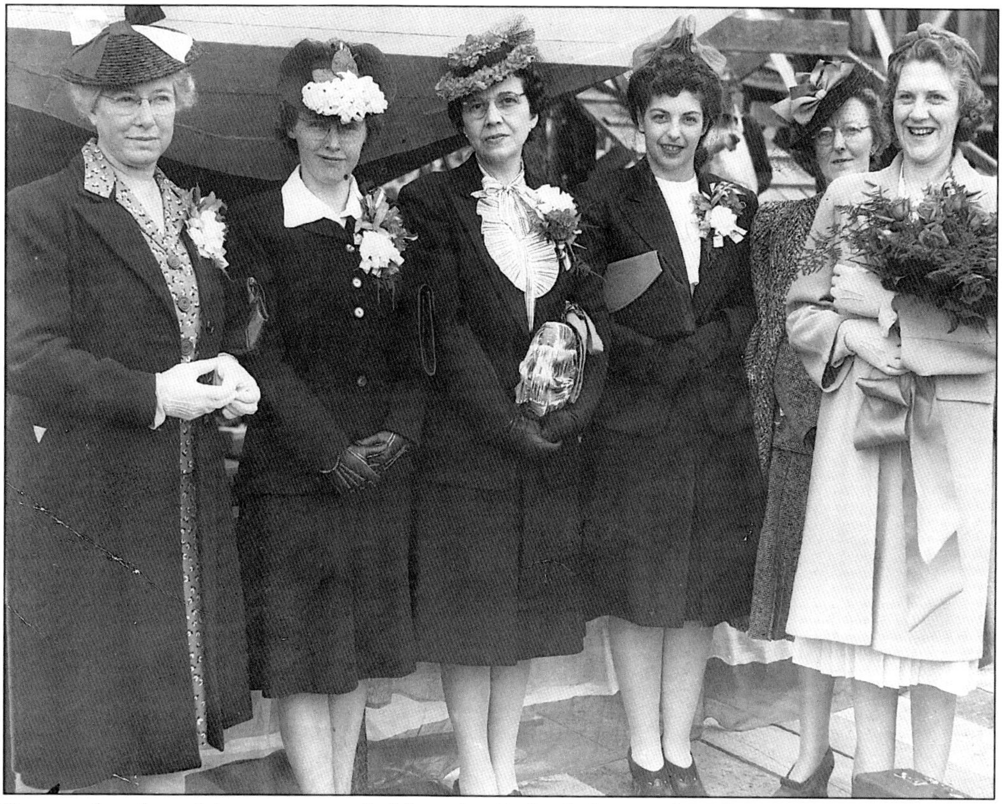

Yet another launching party was held, with all the ladies in their hats. Sometimes the yard worked seven days a week. No one was allowed vacations or allowed to travel, so the launching parties had to make up for it.

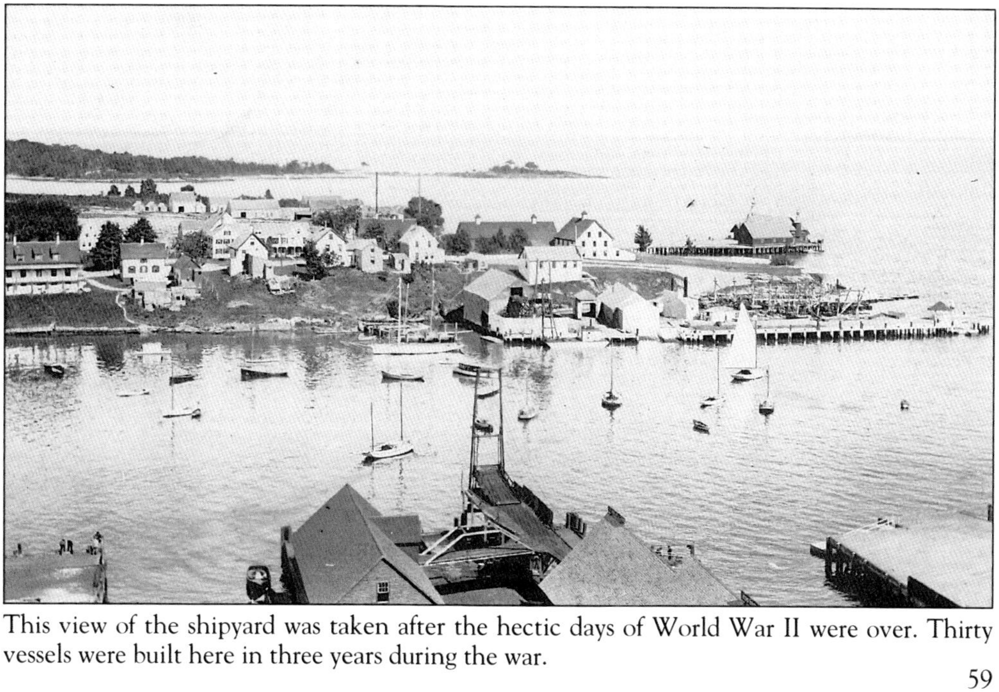

This view of the shipyard was taken after the hectic days of World War II were over. Thirty vessels were built here in three years during the war.

List Of Wooden Ships Built 1941-1945 At Camden Shipbuilding & Marine Railway Co.

Govt. #	Sponsor	Launch Date	Time	Delivery Date	Type of Boat
AMc82	Mrs. Lois Lyman	072641	1:30 p.m.	011242	Minesweeper
AMc83	Mrs. Helene Bok	092041	10:45 a.m.	022742	Minesweeper
CWW	Miss Beverly Manning	031742	–	04--42	Fisherman
APc15	Mrs. Marion Lunt	071842	2:00 p.m.	101742	Troop Transport
APc16	Mrs. Evelyn Stevens	072542	9:00 a.m.	011143	Troop Transport
APc17	Mrs. Helen Parker	080142	3:00 p.m.	010443	Troop Transport
APc18	Miss Hazel Witherspoon	080642	7:45 p.m.	012243	Troop Transport
APc58	Miss Ellen West Childs	101542	3:00 p.m.	050343	Troop Transport
APc59	Miss Barbara Pitman	111042	12:30 p.m.	041443	Troop Transport
APc60	Miss June O. Labbe	120742	10:33 a.m.	051743	Troop Transport
APc61	Mrs. Mary E. Galloupe	010943	1:45 p.m.	052443	Troop Transport
APc62	Mrs. Helen S. Price	020843	1:35 p.m.	062143	Troop Transport
MCc851	Mrs. Eleanor Roosevelt	020843	1:50 p.m.	050743	Coal Barge
MCc852	Mrs. Alice Farnsworth	040743	1:00 p.m.	072243	Coal Barge
APc64	Miss Evelyn L. Mayhew	050443	11:12 a.m.	072443	Troop Transport
APc63	Miss Mary C. O'Brien	050643	12:40 p.m.	070643	Troop Transport
MCc853	Rep. Margaret Chase Smith	060543	1:00 p.m.	083143	Coal Barge
MCc854	Mrs. Mary Louise Bok	070443	12:01 p.m.	091643	Coal Barge
ATR17	Mrs. Evelyn E. Rogers	071343	7:25 p.m.	122043	Rescue Salv. Tug
ATR18	Miss Constance Hitchcock	090143	12:09 p.m.	020244	Rescue Salv. Tug
ATR19	Mrs. Martha Wilson Dean	100143	12:14 p.m.	032044	Rescue Salv. Tug
ATR20	Miss Joy D. Creyk	101643	2:44 p.m.	042444	Rescue Salv. Tug
ATR21	Mrs. Florice Pitcher	122843	10:33 a.m.	052544	Rescue Salv. Tug
ATR22	Mrs. Irene McInnis	013044	3:00 p.m.	071044	Rescue Salv. Tug
ATR74	Miss Edna Fuller	032444	10:45 a.m.	081444	Rescue Salv. Tug
ATR75	Mrs. John Gammage	042444	12:16 p.m.	091144	Rescue Salv. Tug
ATR76	Mrs. Ora Brown	061544	6:46 p.m.	101044	Rescue Salv. Tug
ATR77	Mrs. Allen Payson	080144	8:32 p.m.	110344	Rescue Salv. Tug
ATR79	Mrs. Mary Lyman	090844	3:30 p.m.	120944	Rescue Salv. Tug
ATR78	Mrs. John Willey	103044	9:40 a.m.	010645	Rescue Salv. Tug

Five

CAMDEN SHIPBUILDING COMPANY

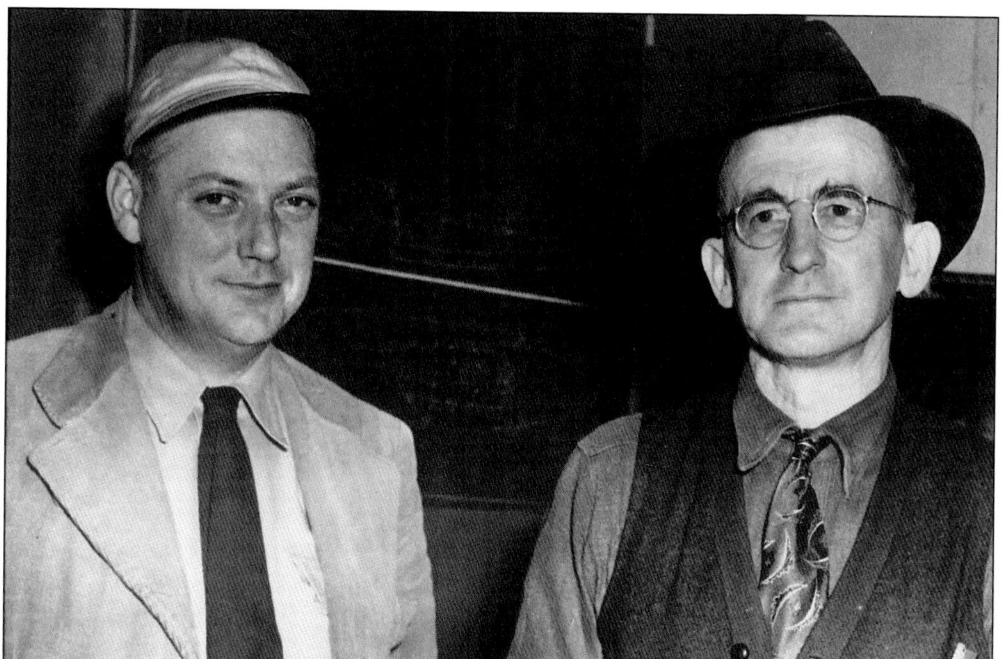

Pictured here are the president of the Camden Shipbuilding Co., Captain William E. Peterson, and master-builder Malcolm H. Brewer. Captain "Pete" first came to Camden to be commander of APc#15 during World War II. He came back after the war to form a partnership with Cary Bok to build yachts. Malcolm was one of the best master-builders around, and had worked in the yard during World War II. Everyone had great respect for him, for both his building and his integrity. He was a quiet man, but when he spoke the workmen listened carefully. We remained friends until the day he died, in the Camden Health Care Center many years later.

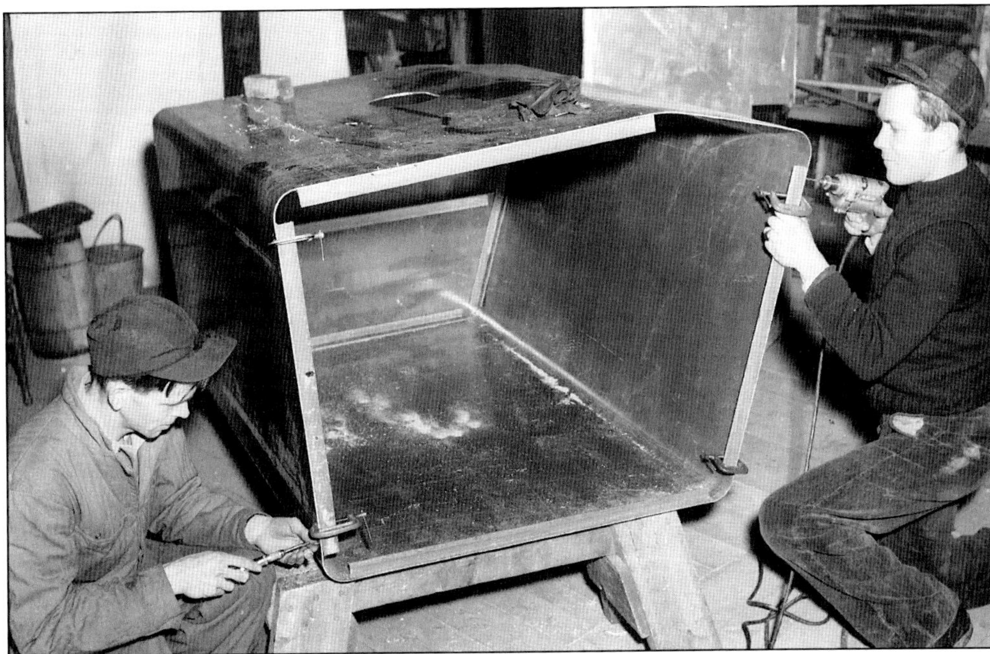

The new yard thought they could build aluminum boats for the public, but the workmen could not get over their love for wooden ones. Pictured here are Jay Hanna and William Goldsmith, who were foremen of the aluminum boat-building department. George Michelson did all the welding work in the shop. Jay Hanna was a noted model maker. They were all talented, but aluminum boats could not be loved in a yard that had always built wooden ones.

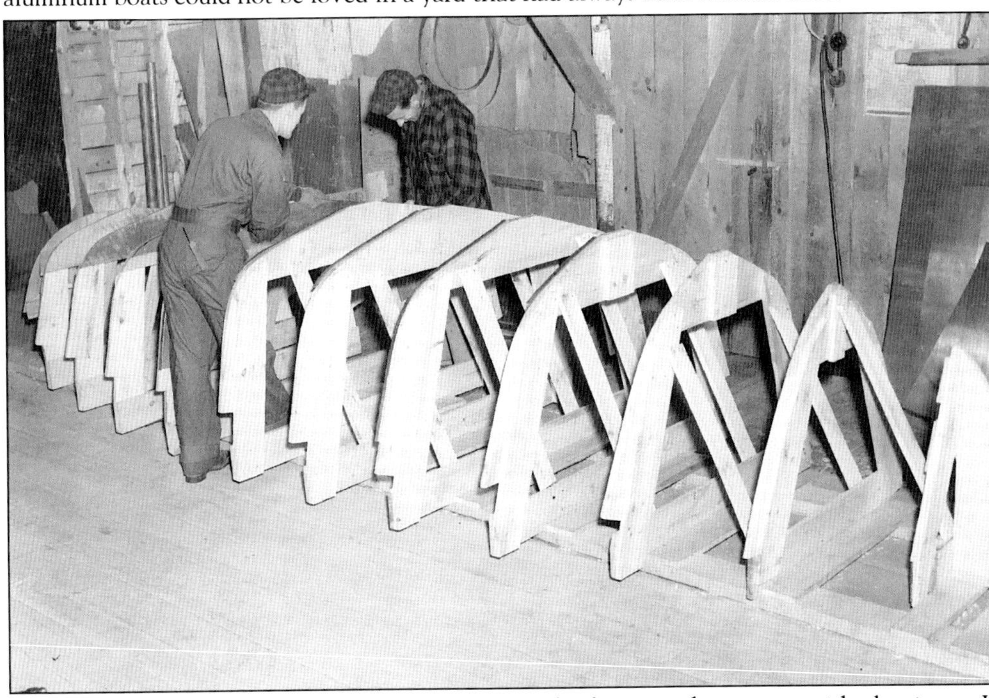

Two of the young workmen are shown here getting the frame ready to cover with aluminum. It had to be done in various stages.

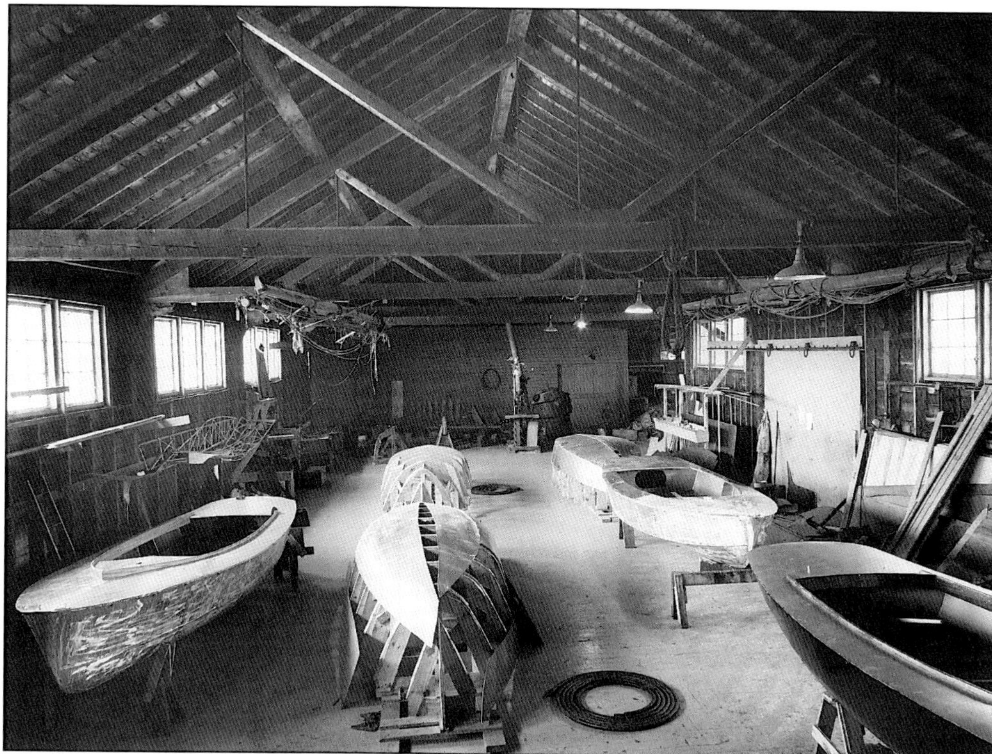

This is the building where the aluminum boats were built. There are several boats shown in the image, all in various stages of completion from beginning to end. The barrel stove in the rear of the building kept it warm enough for the men to work.

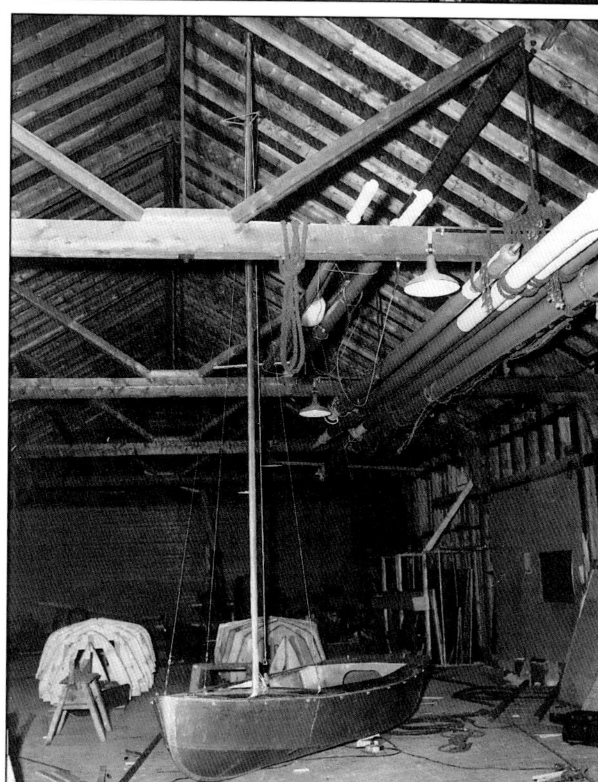

This aluminum boat is nearing completion, and its mast has been placed in it. The two boats in the background are in the beginning stages. Later the yard went back to building wooden boats. The men claimed that aluminum did not last in salt water.

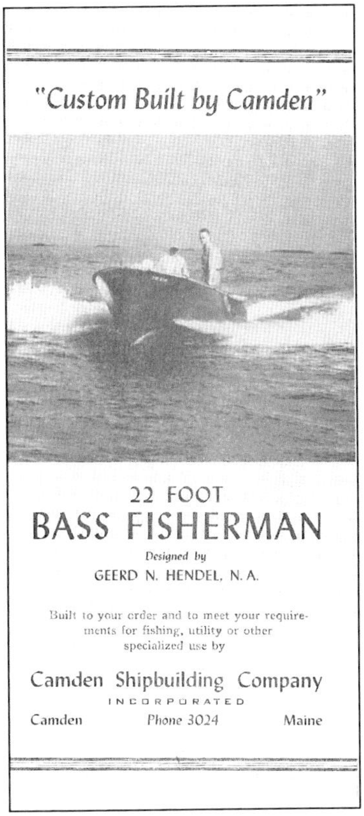

Next the yard built "Bass Fisherman" boats to individual specifications. The keel, backbone, and frames were of selected oak, but the planking was of white cedar. They were all Everdur screw fastened, and were furnished with lights, horns, an anchor, life jackets, and fenders. They could be with or without a cabin. The standard one was delivered with a Chrysler Crown engine, for $3,675.

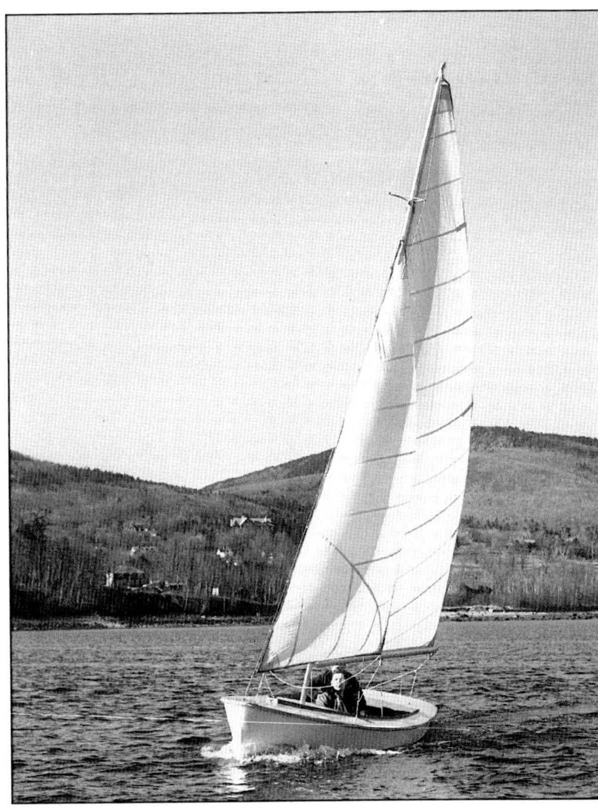

Pictured here is an 18-foot keel sloop, the first of this type built here. Under sail it made a nice small boat for one to use in the harbor or lakes.

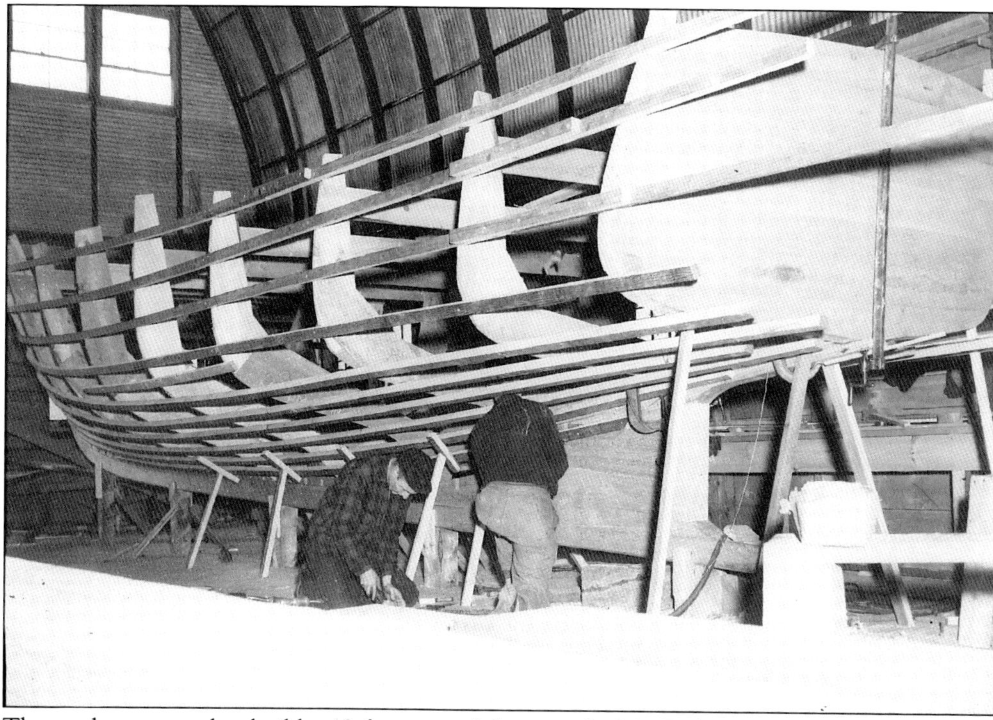

The yard contracted to build a 40-foot sport fisherman for Mr. Earl Boardman. It is shown here in progress, decorated with hammers and "C" clamps. The ribs are in place. The picture was taken in the Quonset hut where it was built.

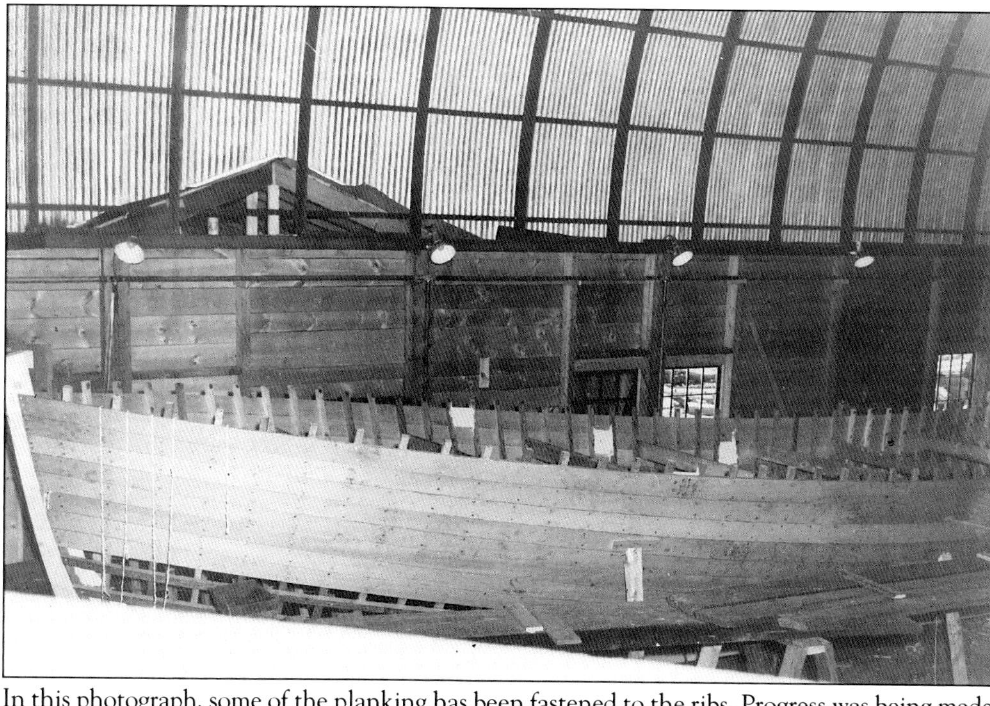

In this photograph, some of the planking has been fastened to the ribs. Progress was being made and the sport fisherman was beginning to take shape.

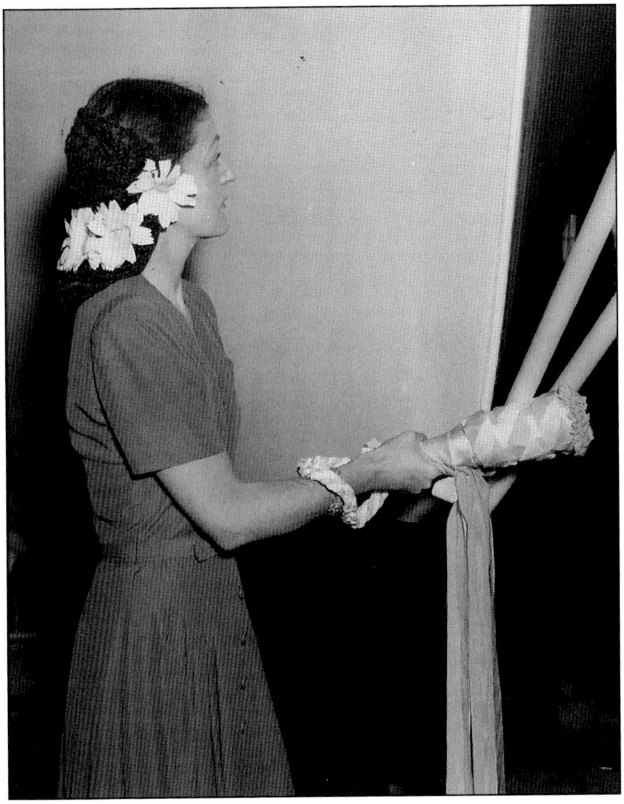

Mr. Boardman's boat, the *Andrea B*, was now ready to be launched. Grace Peterson, wife of the yard president, is shown taking aim to hit the bottle over the bow. As the bottle broke the *Andrea B* was officially christened.

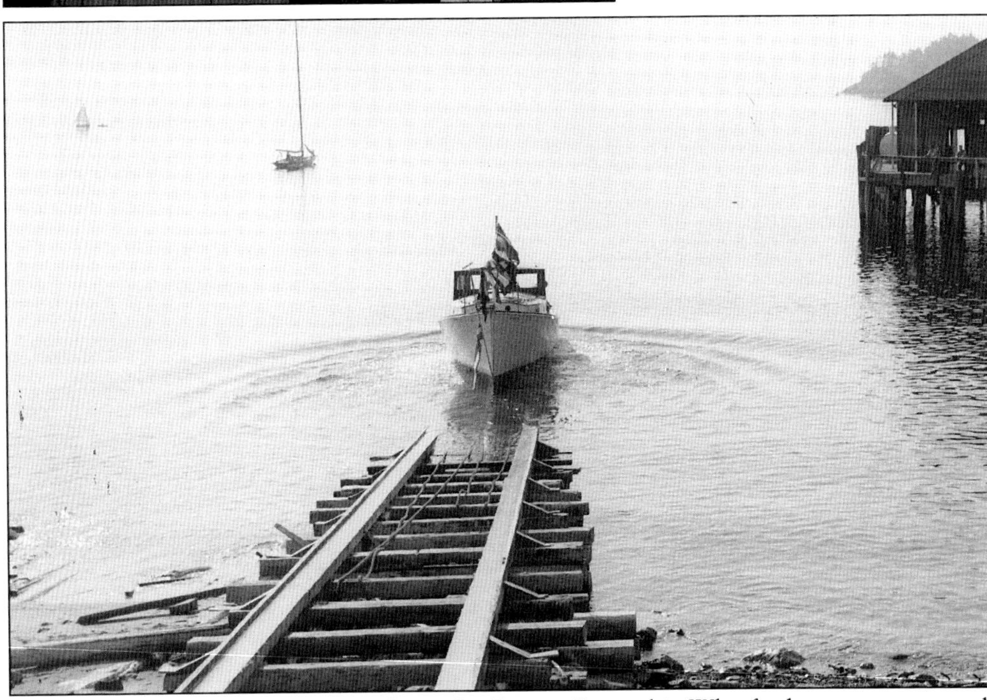

The *Andrea B* slid down the ways and past the Eastern Steamship Wharf, where so many vessels had gone before her. The launching date was in August of 1946.

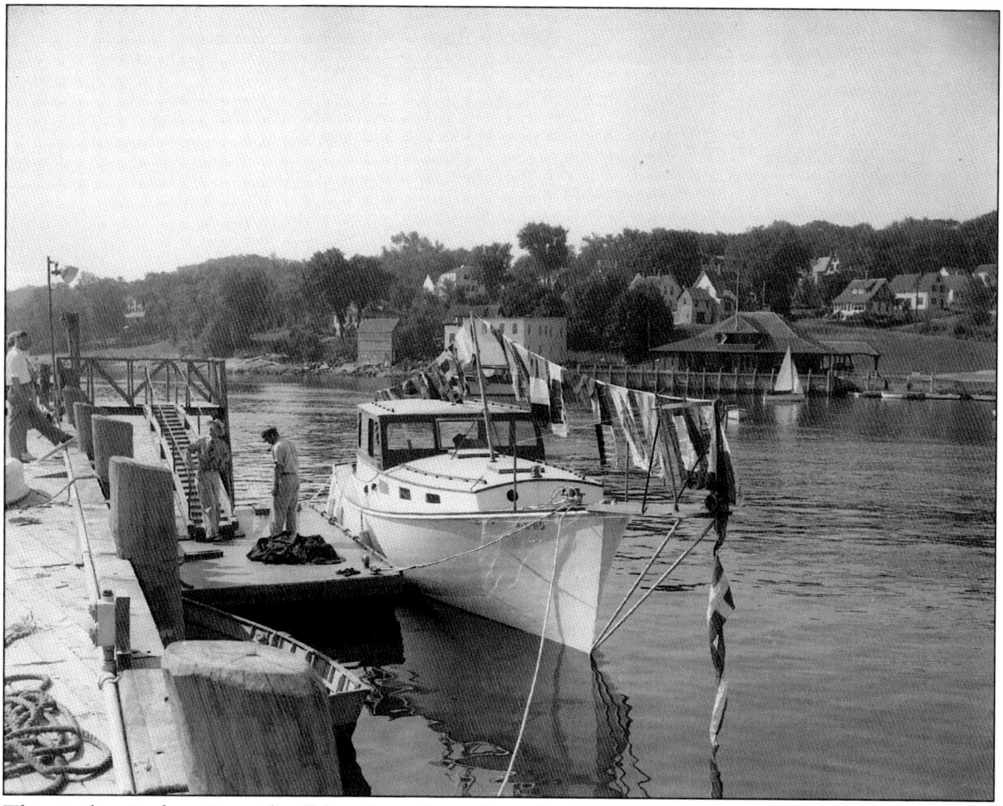

This is the *Andrea B*, with all her launching flags, being towed to the outfitting dock for final touches. It was exciting to see the first custom-built yacht launched by the new company in the post-war era.

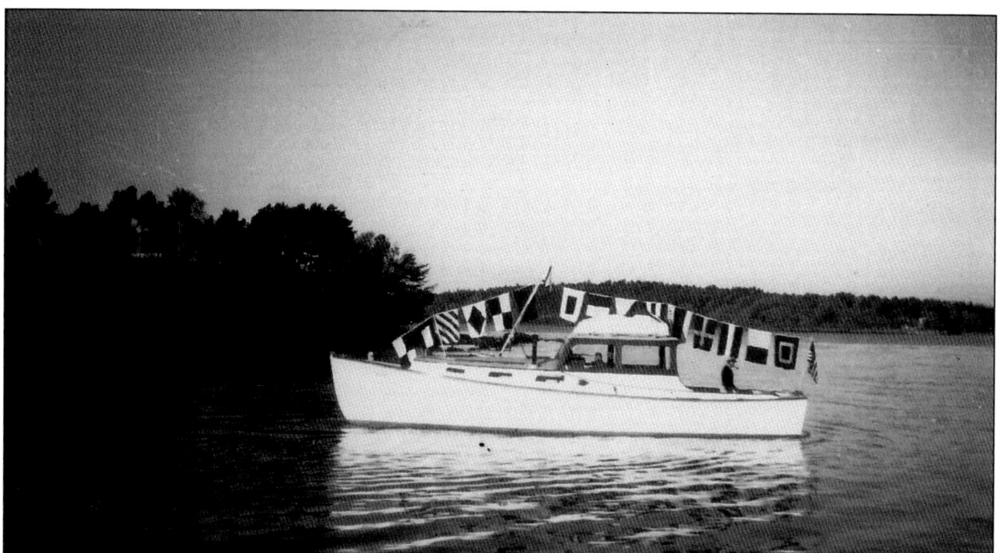

The next boat launched was the *Marbaru*, built for Clinton Lunt. The name was chosen from combination of letters from his wife's and daughters' names. It, too, was a 40-foot sport fisherman, and was launched in October of 1946.

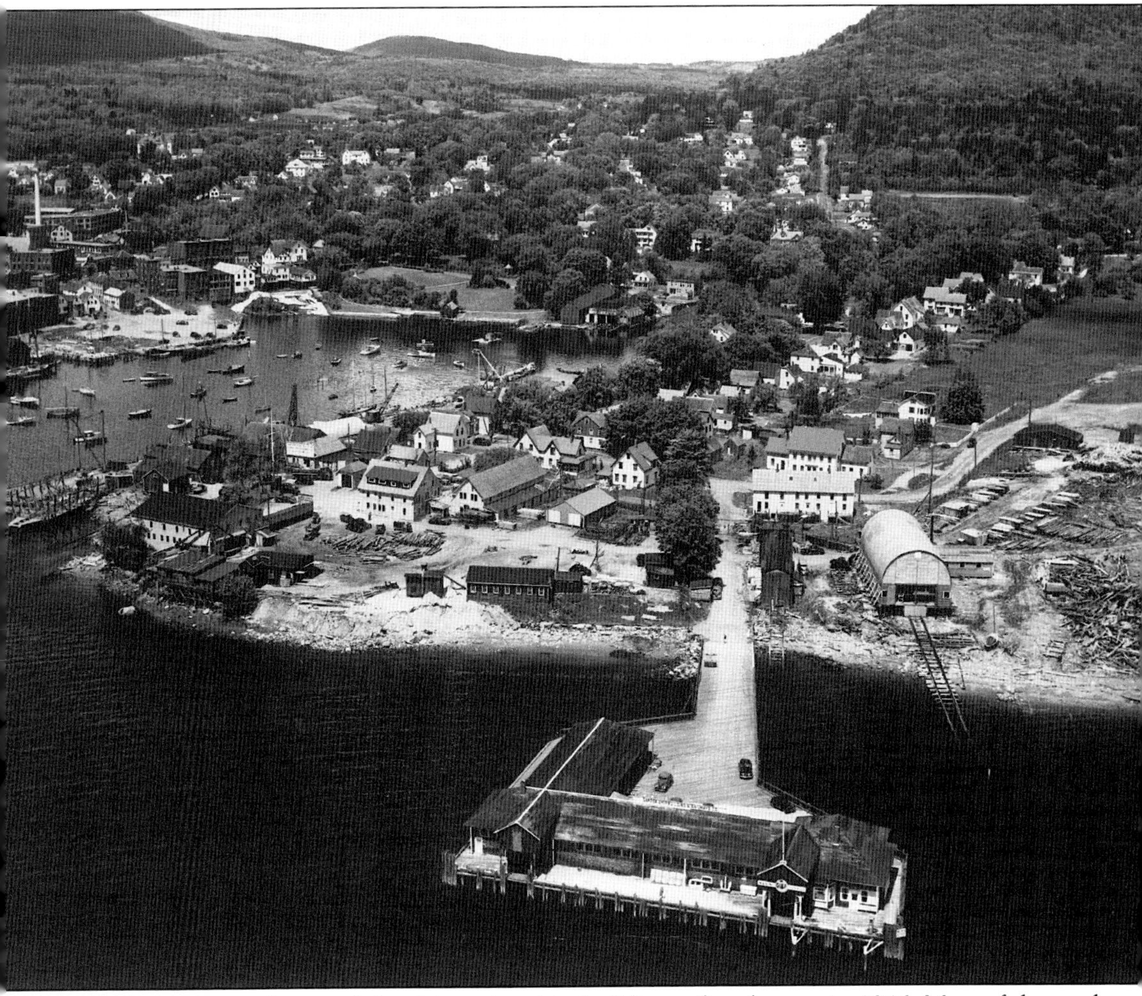

This is an aerial view of the shipyard and its buildings after the war in 1946. Most of the yard buildings are now gone. Many of them were burned by fires of unknown origin. The Eastern Steamship Wharf began to show deterioration, but lasted another 13 years.

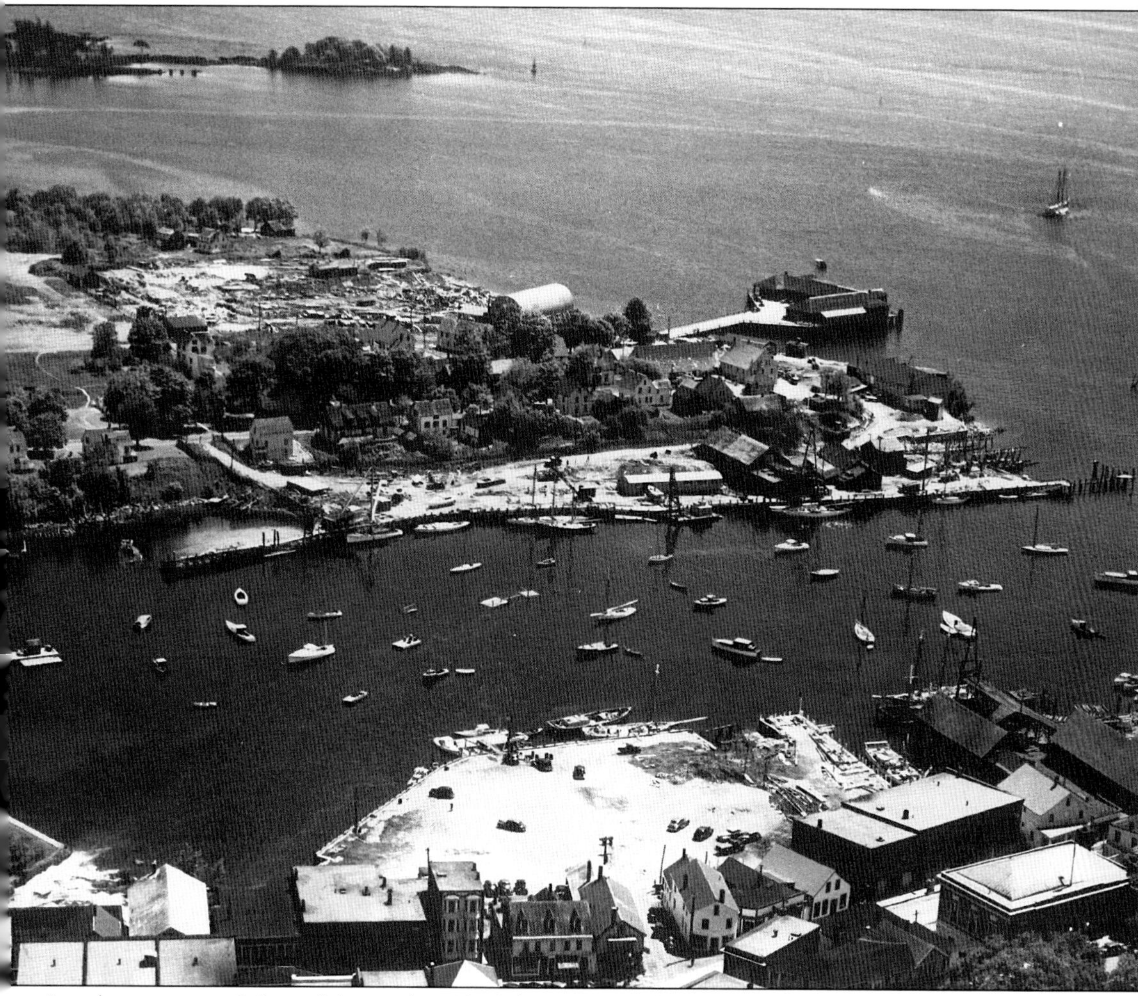

Another nice aerial shot of the yard in 1946 shows a view from the inner harbor. It brings back memories to see the way that everything looked 50 years ago. The old buildings have gone and new ones have replaced them, both bigger and better.

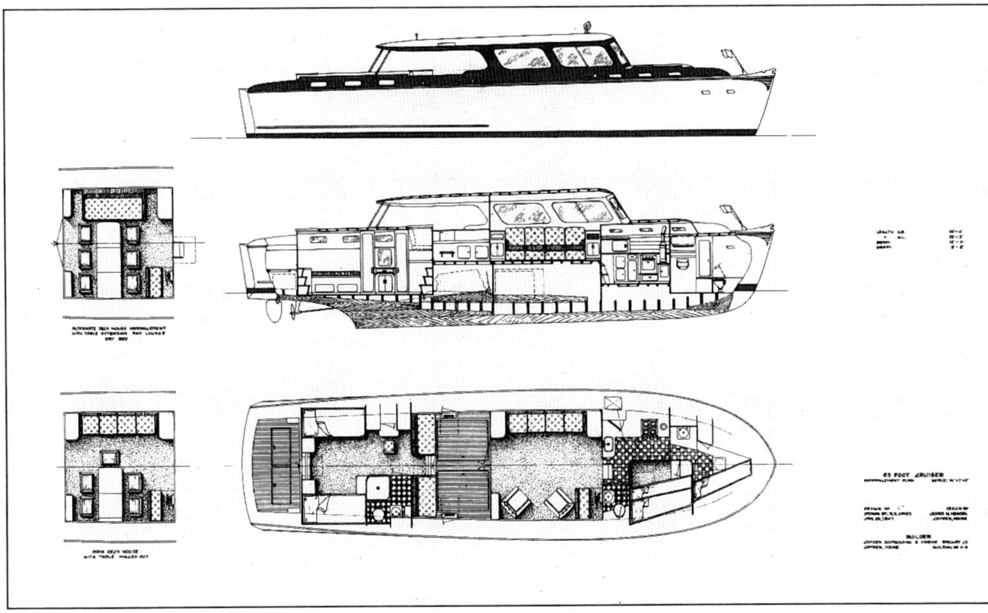

A 55-foot cruiser was built for Cary W. Bok. The interesting arrangement plan shows how she would look, inside and out, when completed. Mr Bok named his cruiser the *Northern Cross*.

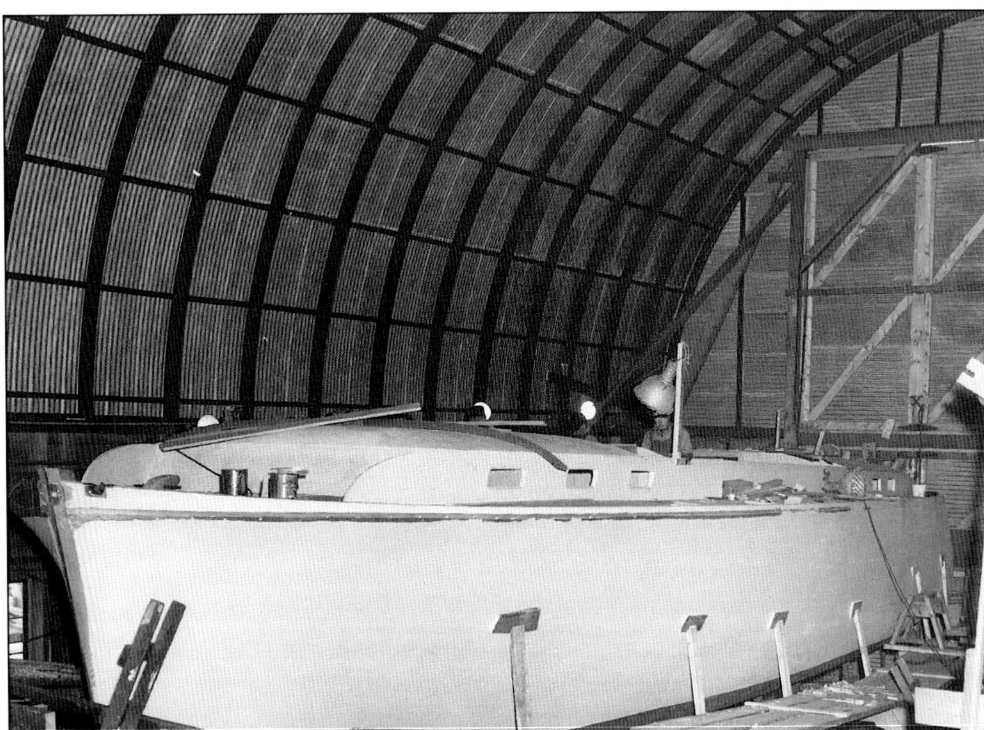

The *Northern Cross* is shown here under construction. One could never imagine all the detail work that went into a yacht like this, unless they followed its building from laying the keel until it was launched. The *Northern Cross* was launched on June 27, 1947.

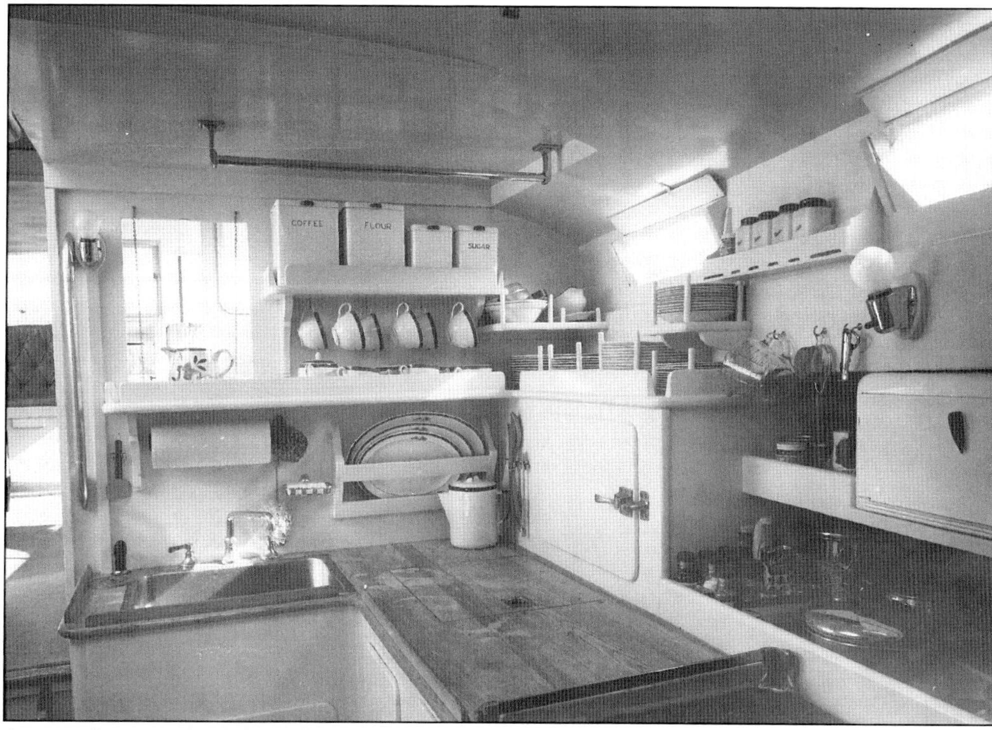

A nice photograph of the galley in the *Northern Cross* shows everything in place. It took a great deal of planning to fit things in small spaces. Also, care had to be provided so that nothing could fall off the shelves, when the sea was rough. It was much more difficult, in every way, to build a yacht than a house. Spaces were much more compact.

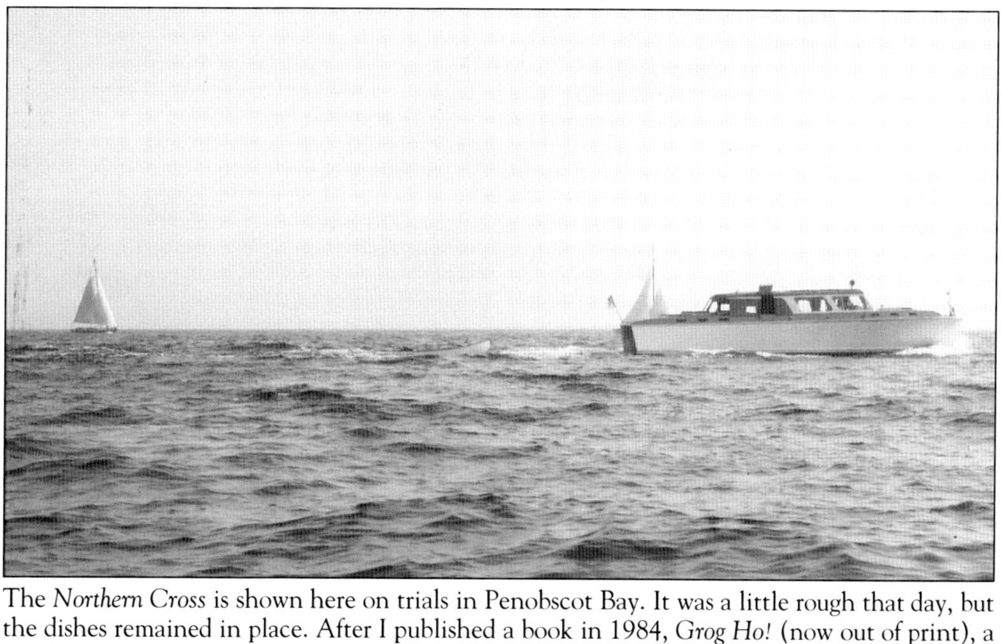

The *Northern Cross* is shown here on trials in Penobscot Bay. It was a little rough that day, but the dishes remained in place. After I published a book in 1984, *Grog Ho!* (now out of print), a gentlemen wrote to me sending a picture of the yacht at that time. It was in hard shape and he planned to restore it and make it his home. Did it happen? I never heard from him again.

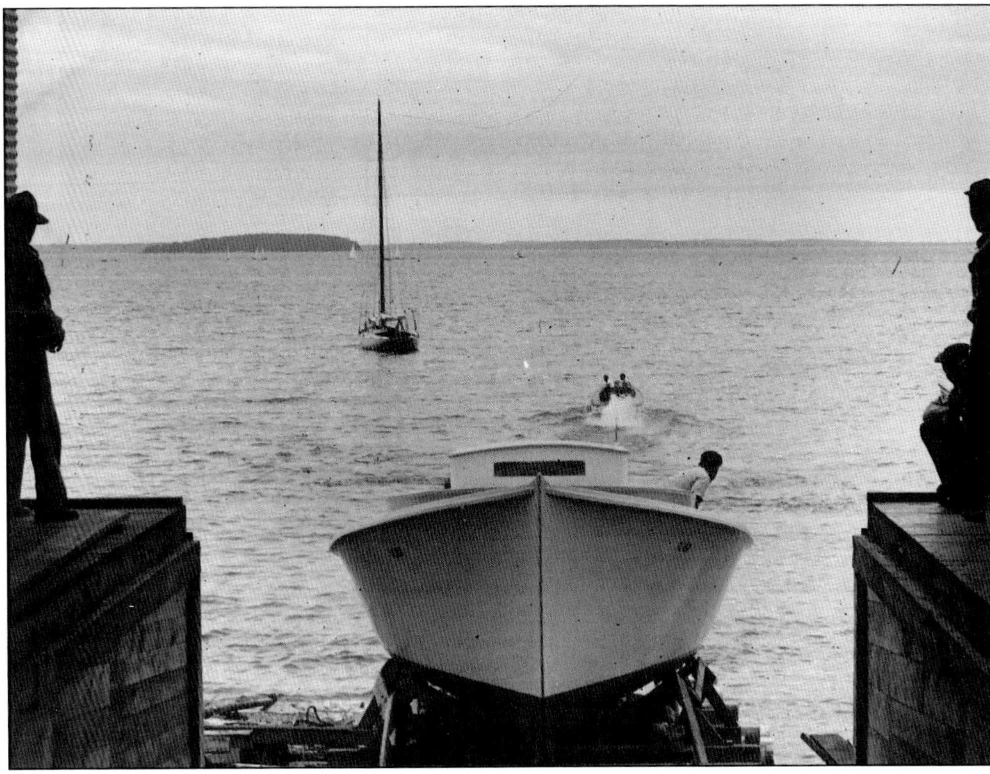

A 13-foot lobster boat was built for Mr. Bradbury Young. She had to be sturdy and very seaworthy in order to haul lobster traps in any weather. She was also launched in 1947 and put to good use out on the island where Mr. Young lived.

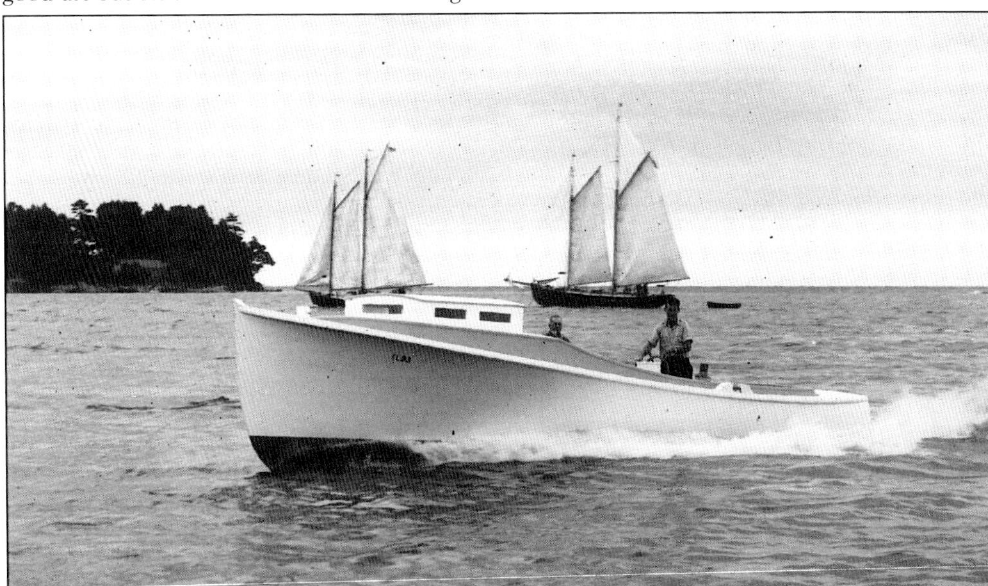

Mr. Young called his fishing boat the *Madelyn E*. She is shown here on trials in the bay. It looks as if they opened the engine to see how fast she would travel. Two two-masters are in the background watching the new fishing boat perform.

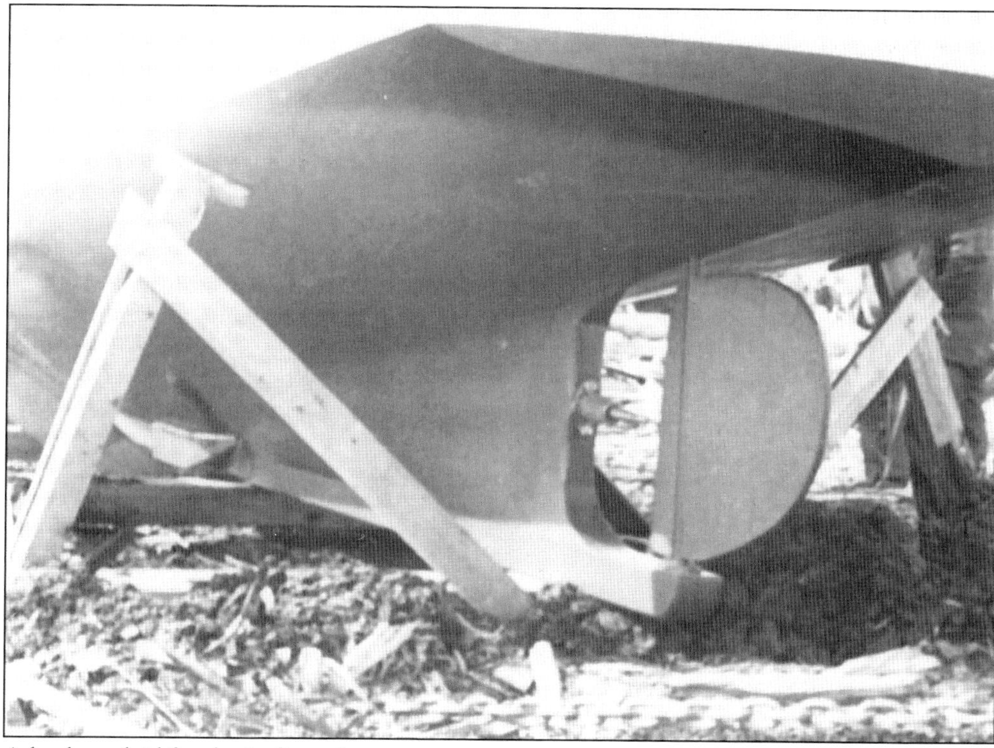

A keel was laid for the *Lydia and Dick II*. It was a contract for a 32-foot lobster boat for Harold Ames. He also wanted it for his working boat.

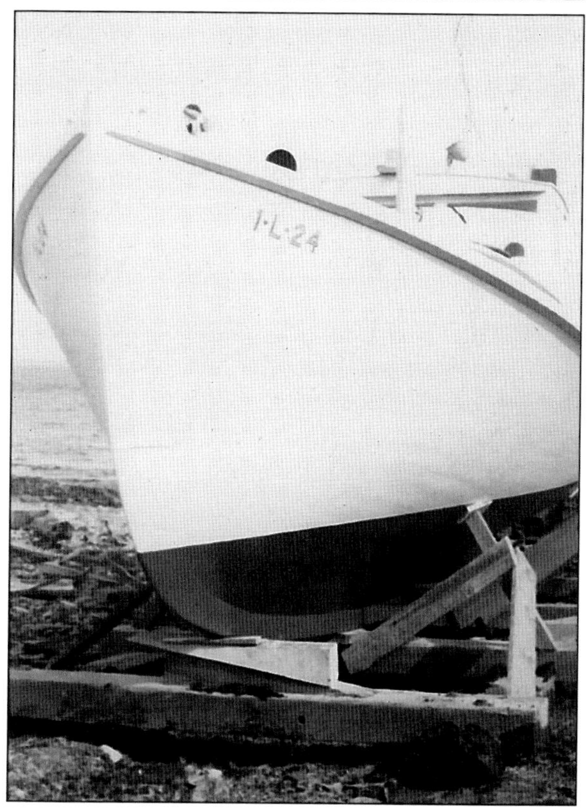

This picture shows the bow of the boat while under construction. The owners of these boats visited very frequently to watch the progress of the boat that they would depend on to make a living. Their lives were also dependent on a sea-worthy boat.

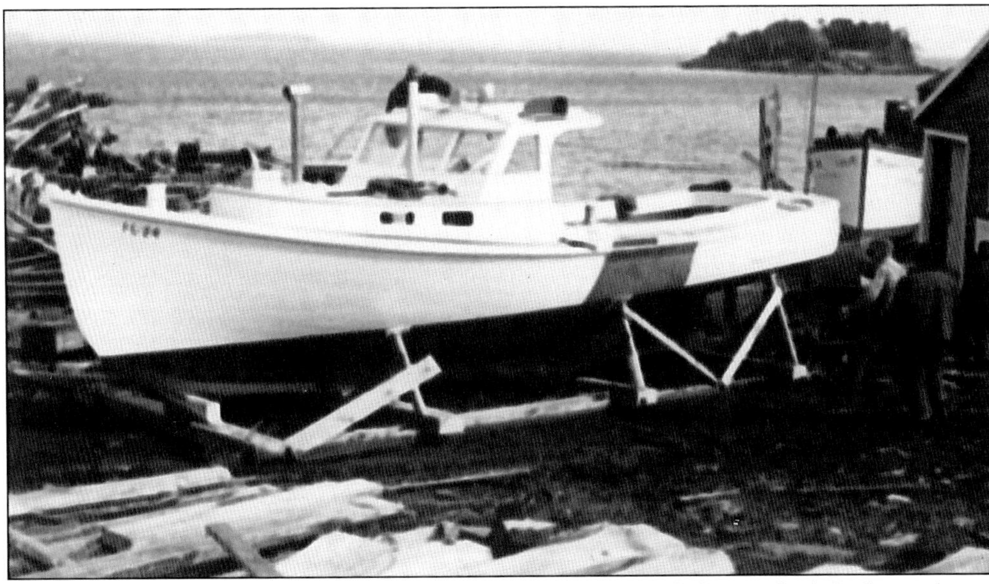

This is another view of the *Lydia and Dick II*. It shows the whole boat, which had its cabin in place.

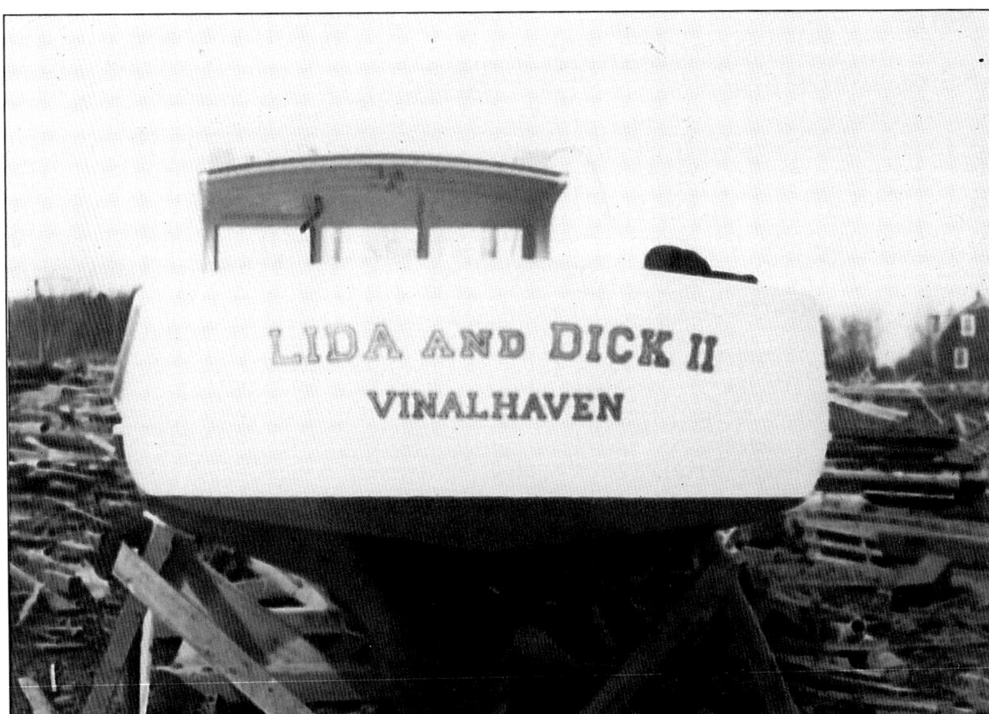

The stern of *Lydia and Dick II* plainly shows her name. She was in the cradle that would launch her.

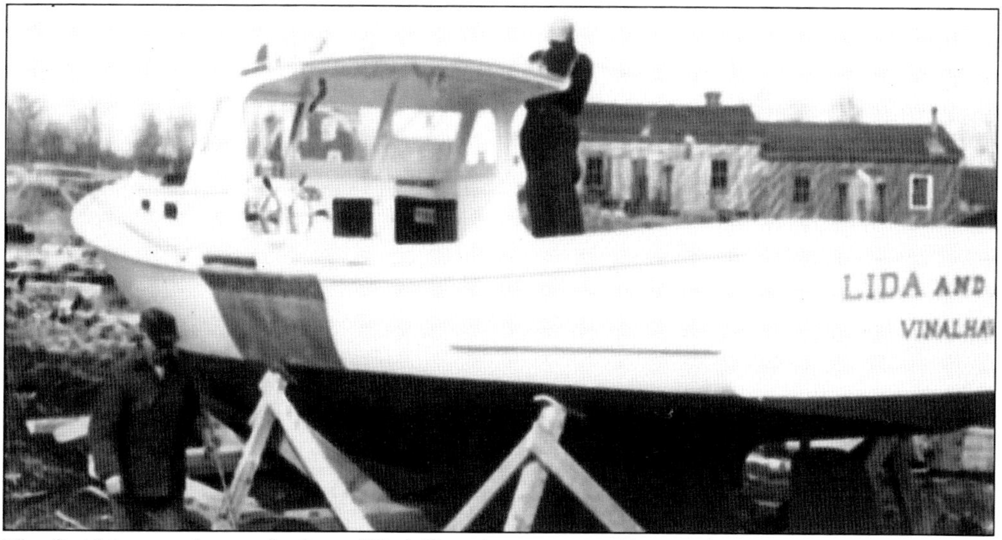

The finishing touches on *Lydia and Dick II* are being made. She was launched on April 20, 1948. She was an excellent workboat for her owner and served as such for many years.

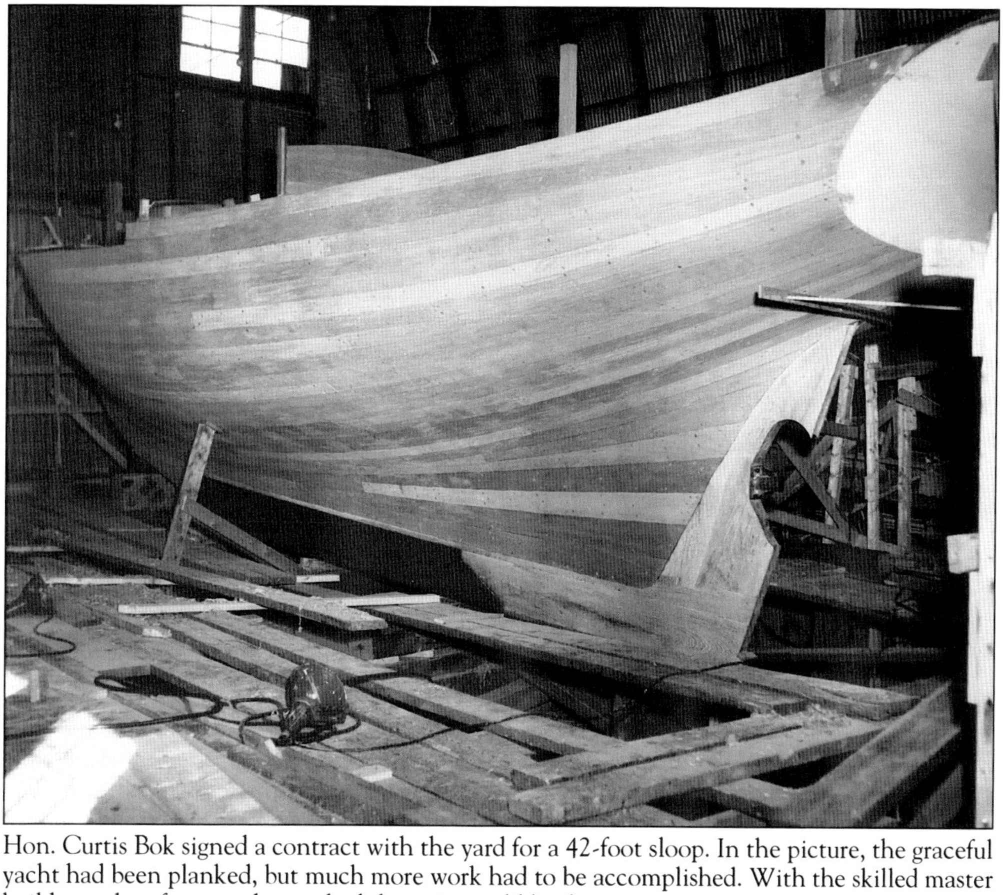

Hon. Curtis Bok signed a contract with the yard for a 42-foot sloop. In the picture, the graceful yacht had been planked, but much more work had to be accomplished. With the skilled master builder and craftsmen who worked there, it would be done.

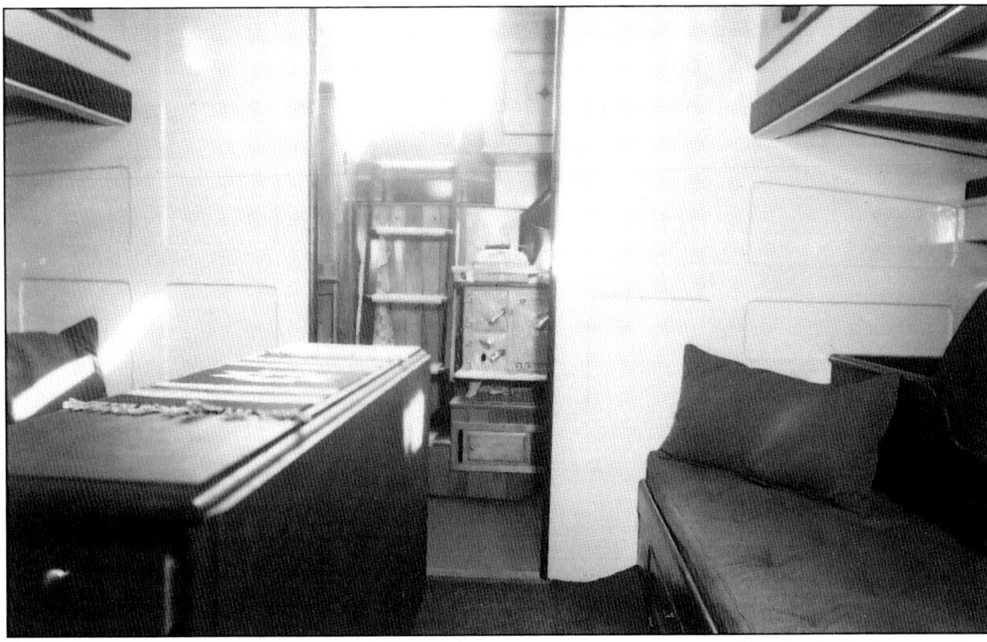

The interior of the yacht *Alphard* is shown here upon its completion. She had all the comforts of a large yacht. The *Alphard* was going to be sailed frequently by the judge. He had great plans for her, and did enjoy his sloop.

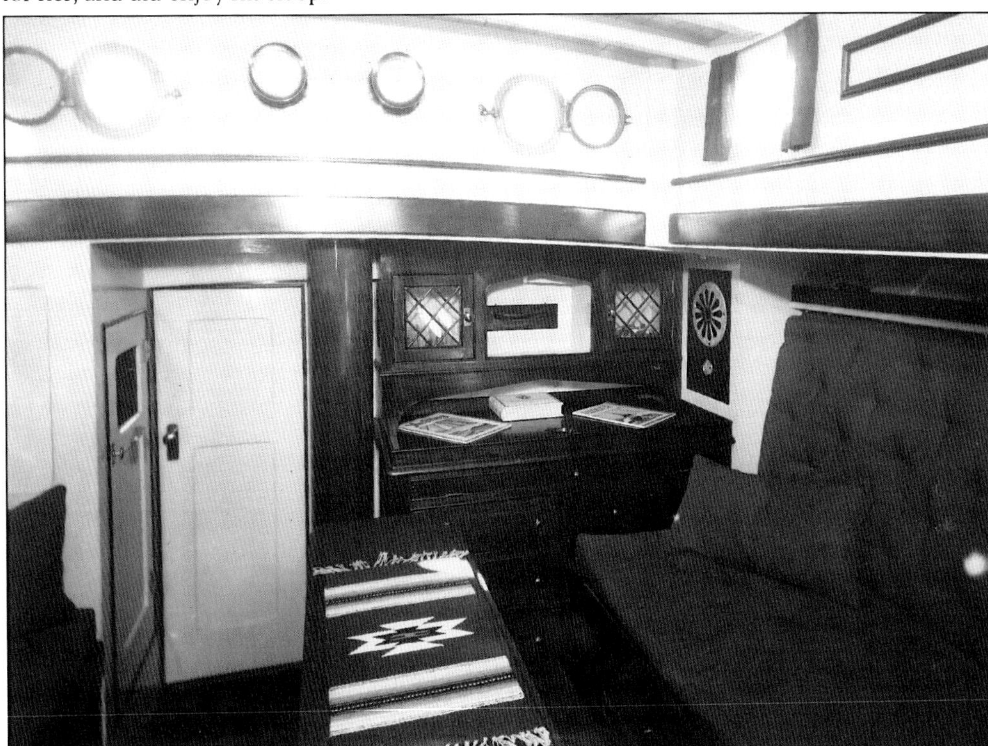

Another photograph shows the interior of the *Alphard* from a different angle. It was a nicely decorated lounge for reading, writing, eating, resting, or whatever.

The *Alphard* is shown here completed. The launching flags are in place, and Mrs. Curtis Bok, wife of the owner, christened it on May 29, 1948. It was an exciting day for the owner, his friends, and the workmen who built the lovely sloop.

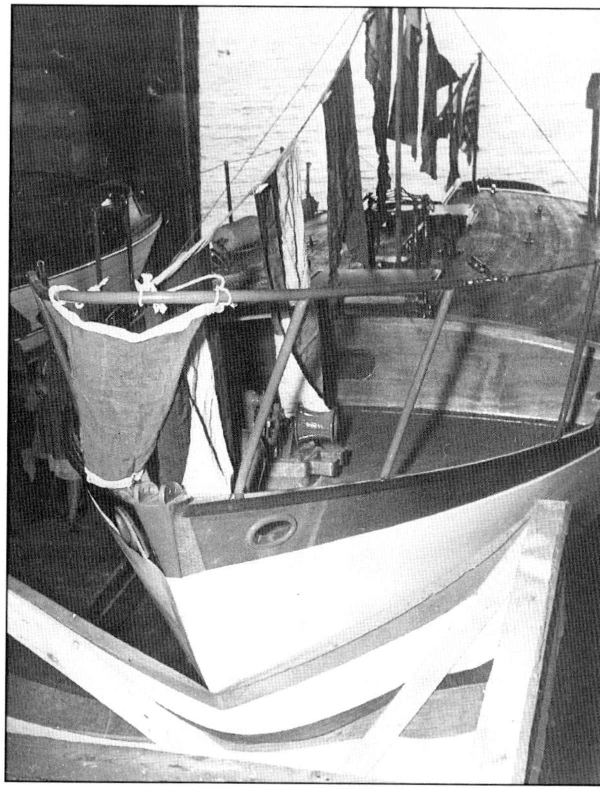

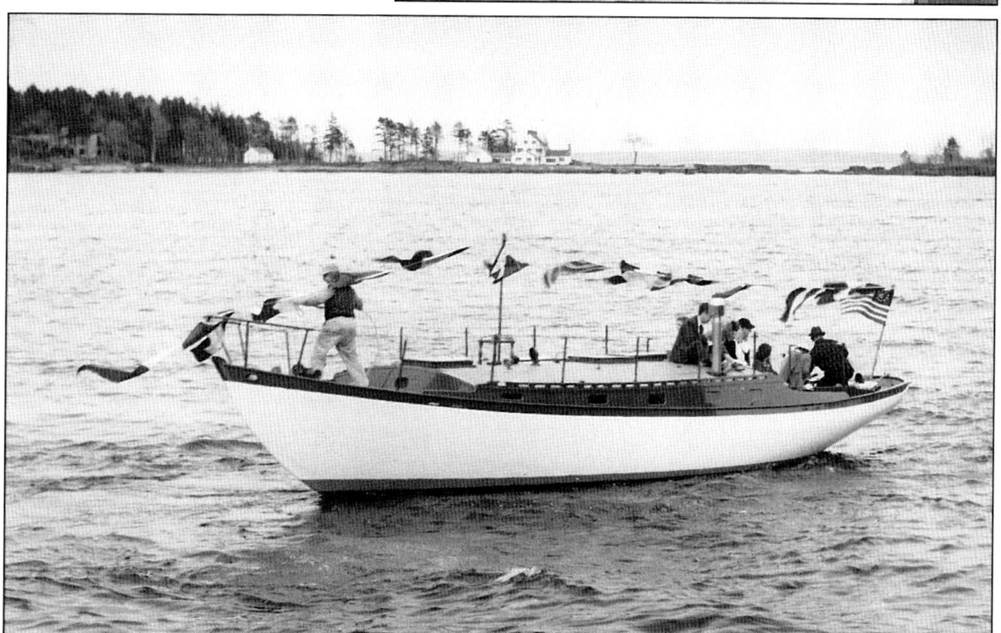

The *Alphard* is in the water, but the mast was not stepped. That would be the next thing to be done, after she was docked. It would take one of the derricks and several of the workmen to put the mast in place. Some sailing yachts have a coin placed under the mast, before it is put in place.

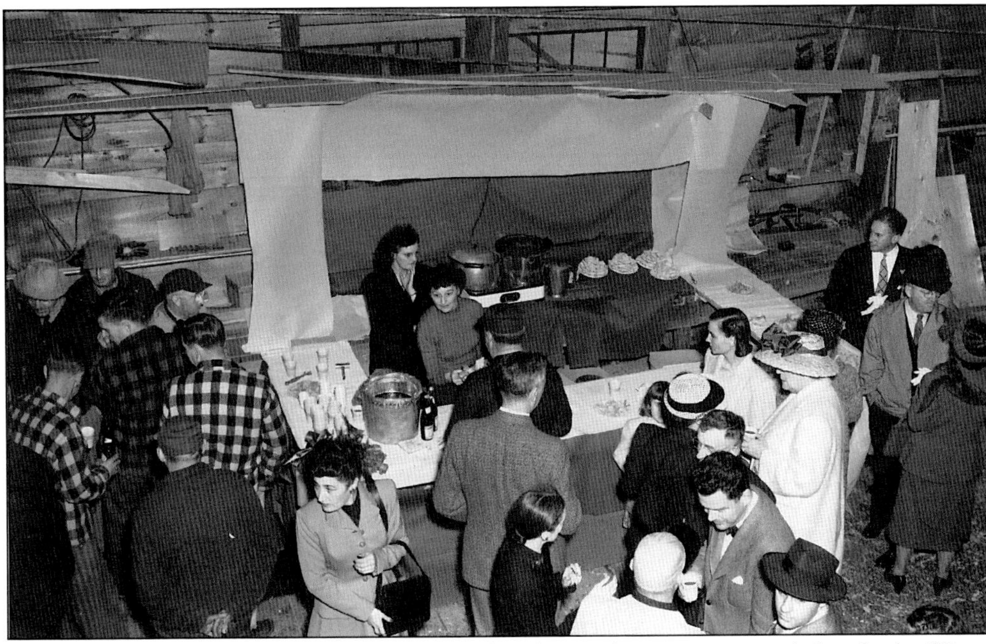

A launching party was held by the owner for the workmen, in one of the sheds. "Spot" Wadsworth, a well-known Camden caterer, was hired for the party. George H. Thomas, a much-loved Camden businessman and longtime friend of Curtis Bok, is to the right with his felt hat. Richard Lyman's mother is in the straw hat, with Richard's pretty wife beside her. Clinton Lunt is wearing the felt hat in the right foreground. Richard Lyman is talking to William and Grace Peterson.

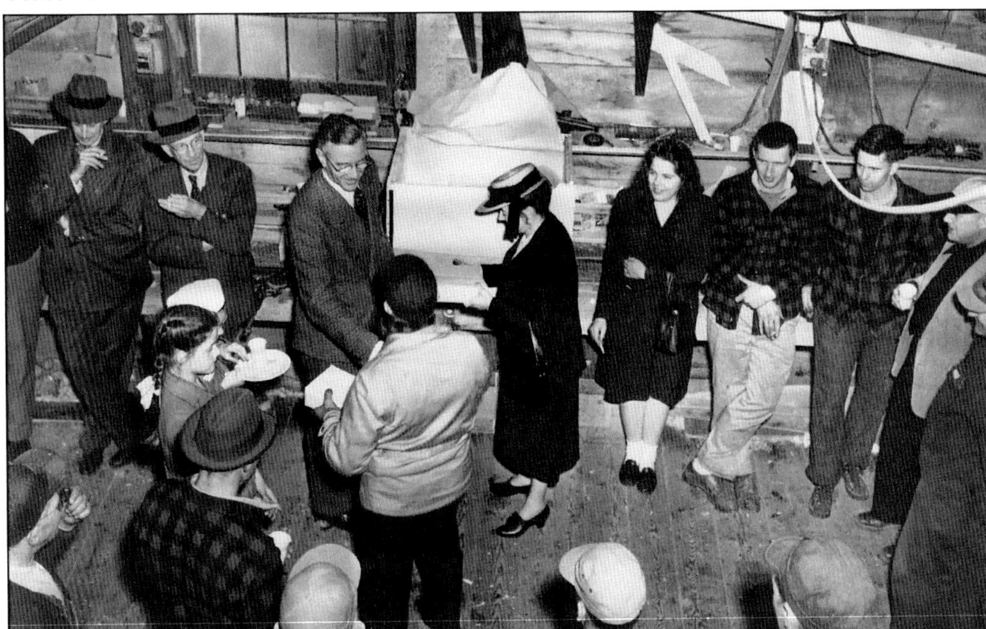

Judge Curtis Bok and his wife, Nellie Lee, shake the hands of the employees who worked on the *Alphard*. Behind Nellie Lee are Catherine and Bill Karl, painter, as well as Robert Jones. Behind Curtis Bok was "Pete" Mayhew, purchasing agent, and Guy Benner, accountant.

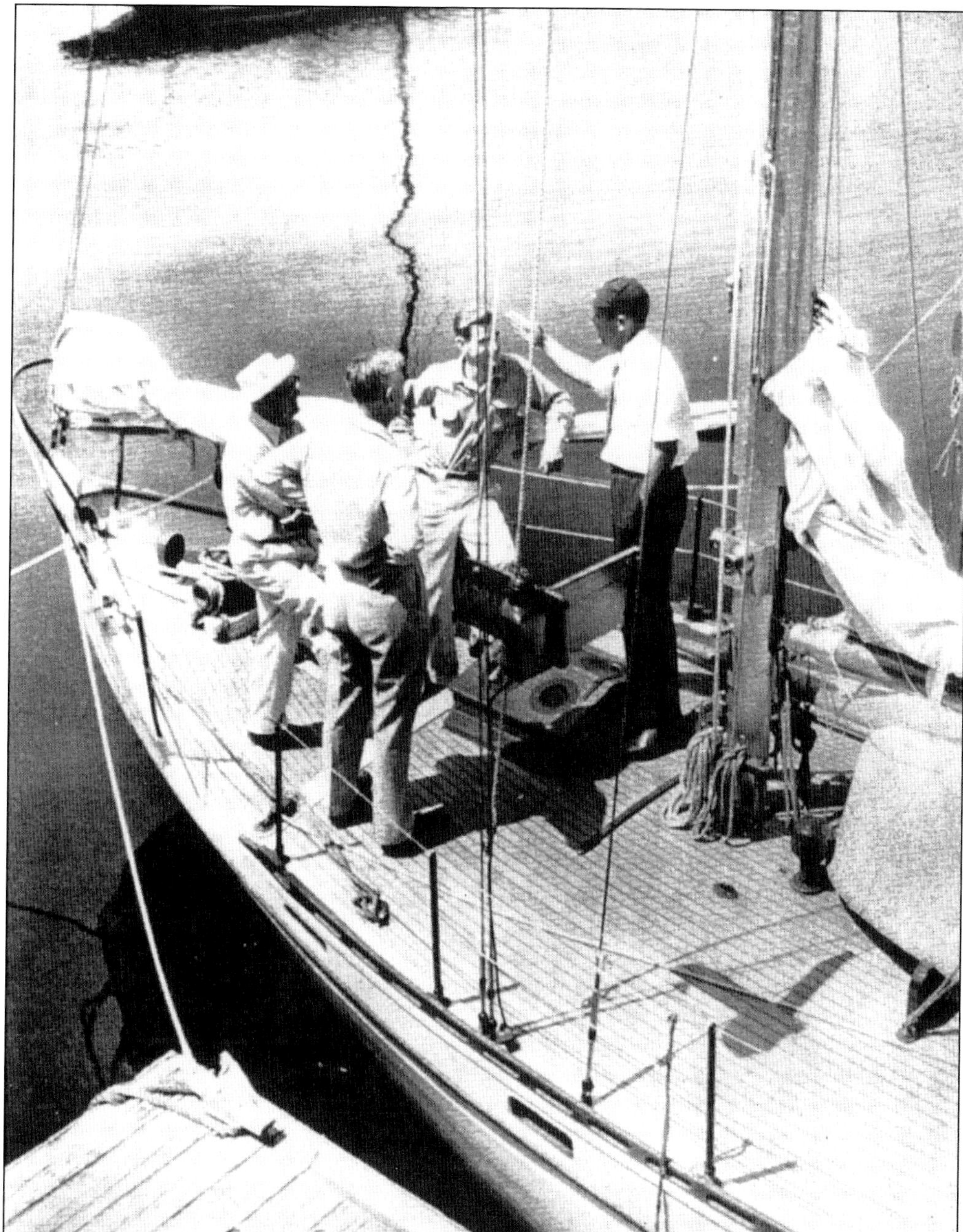

Judge Bok decided to sail the *Alphard* to Plymouth, England. It was a six-week voyage with his crew of four. The crew were his son Ben, of California; Dr. Morton Kravitz of Pennsylvania; Norris Hoyt of Rhode Island; and Frank Crowley of Massachusetts. A cocktail party was held in the lounge at Camden Shipbuilding to wish them a "Bon Voyage." The picture shows them on their way. The first leg of the trip took them to Halifax, Nova Scotia, then St. John's, Newfoundland, and on to 2,000 miles of open water to Plymouth, England. The dream was accomplished.

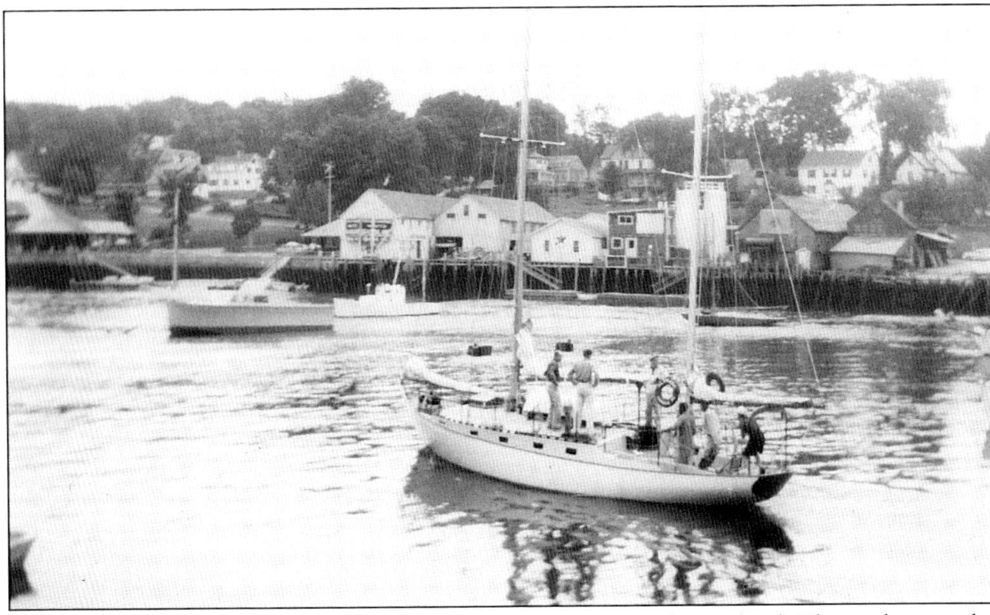

The *Alphard* sails out of Camden harbor on its way to Plymouth, England. The yacht was also in a race to Spain in 1957. It was an extremely rough trip and *Alphard* was demasted in a storm. For several days it was believed that all hands aboard were lost, but good news came that they were safe. The Judge was appointed as a Pennsylvania Supreme Court Justice in 1958. After his death in 1964, the vessel was purchased by a good friend, Carol Wetzel.

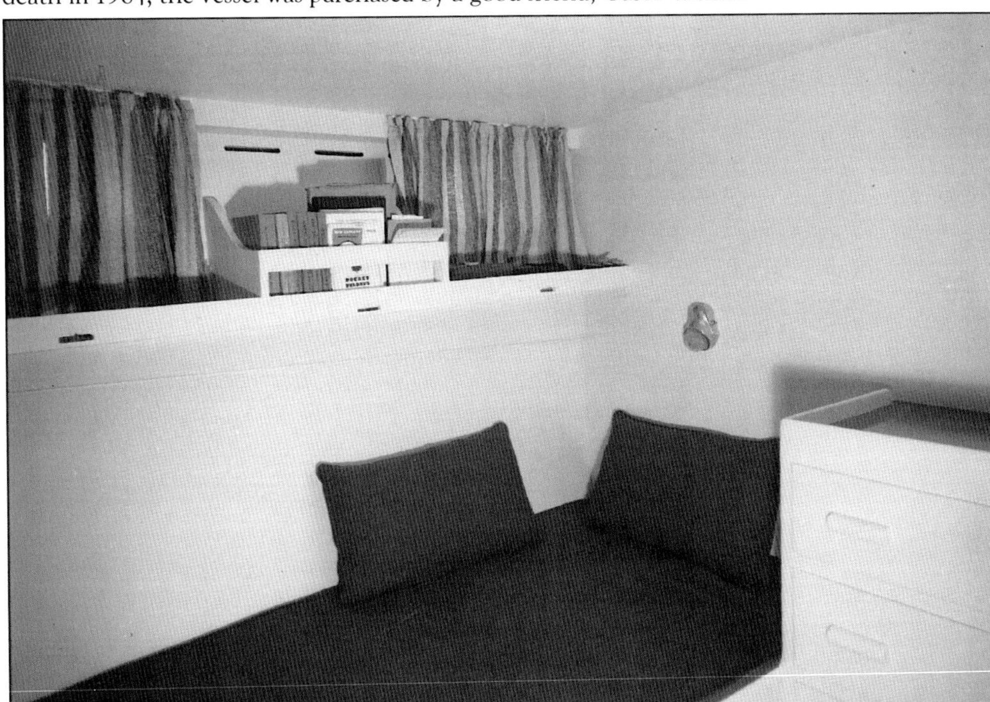

Mr. Saul Brodsky signed a contract with the yard for a 50-foot sport fisherman, designed by Sparkman & Stephens. This is part of the finished interior.

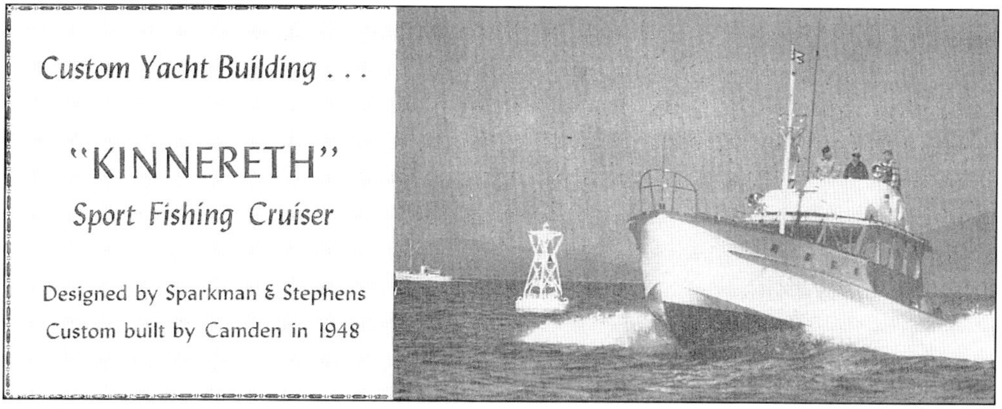

Another picture used as an advertisement for the yard shows the *Kinnereth* under way. She was launched on October 2, 1948. The name of the yard was changed that year to the Camden Shipbuilding Company.

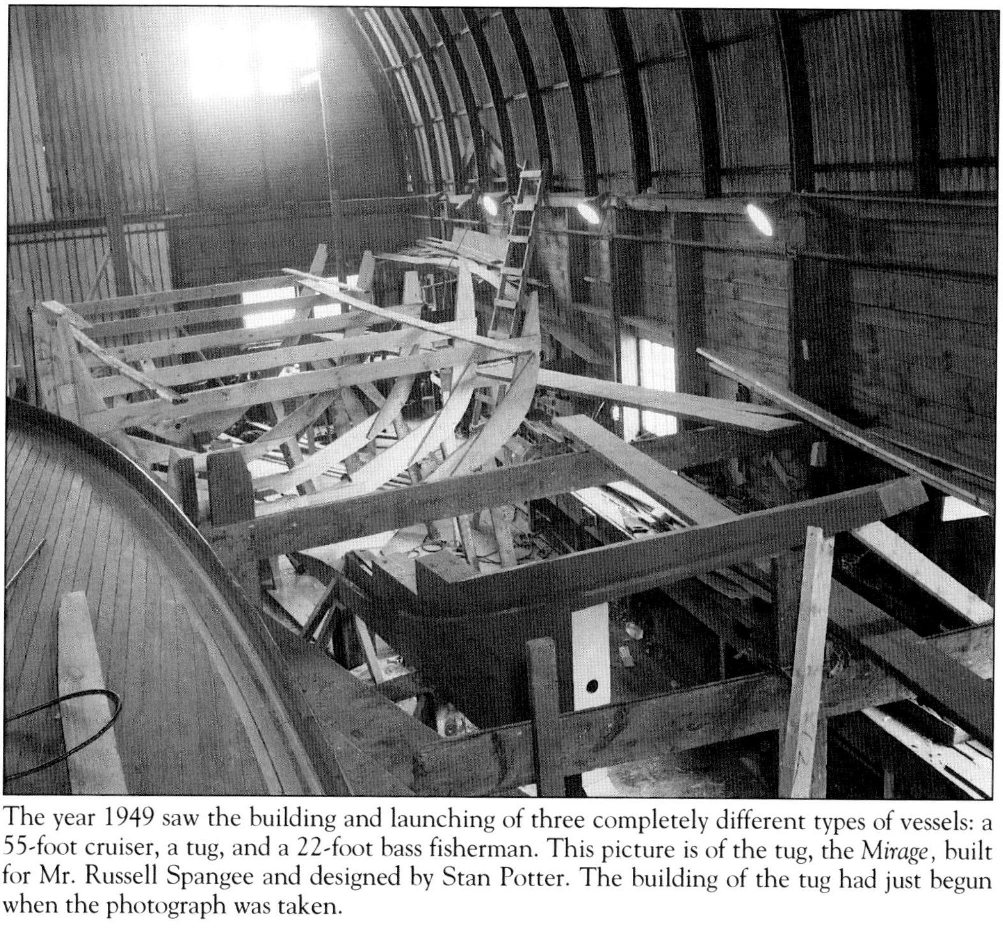
The year 1949 saw the building and launching of three completely different types of vessels: a 55-foot cruiser, a tug, and a 22-foot bass fisherman. This picture is of the tug, the *Mirage*, built for Mr. Russell Spangee and designed by Stan Potter. The building of the tug had just begun when the photograph was taken.

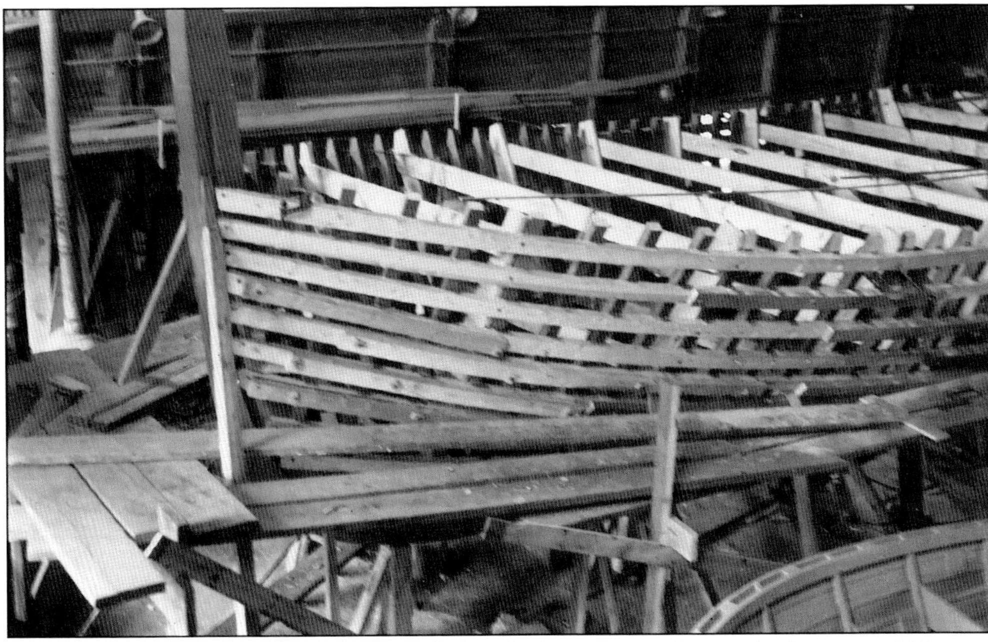

The *Mirage* is shown here framed and ready for planking. I never knew whether it would be used as a working boat or as a pleasure boat, for some people like the looks of a tugboat.

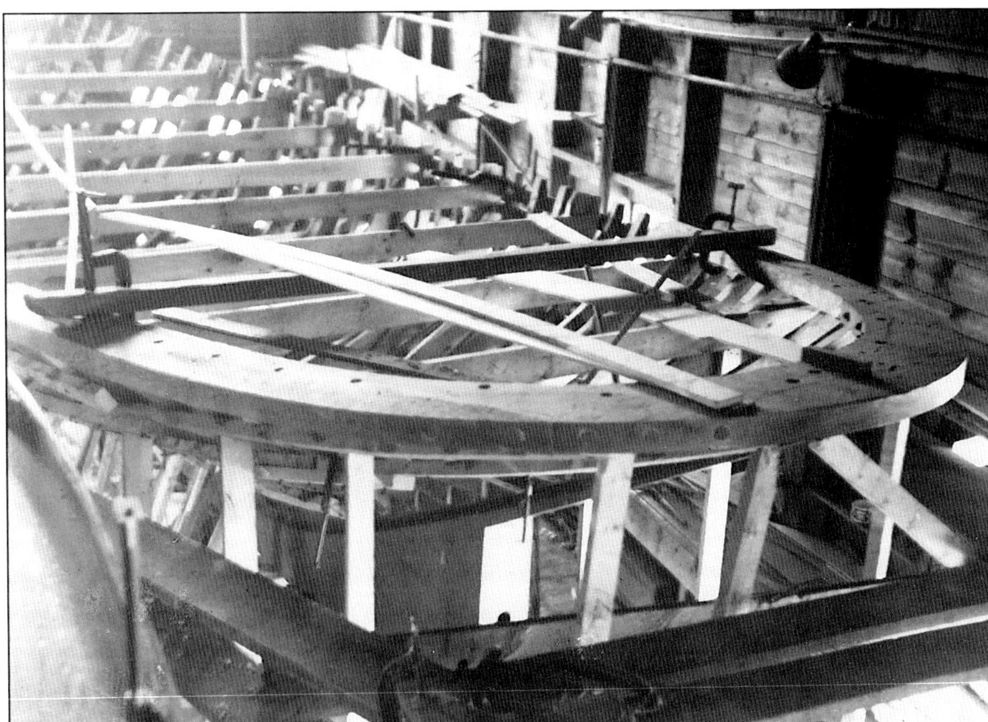

The tug was beginning to take shape. The construction and preparation for where the pilothouse would be located is shown here.

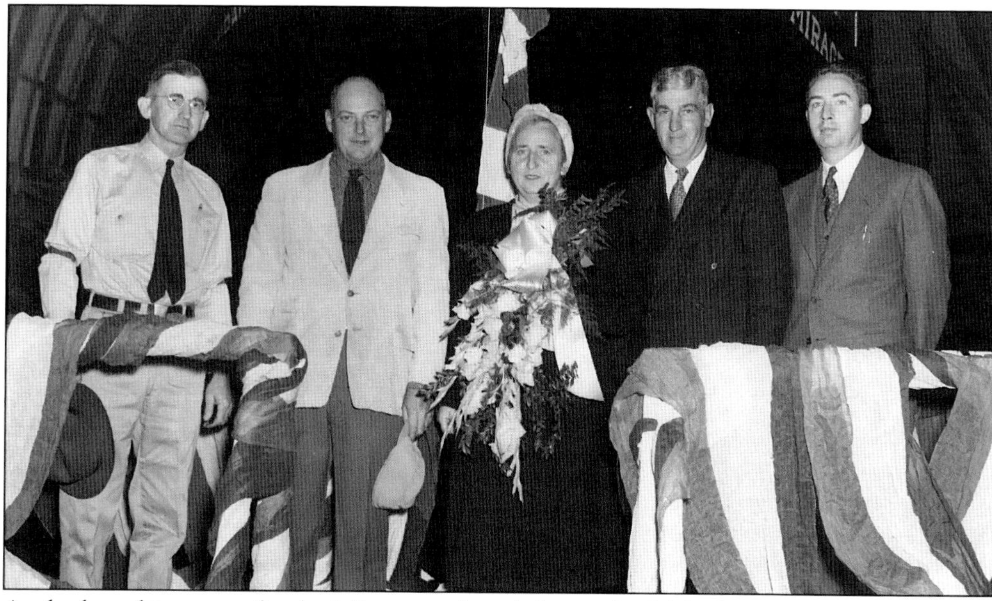

At the launching party for the *Mirage* are, from left to right, Malcolm Brewer, master builder; William E. Peterson, president of the Camden Shipbuilding Co.; Mrs. and Mr. Russell Spangee, owners; and Stan Potter, naval architect.

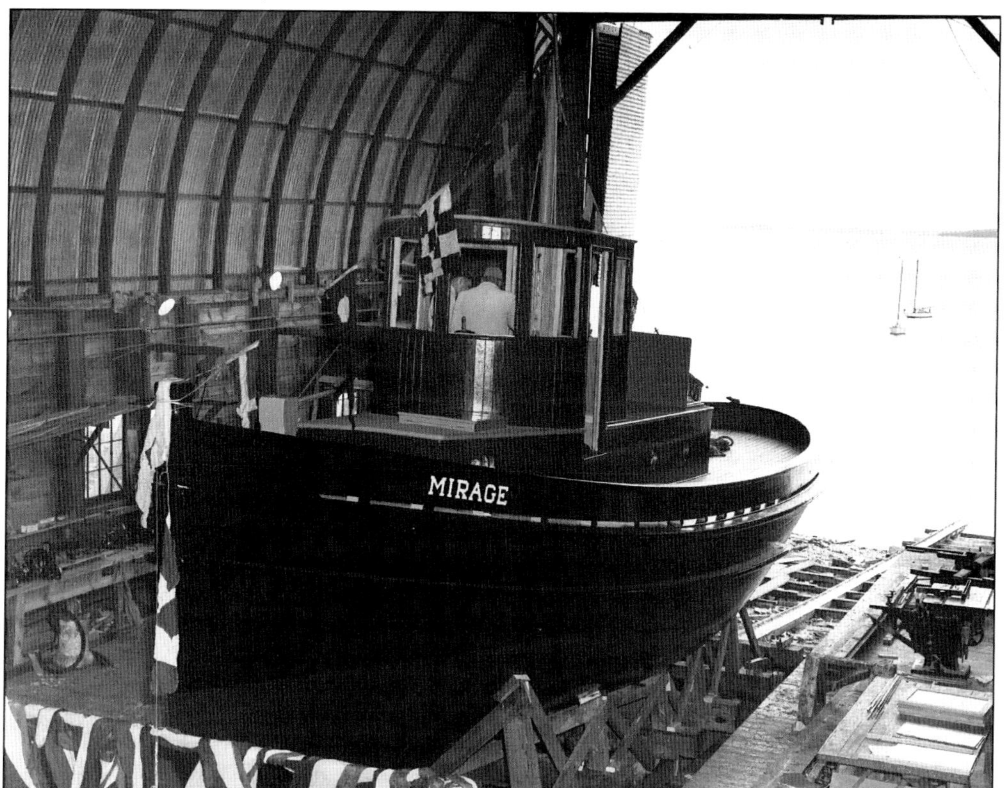

The *Mirage* was finished and ready to slide down the ways on July 22, 1949. She was a very sturdy workboat, or toy as the case may be.

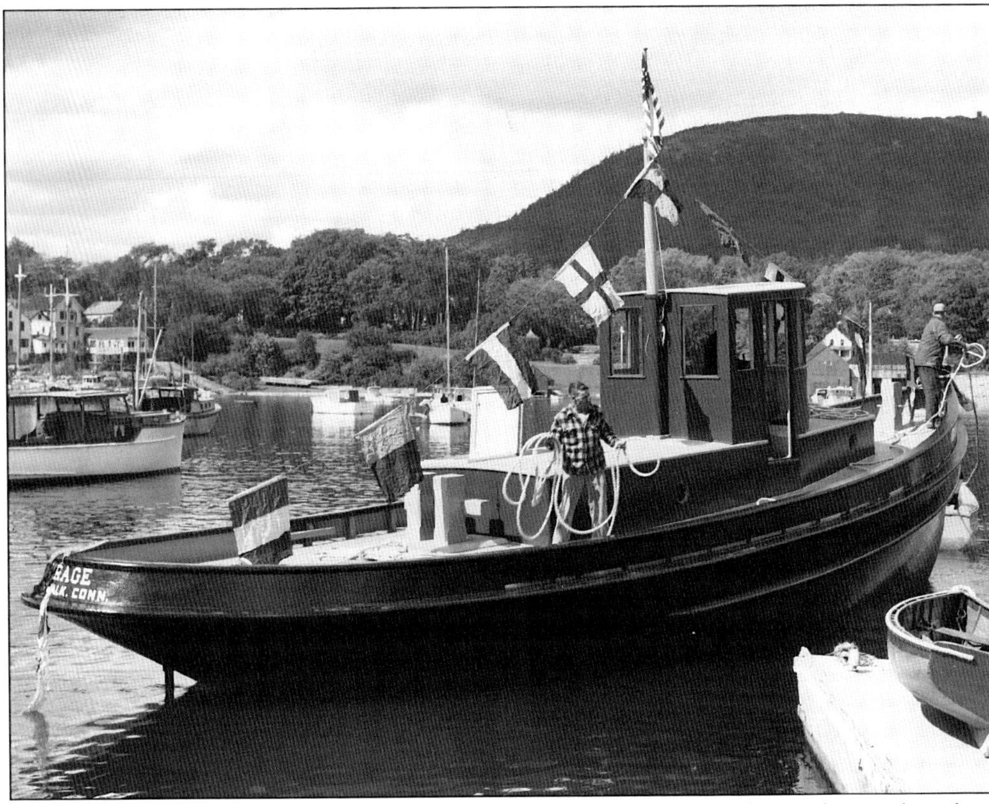

This is the *Mirage* in full view, being towed to the outfitting dock. The workmen aboard are ready to cast the lines ashore so she could be tied there and finished.

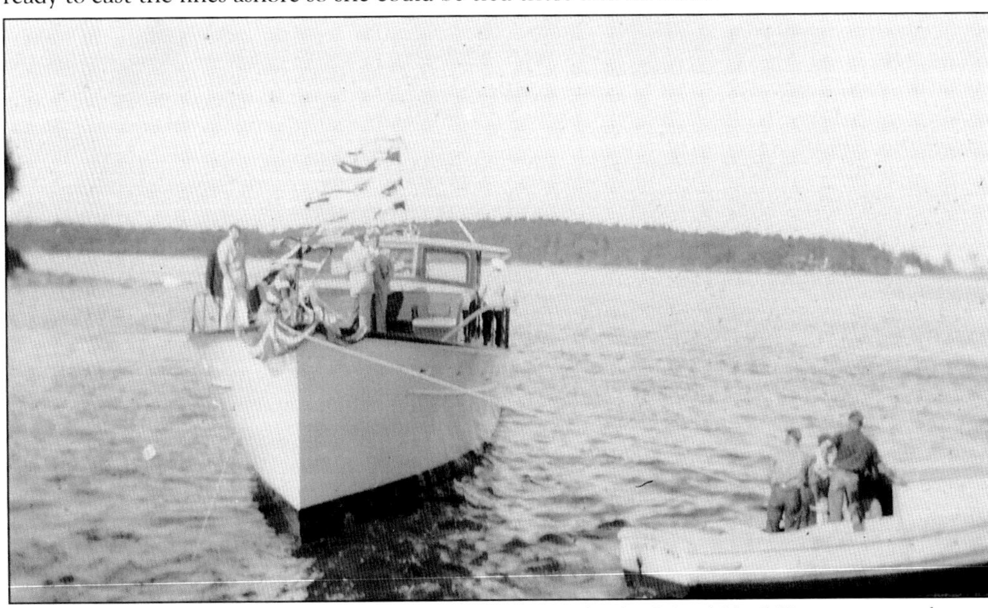

Geerd N. Hendel designed a 70-foot diesel luxury yacht for Mr. Alfred Epstein, president of the Pfeiffer Brewing Company of Detroit. This beauty was my favorite. It was the largest motor yacht to be built in Maine in several years. The picture shows her being towed after launching.

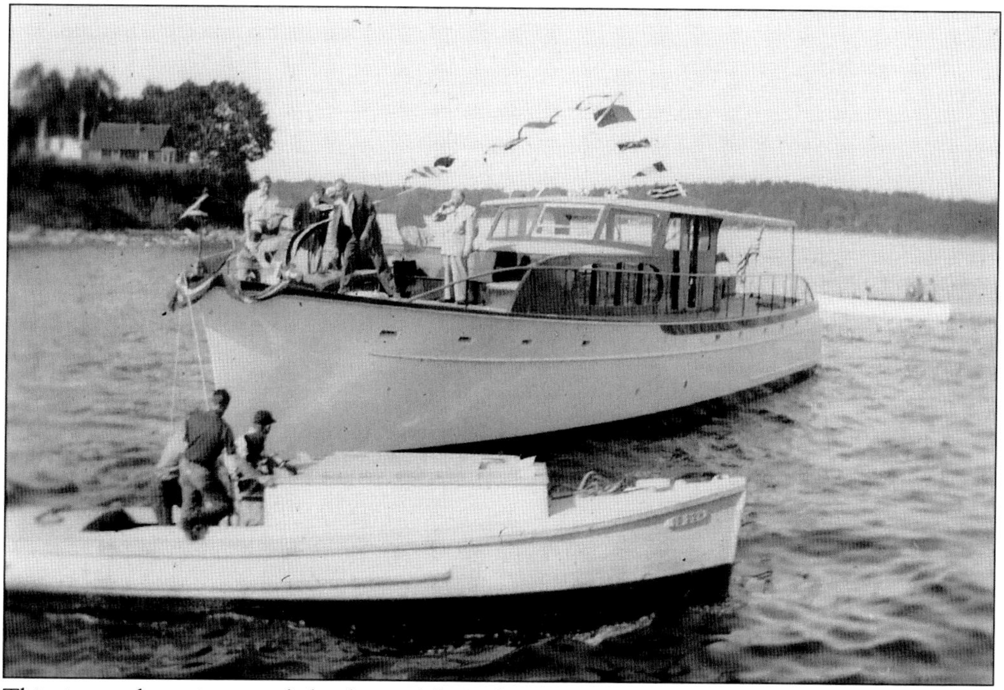

This is another picture of the beautiful *Anahita IV*, after her launching. She had double staterooms aft with a bath for the owner. Forward was the captain's stateroom and one for the crew, each with their own bath. She had hot and cold running water for all, and was one of the fastest yachts afloat, with twin GM diesels of 800 horsepower. She had a top speed of 17 knots. The luxury yacht was double-planked—the inner of cedar and the outer of mahogany—and had Everdur fastened throughout.

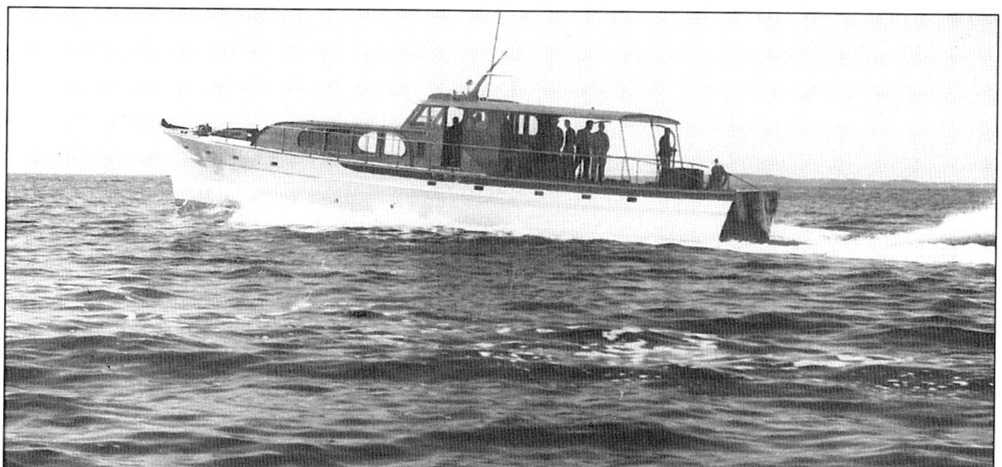

Anahita IV's paneling was of beautifully grained mahogany, trimmed in black walnut. The dining saloon was of natural blonde mahogany, and she had decks of teak. There was red carpeting throughout and white silk curtains hung from the windows. After 27,000 man-hours and many dollars invested, the vessel was ready to leave Maine. She was headed for Florida, the Great Lakes, and the Bahamas. The launching party floated in Pfeiffer beer. It was in June of 1952 that the vessel returned to the yard, while cruising Maine. It had a new owner and new name, the *Murlyn II*.

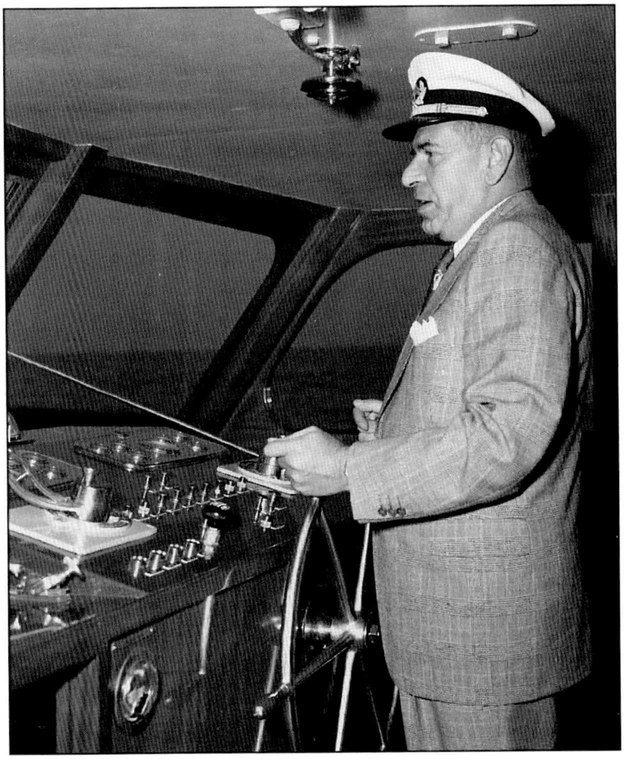

Mr. Alfred Epstein is pictured at the helm of his new boat in 1950, ready to cruise.

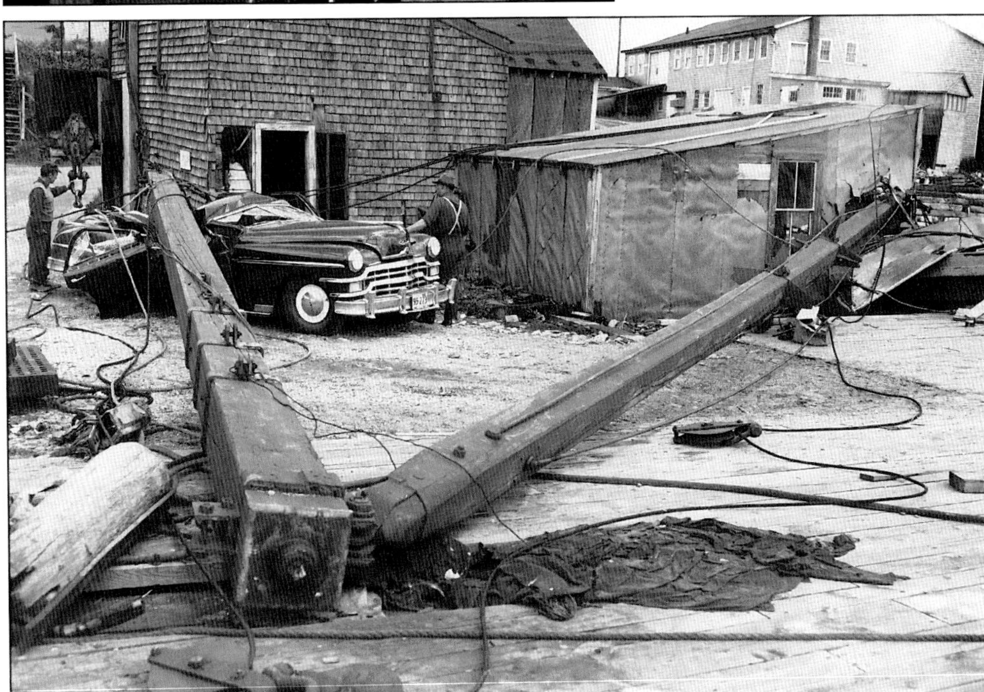

Meanwhile, the derrick on the dock let go and fell on Captain MacDonald's car. No one was in it, but the car was completely demolished. Workman Ken Alley is shown here looking over the wreck.

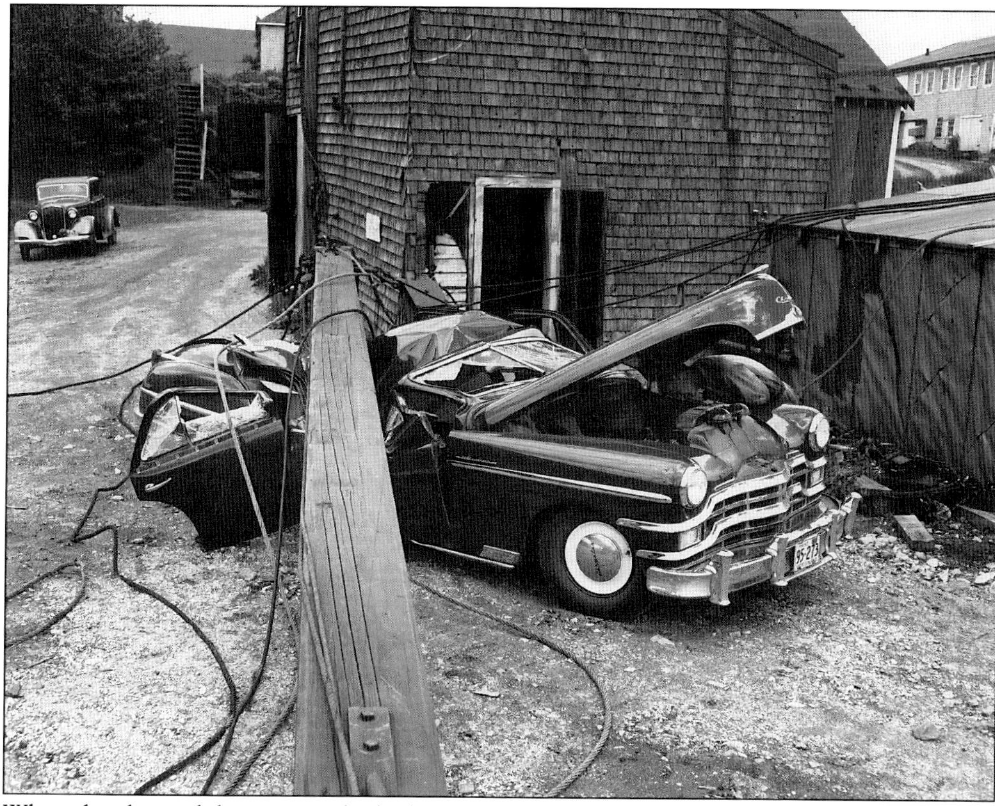

When they located the owner, who had parked it there, he did not seem to be disturbed. He just wanted to know if the "fifth" in the back seat had been broken. Workman Milton Wheaton is looking in on the engine. Being a mechanic, he was interested.

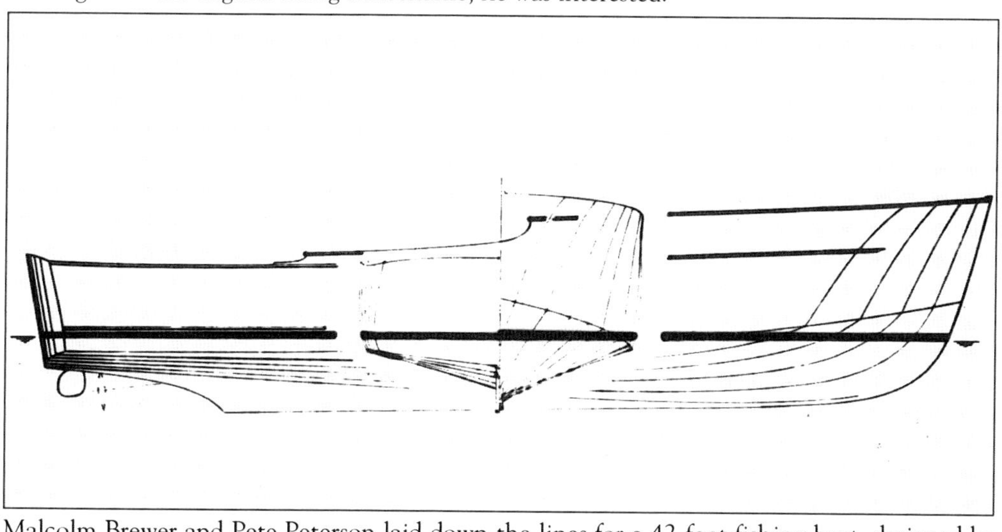

Malcolm Brewer and Pete Peterson laid down the lines for a 42-foot fishing boat, designed by Geerd Hendel. It was built to provide the owner with a high-speed sport fishing cruiser for off shore in the Gulf Stream and Florida Keys. It was designed for a crew of two. Four fishing chairs and one fighting chair were located in the cockpit. Two monel boxes were built flush with the deck, one for fish and one for bait.

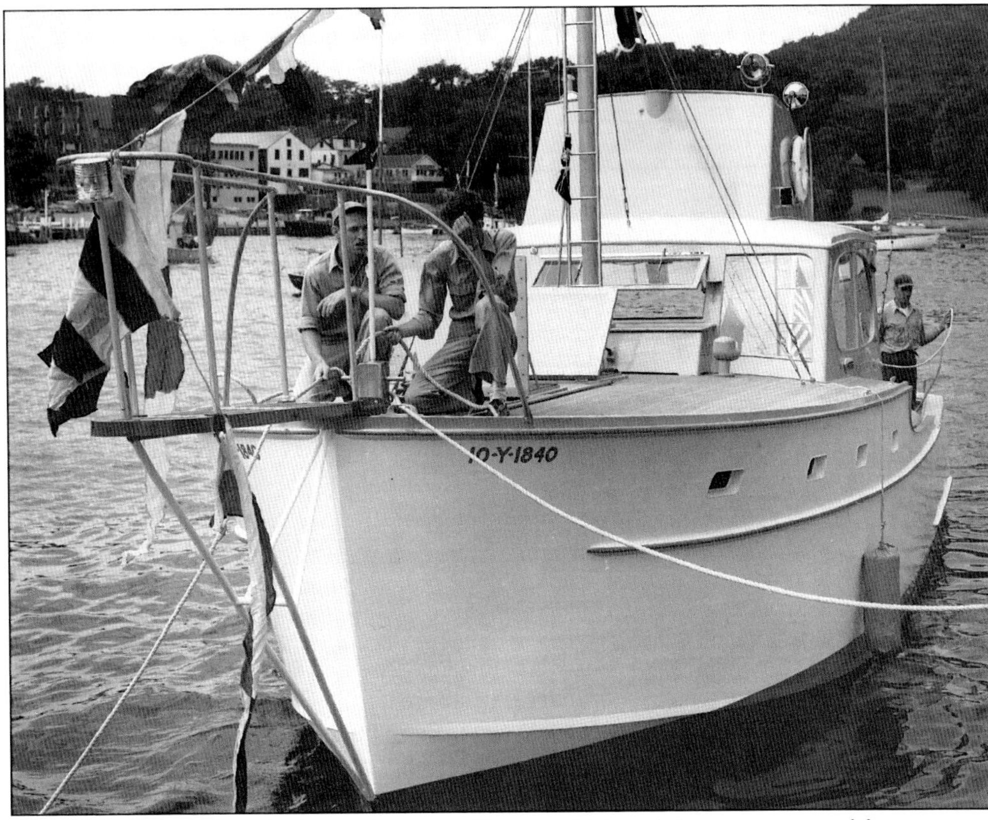

The estimated speed of the fishing boat was 26 knots. Although it was contracted for one party, it was sold instead to Mr. Ferdinand Eberstadt as the *Wild Goose* and launched on August 20, 1951.

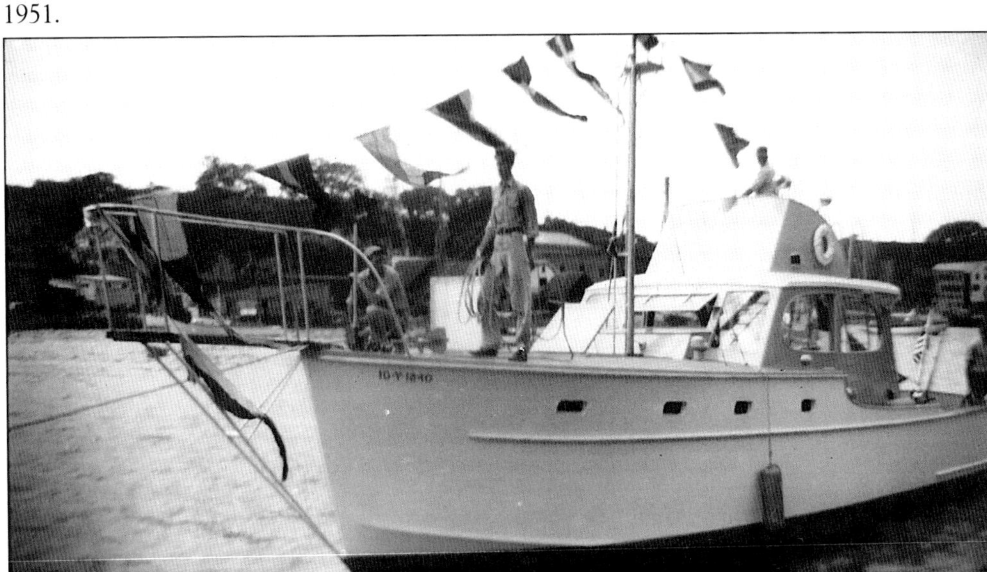

Shown in this launching picture is the deckhouse (located over the engine room), which featured a radiotelephone, helmsman's chair, and portable dining table.

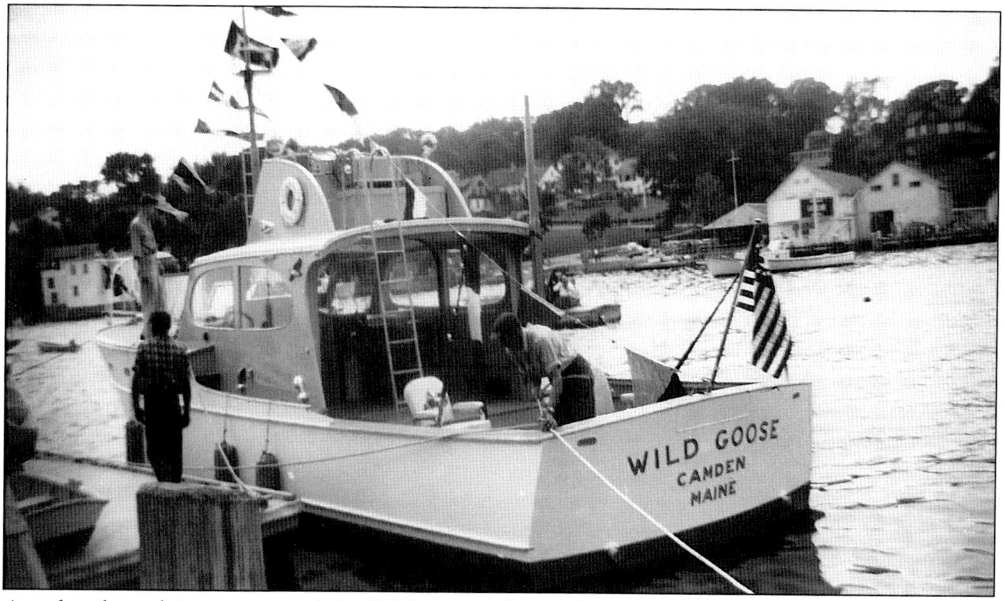

Another launching picture of the *Wild Goose* shows that the after end of the deckhouse was open to the cockpit, but could be protected by canvas curtains running on a sail track.

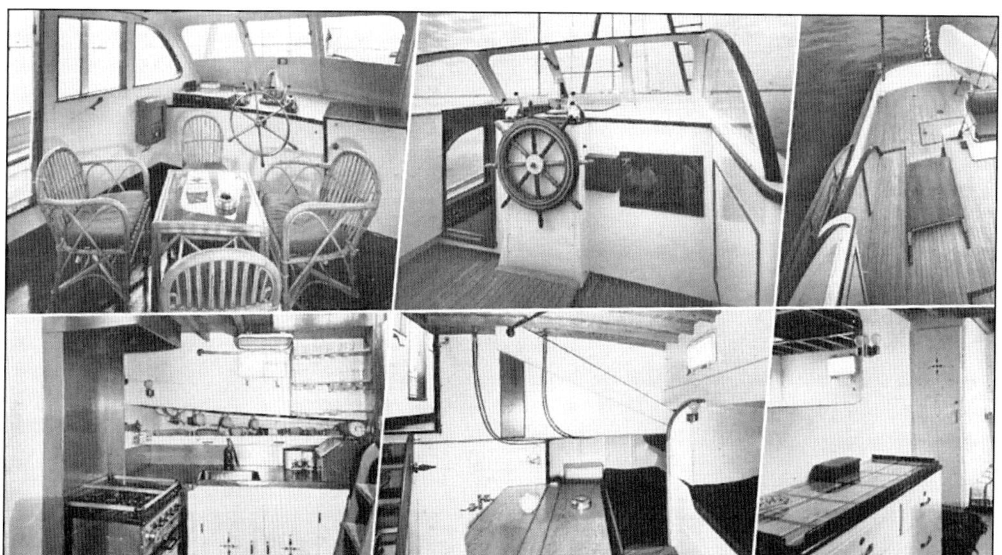

In July of 1952, a 60-foot sport fisherman was launched for Mr. Allison Laytham of Passaic, New Jersey. It was christened by his wife, the former Betty Lark, who had summered in Camden. Pictures of the inside are shown here.

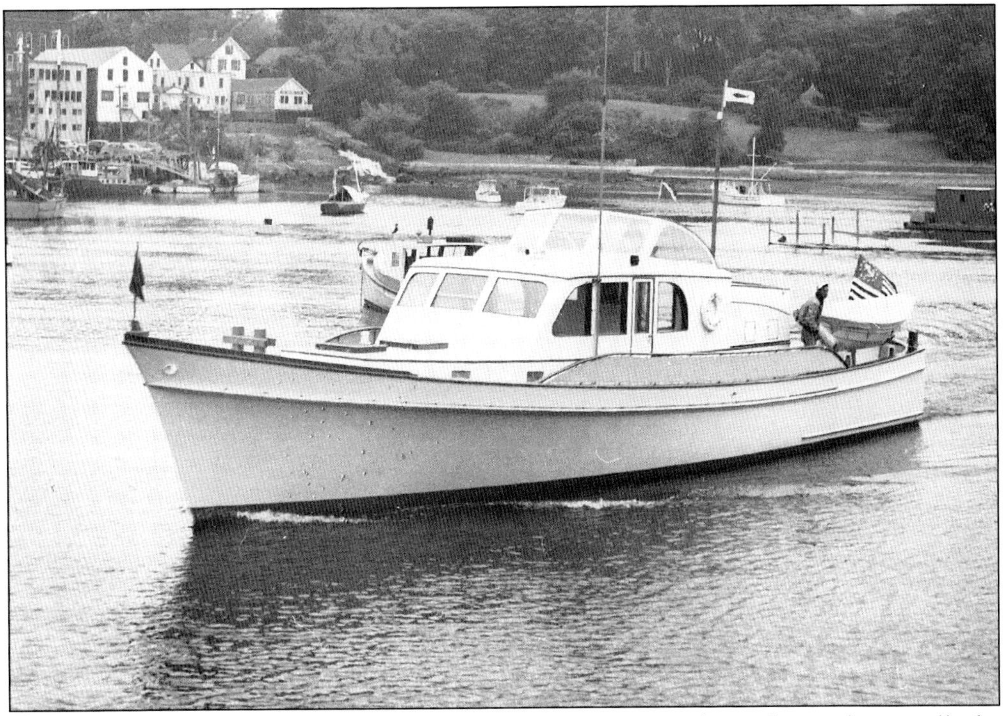

Mr. Laytham was an experienced sword fisherman and the vessel was designed especially for sport fishing on the East Coast. The keel, backbone, and frames were of oak, double-planked Philippine mahogany over cedar, and the decks were teak. He named the vessel the *Porpoise*.

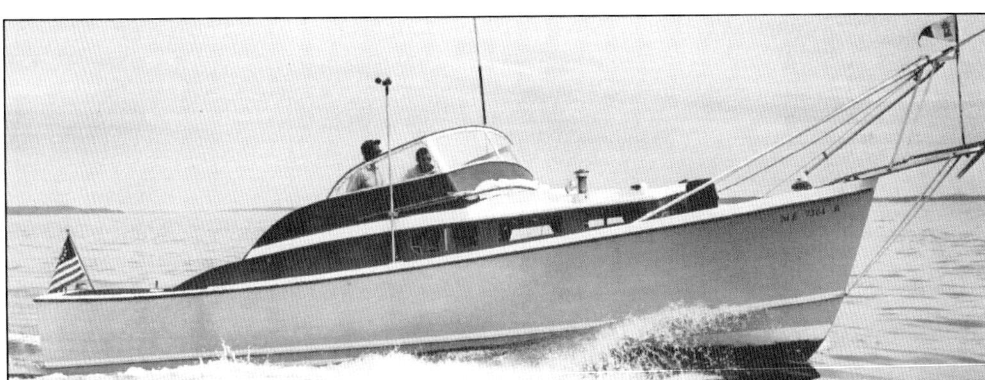

The *Porpoise* had quite a bit of deck space, with wide walkways. The exceptional yacht made the November 1952 cover of *Rudder Magazine*. That was excellent advertising for the Camden Shipbuilding Company.

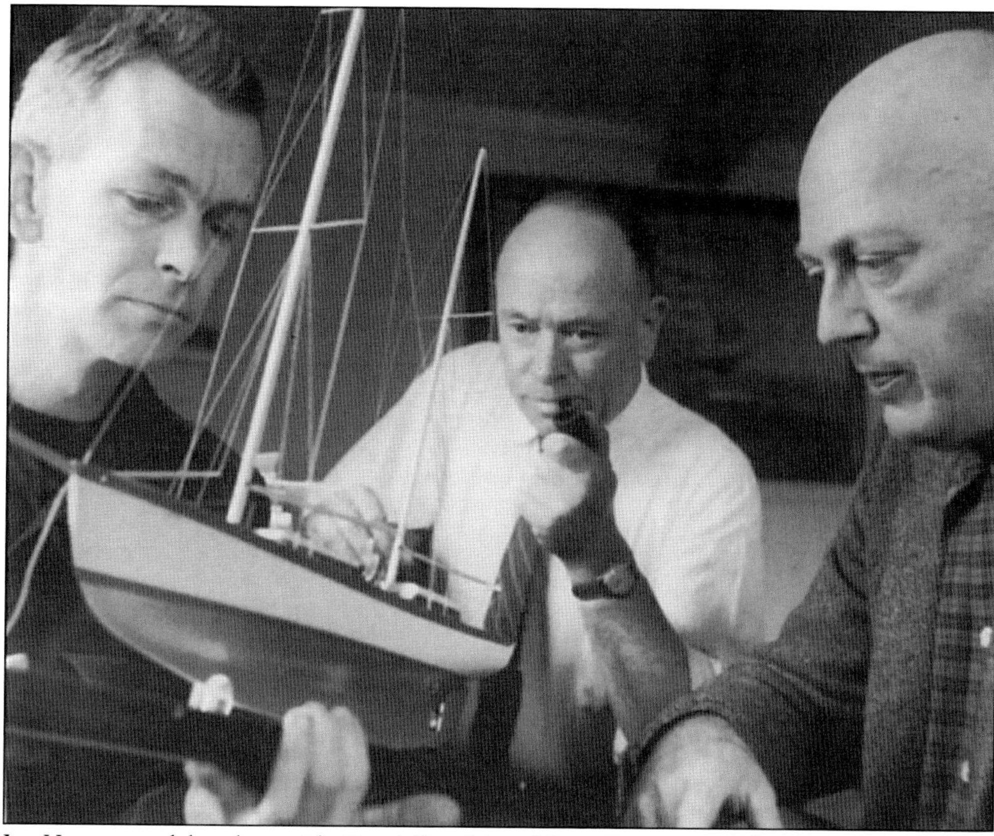

Jay Hanna, model maker, with Geerd Hendel and Pete Peterson are shown studying a ketch they were contemplating for future construction.

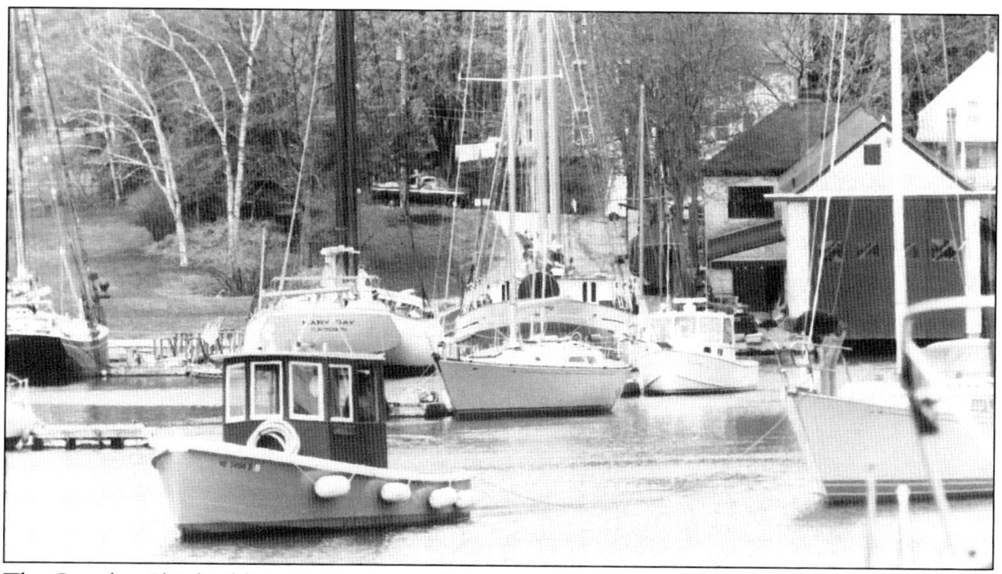

The Camden Shipbuilding Company needed a tug of their own to take boats from launching to outfitting, and also to put yachts back and forth on moorings. They built a sturdy little one that is still in operation. She was named the *Barbie D.* for their office worker.

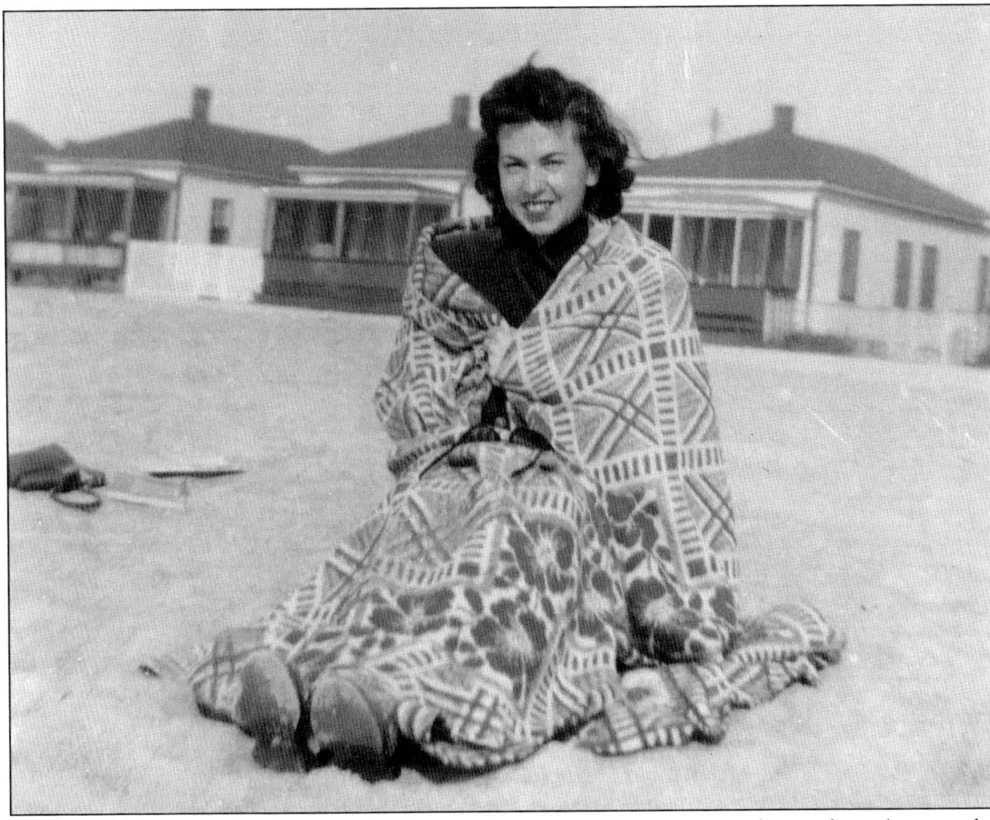

Pictured here is the other *Barbie D.*, making sure that all the paper work was done (or was she resting on the beach?). She only survived at the job for 44 years, so she was slightly outdone by the tug.

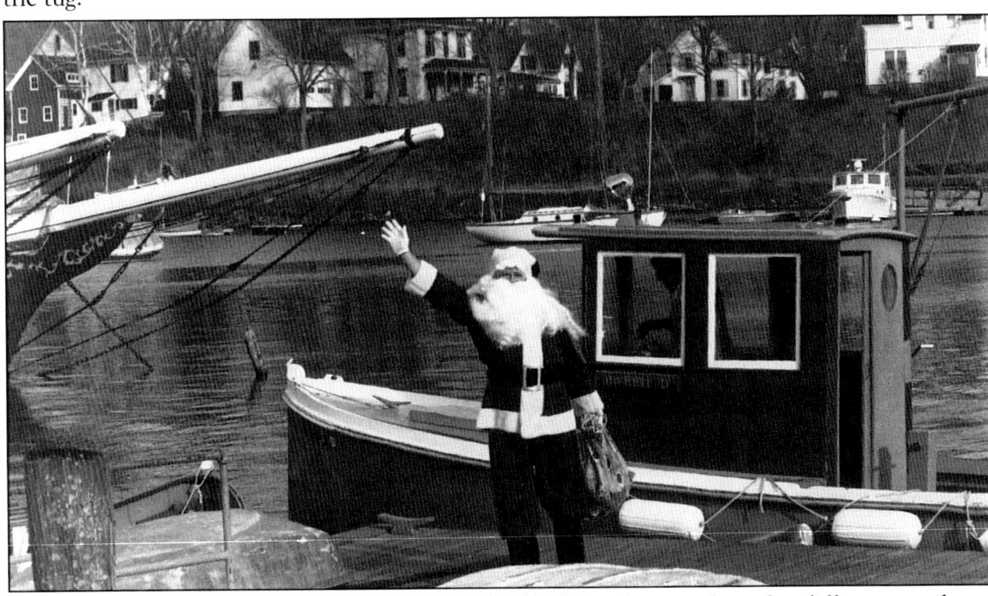

Santa used to arrive in Camden via the *Barbie D.* Now he gets here by different modes of transportation. Santa Claus does manage to find Camden every Christmas, one way or another.

Little Miss Brown was prepared to sponsor her father's lumber tug. William Brown contracted a vessel from the Camden Shipbuilding Company to be used by his Knox Lumber Company for towing lumber rafts and scows in Penobscot Bay. The vessel was 40 feet long and was launched in 1952. Mr. Brown called her the *Joseph H. Stuart*. Murray G. Peterson, N.A. of South Bristol, Maine, designed the vessel.

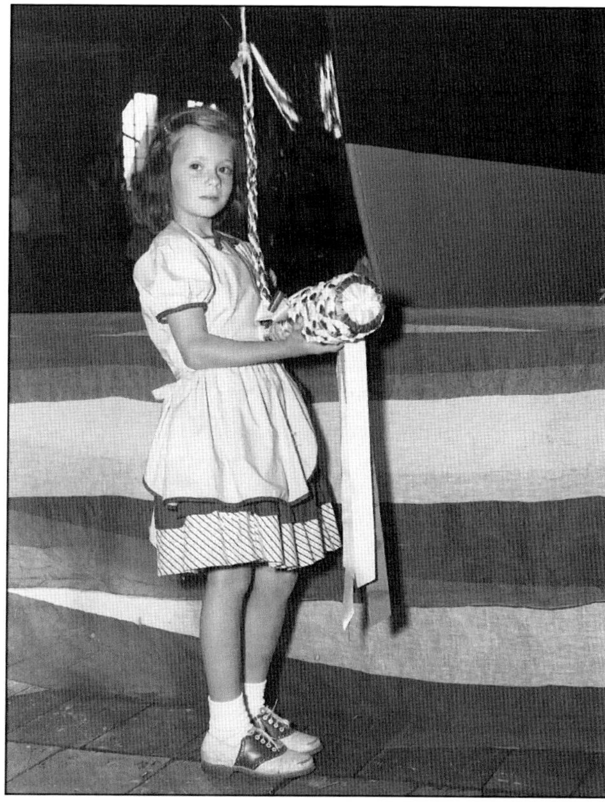

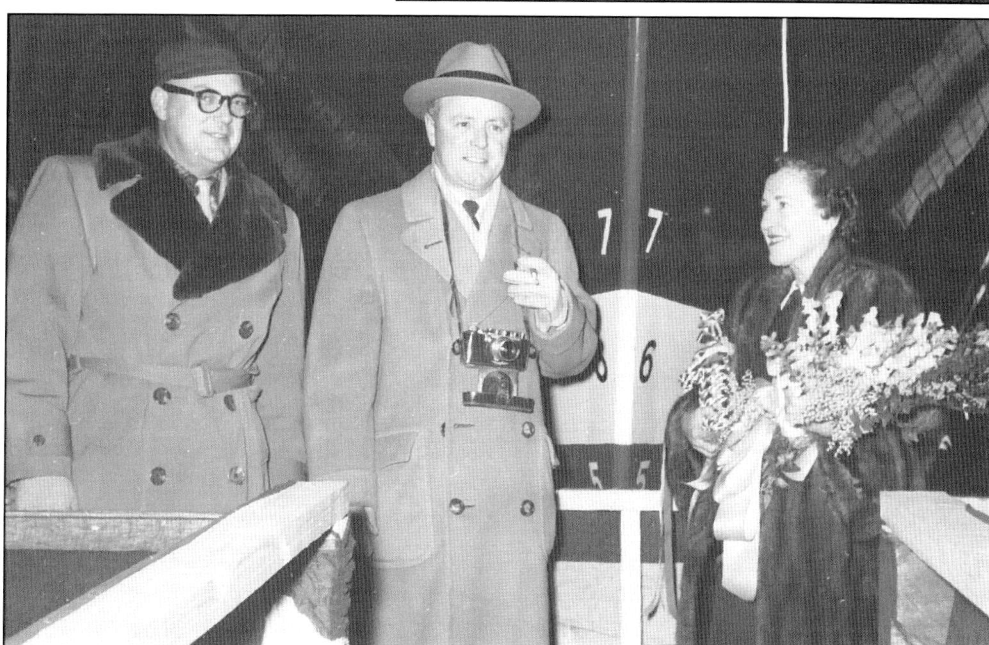

Mr. E. Julian Davis of Oklahoma contracted to have a 68-foot diesel yacht built by the Camden Shipbuilding Company and designed by Geerd N. Hendel. Capt. William E. Peterson, E. Julian Davis, and Mrs. Davis prepared to christen the yacht, which he called the *Sooner*.

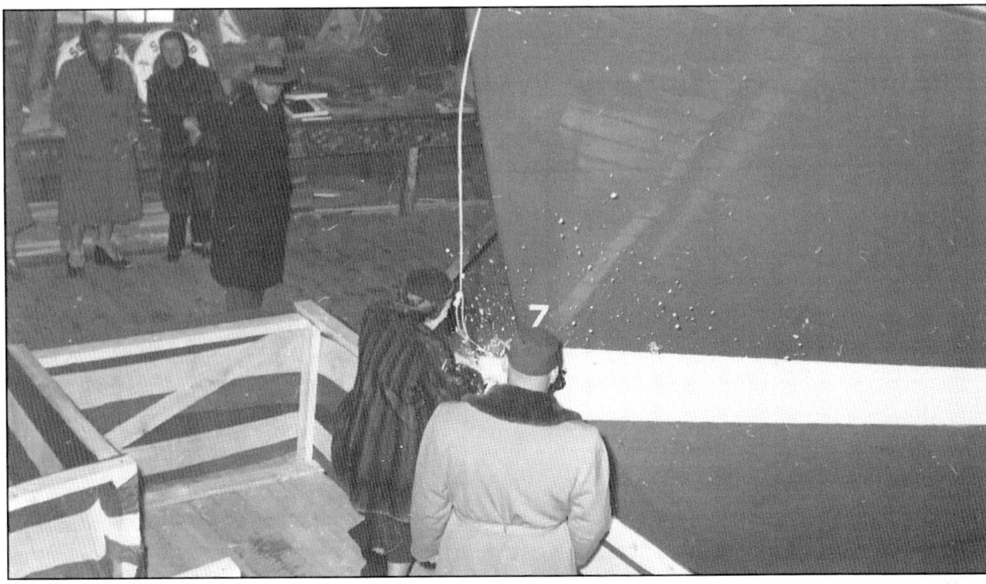

Mrs. Davis has just hit the bow of the boat, smashing the champagne bottle, while William Peterson looks on.

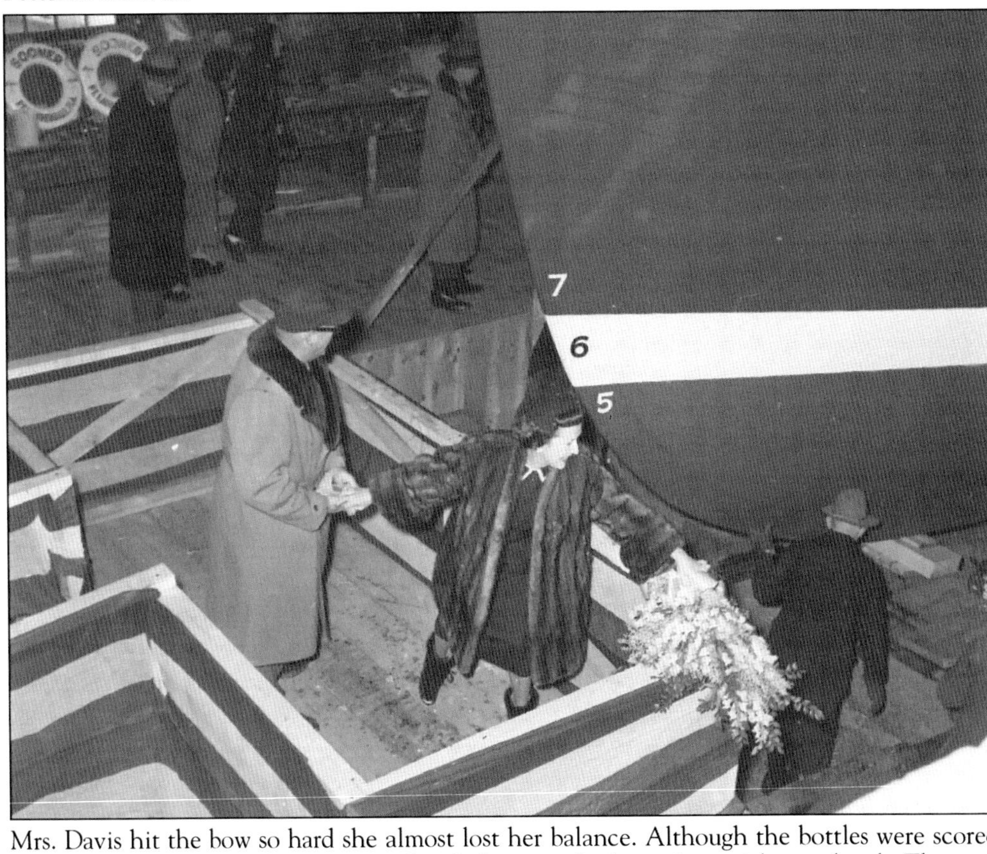

Mrs. Davis hit the bow so hard she almost lost her balance. Although the bottles were scored before wrapping, unless they contacted with force on the bow, they might not break. That was considered bad luck.

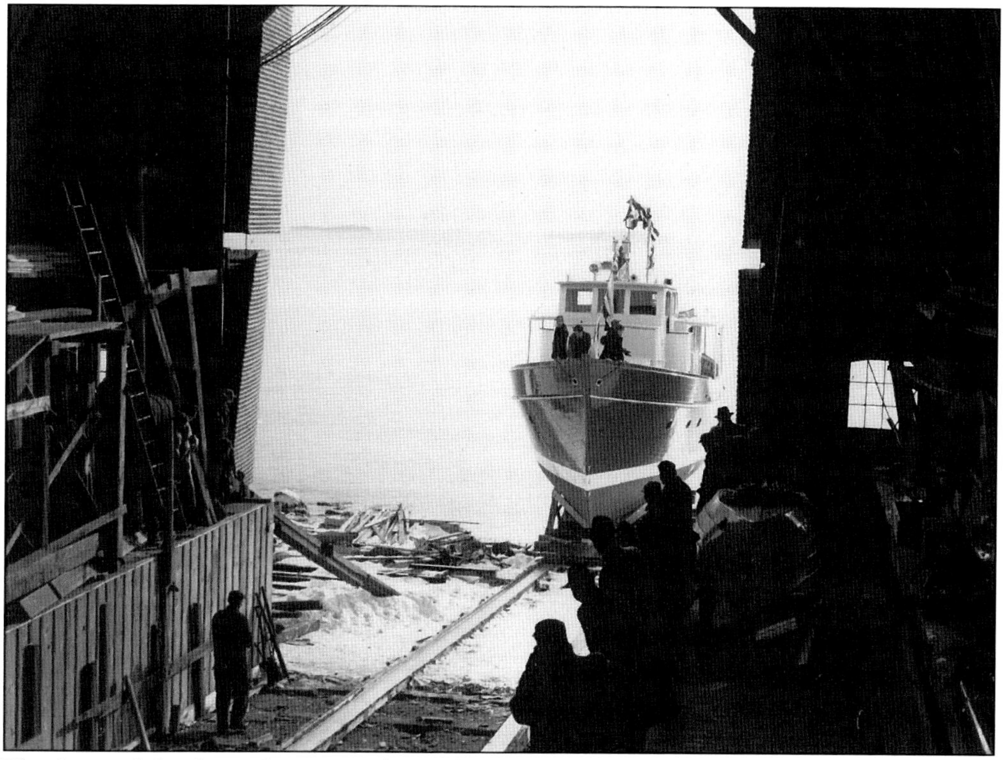

The *Sooner* slides down the ways and into the water.

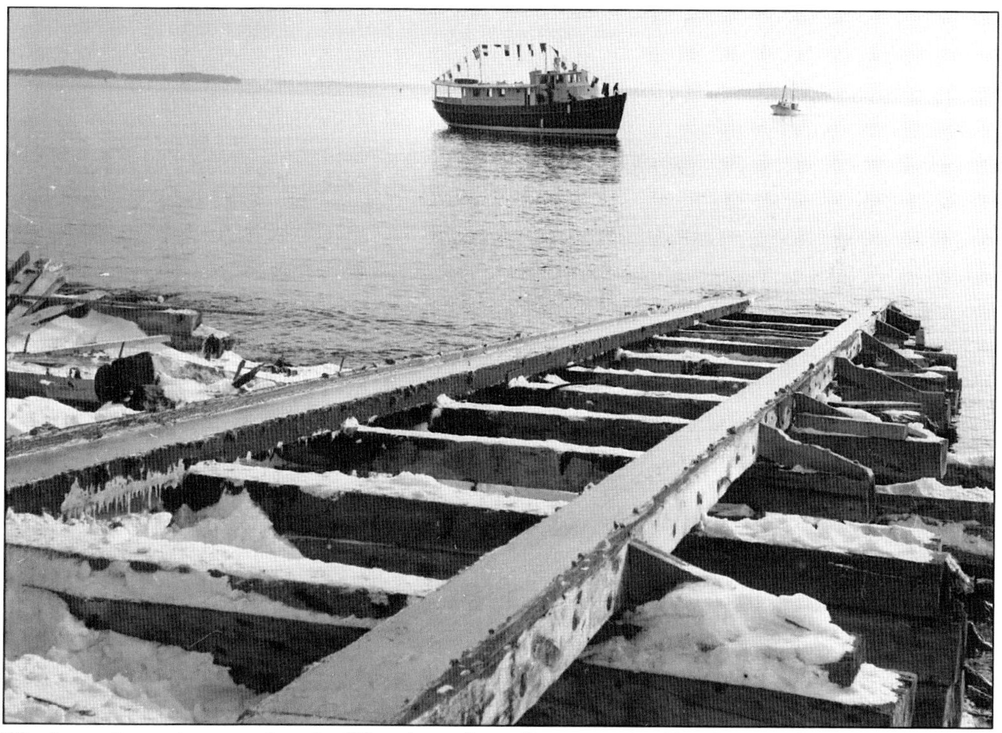

The houseboat, decorated with all her launching flags, was finally afloat in the water.

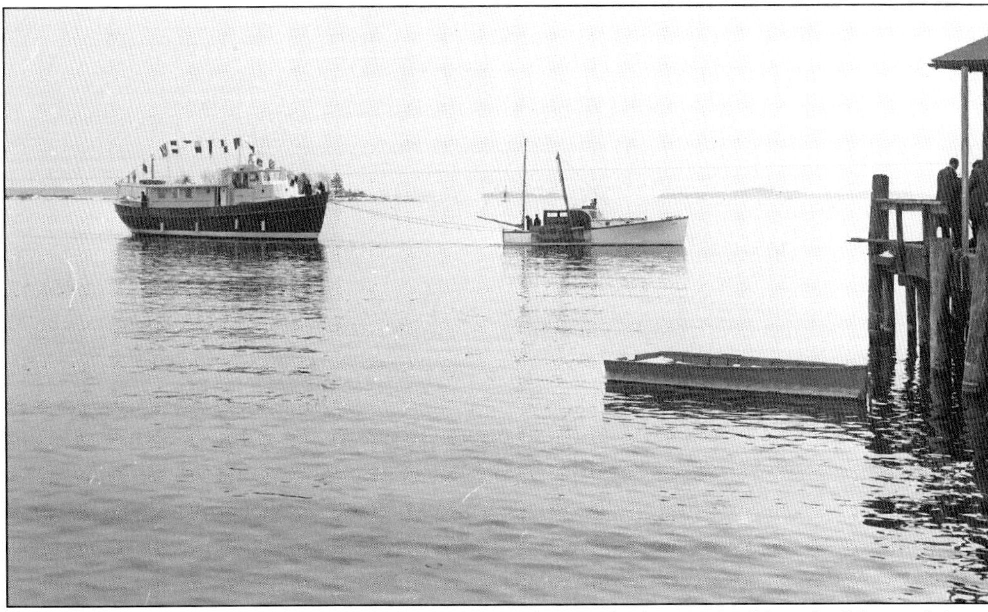

A boat has the *Sooner* in tow, headed for the outfitting dock. Her building had been delayed for several months due to the loss of the yard joiner shop to fire on September 10, 1953. Much of the finish work and cabinets were custom made in that shop. Within 30 minutes, fire had leveled the two-and-a-half-story, 60-by-40-foot wooden building. Many workmen lost their tools, which had been collected over the years.

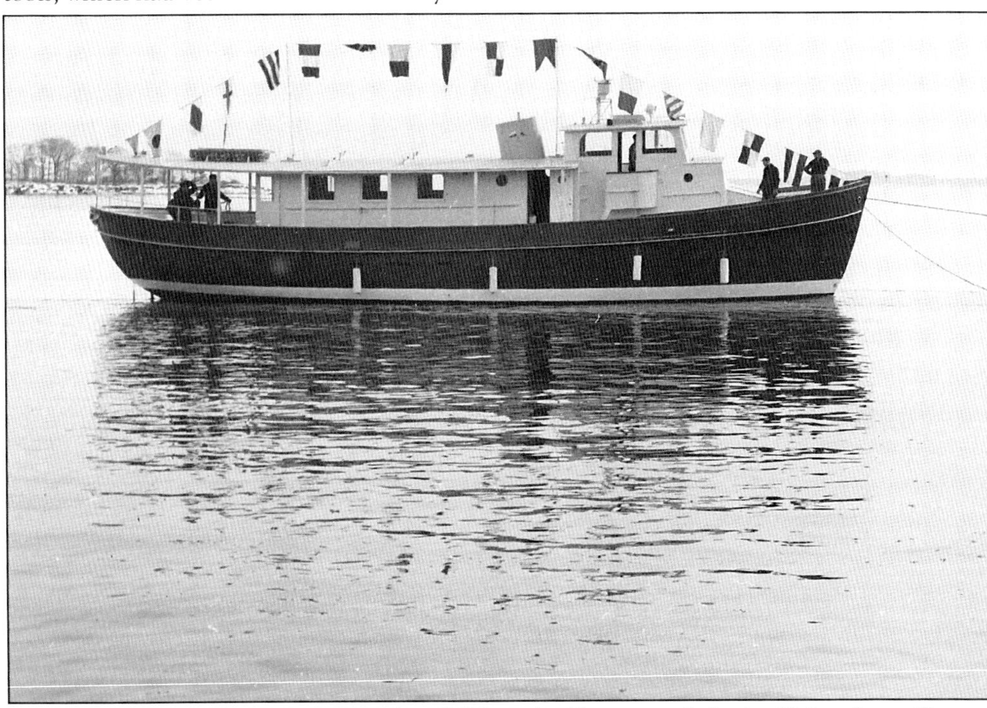

Another picture of the *Sooner* shows her full length. She certainly looks 68 feet long. She was spacious enough for three double staterooms, plus quarters for a crew of four. The vessel was built for off-shore cruising.

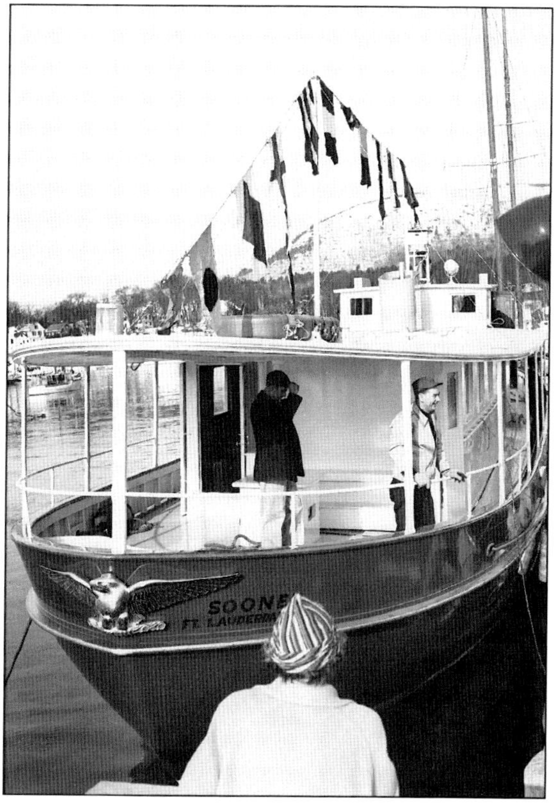

This close up of the stern shows a good view of the carved eagle, along with the vessel's name and hail.

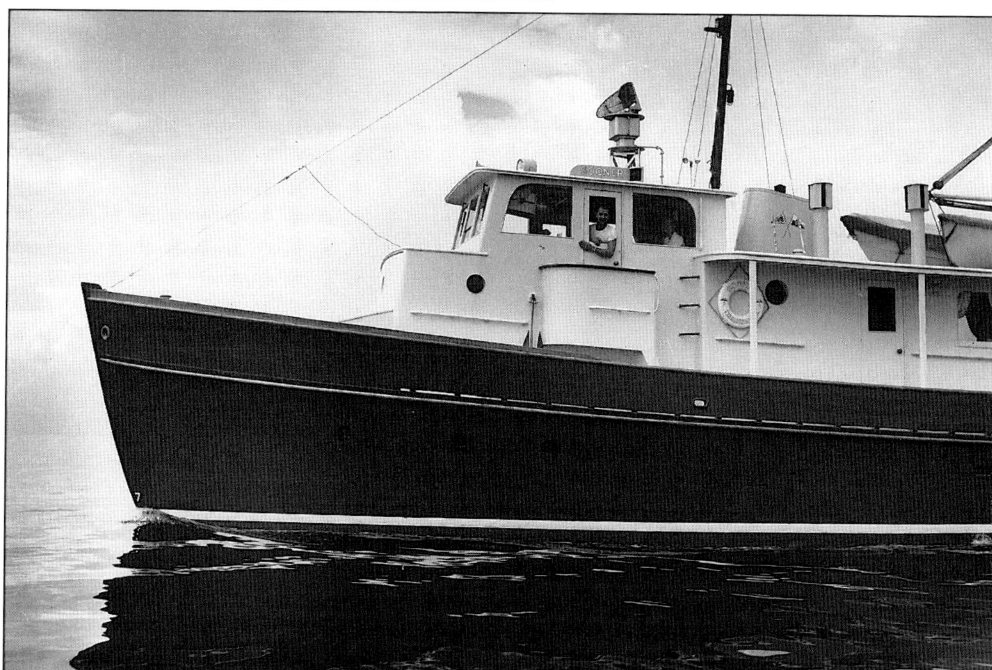

Shown here on trials in Penobscot Bay in 1954, the *Sooner* performed admirably. The captain, at the helm, looks very pleased.

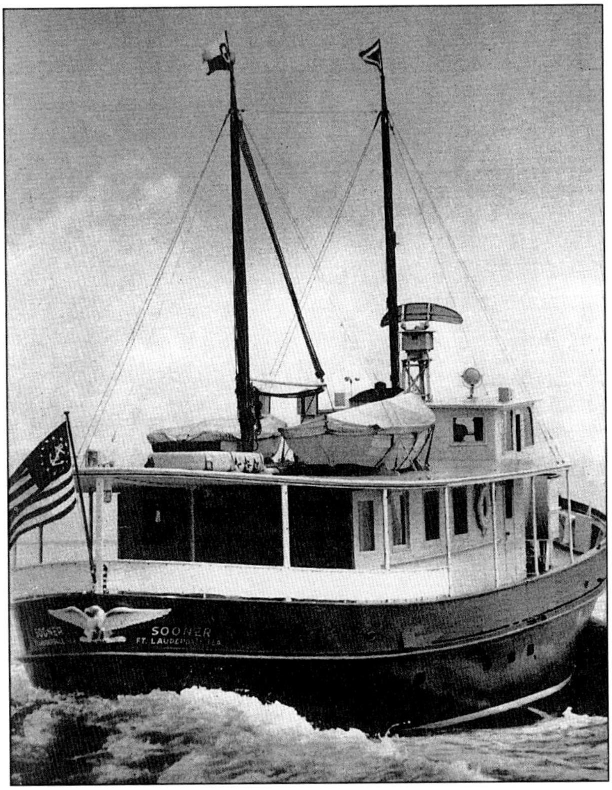

This photograph of the *Sooner* was used in a Camden Shipbuilding Company's advertisement in which it was stated that the *Sooner* had cruised from Maine to South America—to Alaska and beyond.

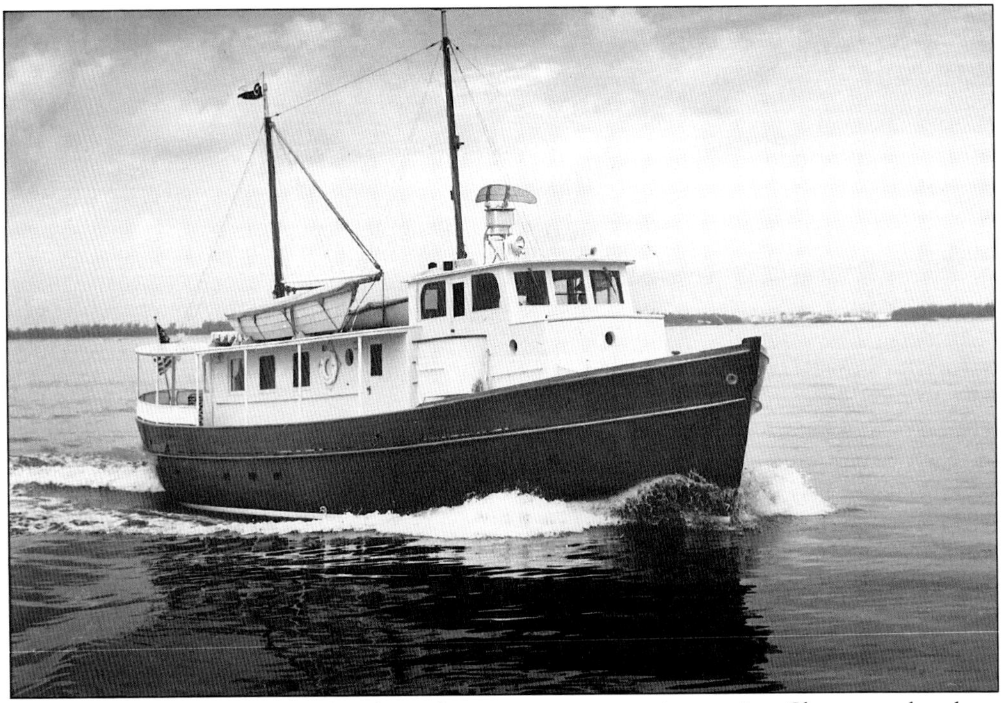

The *Sooner* from a side view, breaking the waves, was quite impressive. She seemed to be a floating house, but built with speed and able to handle the seas.

The Marine Development Company of Providence, Rhode Island, contracted for the Camden Shipbuilding Company to build a 71-foot high-speed cruiser. She was designed by Geerd Hendel and her hull size was determined after a series of tests at the Stevens Institute of Technology. Steering was done from a flying bridge, and she featured a Sperry automatic pilot and hydraulic steering by Crowell Designs. There were accommodations for four, plus a crew of three. The story was told that one of the wives had always wanted a pearl necklace, but each time her husband came up with something else, such as this vessel. It was appropriately named the *Pearl Necklace*, and was launched in 1957.

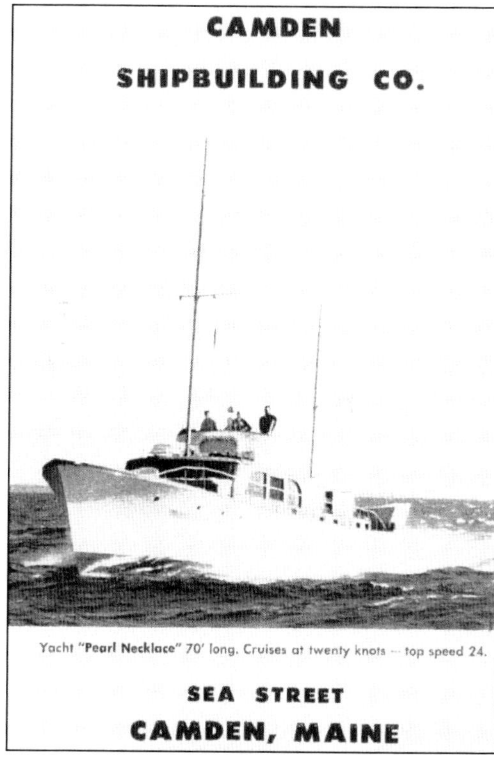

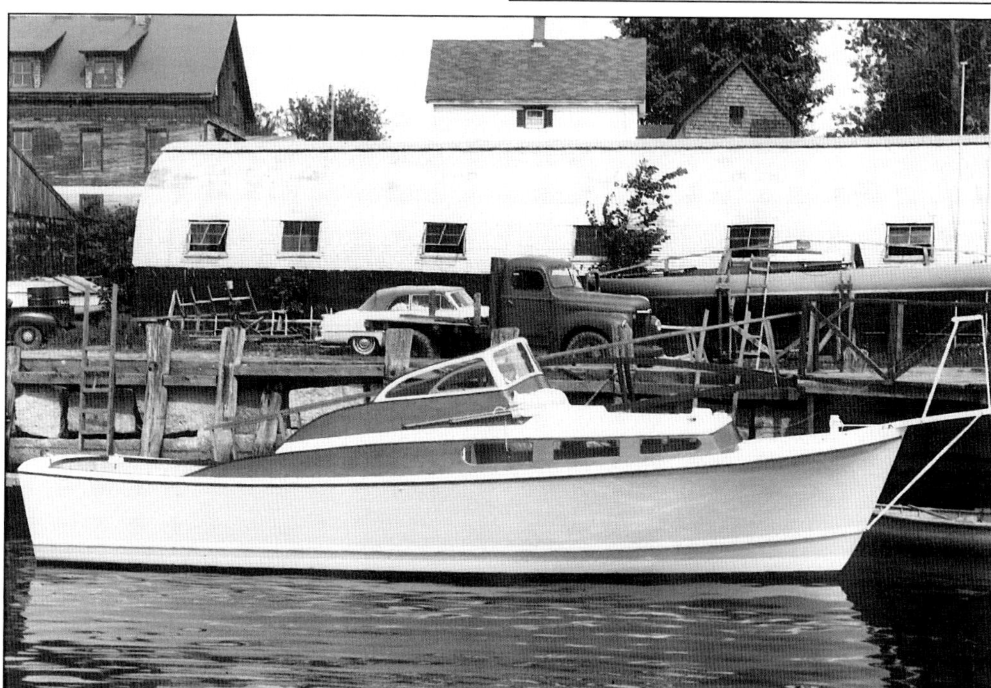

Another sleek cruiser, the *Sabina,* was launched in August of 1960. She was built for Dr. Paul Jones of Union, Maine. Fiberglass boats were becoming popular around this time, as they were easier to maintain. But Camden Shipbuilding kept building the wooden ones that they loved.

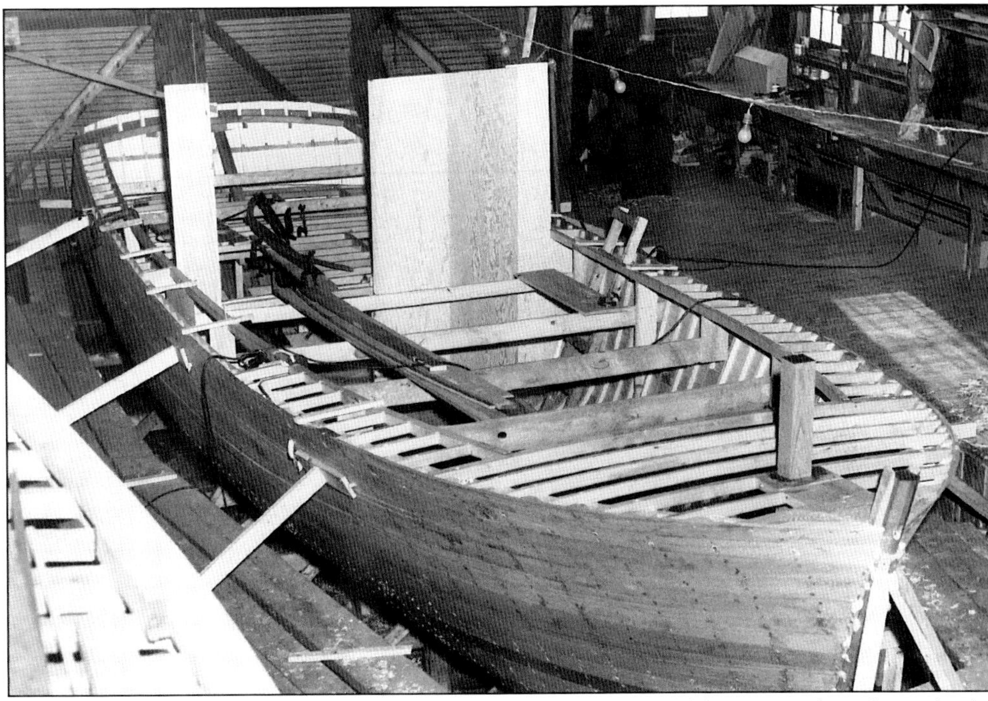

Andrew J. Winslow of Boston commissioned the yard to build him a 40-foot flying bridge sport cruiser. The vessel, built of mahogany planked with teak decks, is shown here under construction.

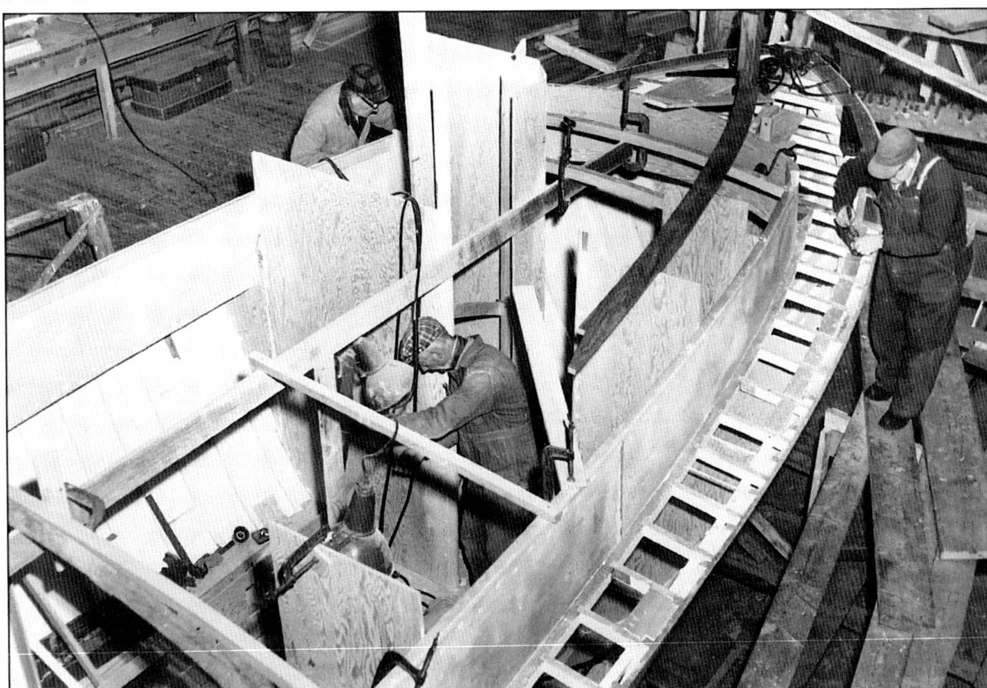

This photograph shows workmen all working on different parts of the vessel. She had accommodations for four, gas cooking, and electric refrigeration.

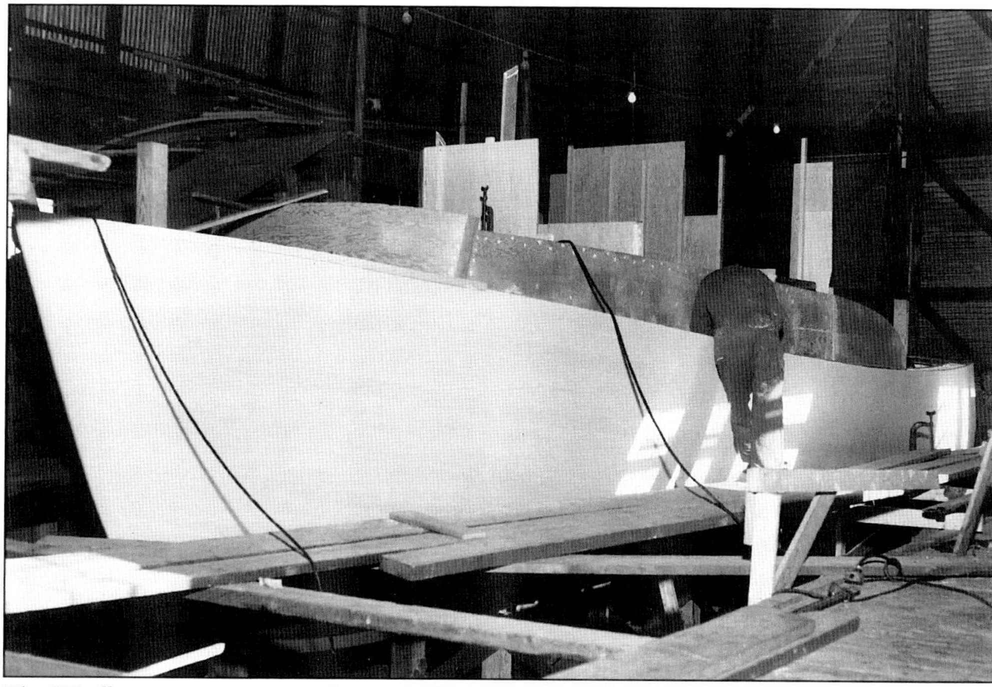

The *Windless* was nearing completion in this photograph, but a great deal of detail work had yet to be done.

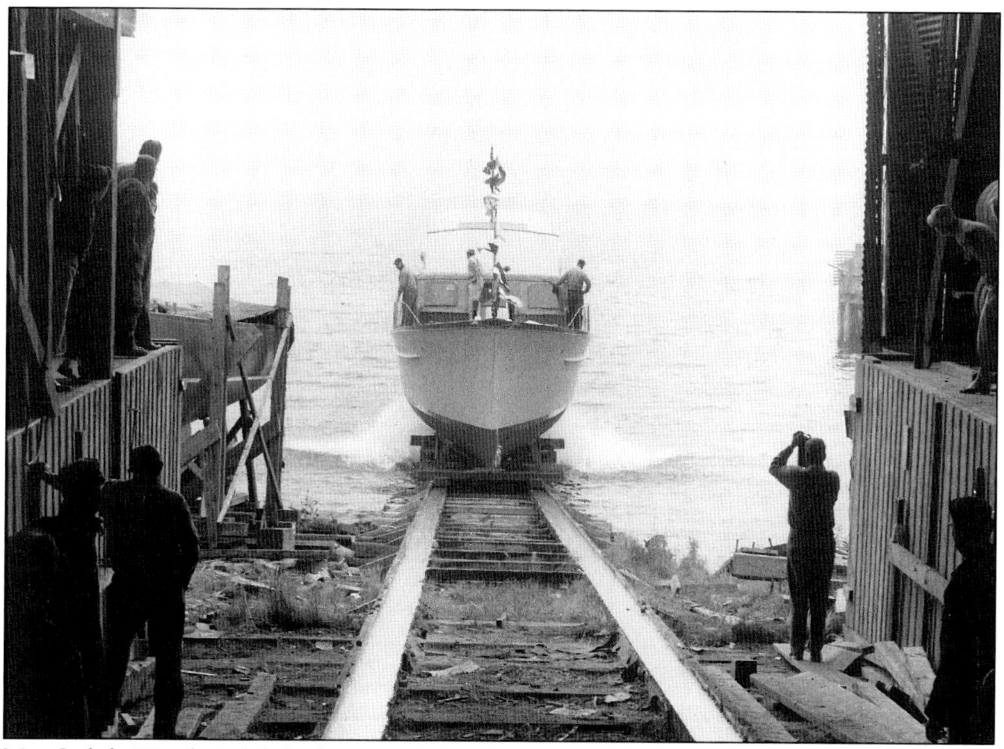

Miss Judith Winslow did the honors of christening the *Windless*. This photograph shows the yacht sliding down the launching ways, into the arms of the sea.

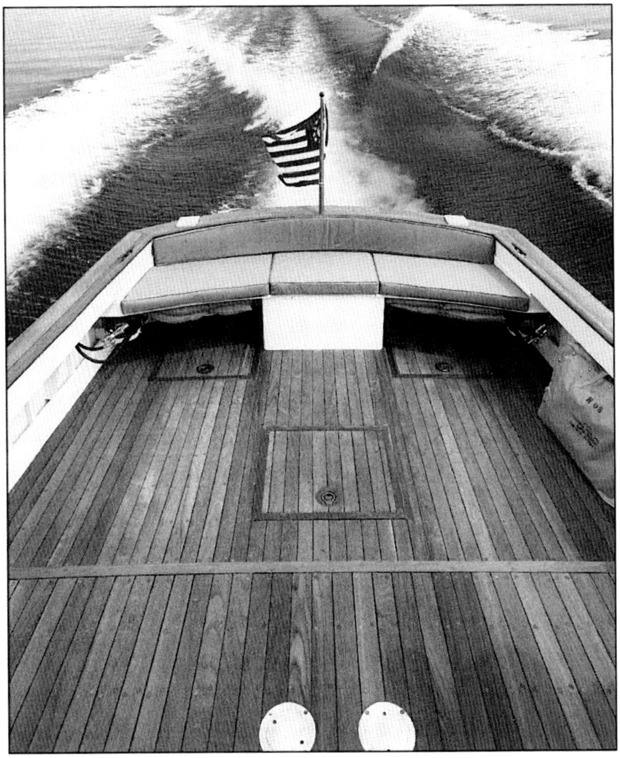

On trials, this view was taken from the stern of the yacht. Great waves were churned up as the *Windless* plowed through the water at high speeds.

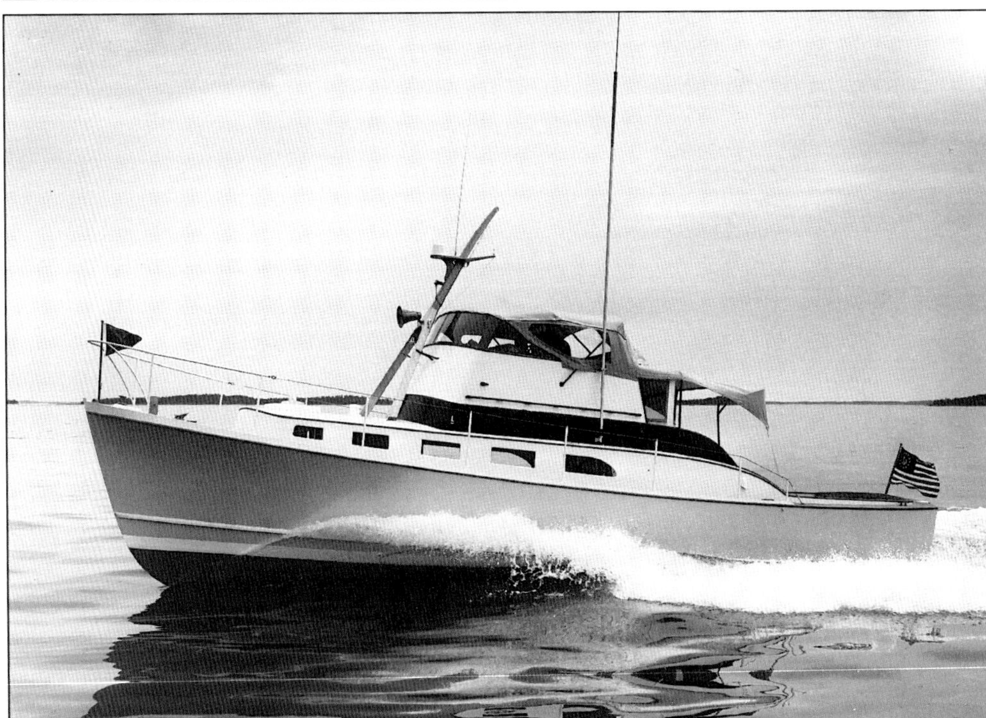

Another photograph of the *Windless* was taken on trials as she tried out Penobscot Bay. She was a sleek boat and is shown here broadside.

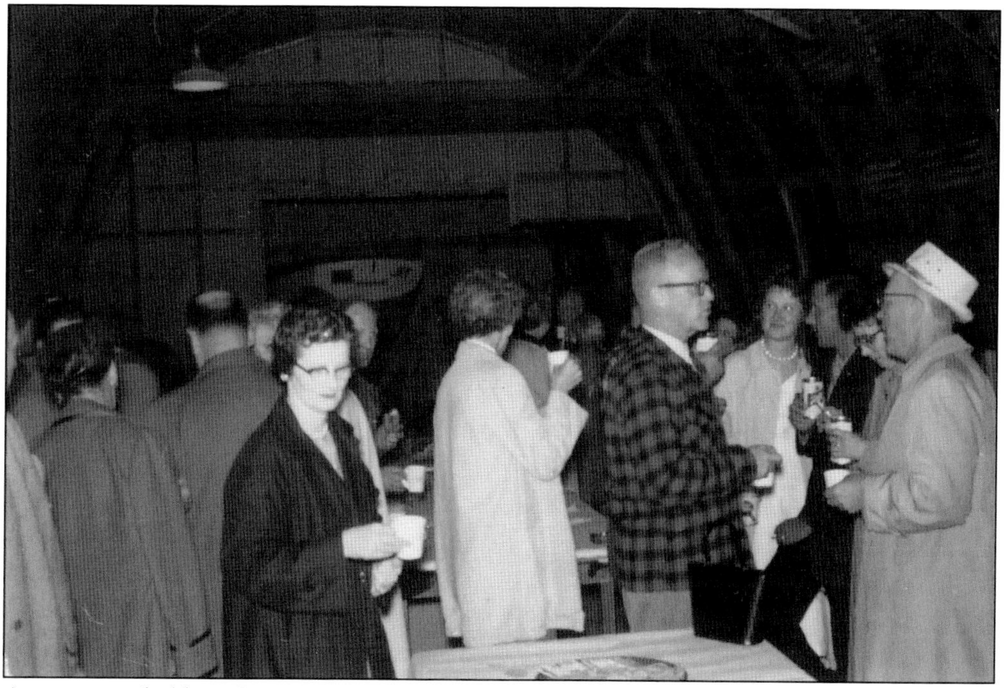

A party was held on June 24, 1961, after the launching. In the foreground is Dot Dean of Camden National Bank; in the plaid shirt is Clarence Waterman, store keeper at the Camden Shipbuilding Company; and on the far right is Charles Dean, paint foreman.

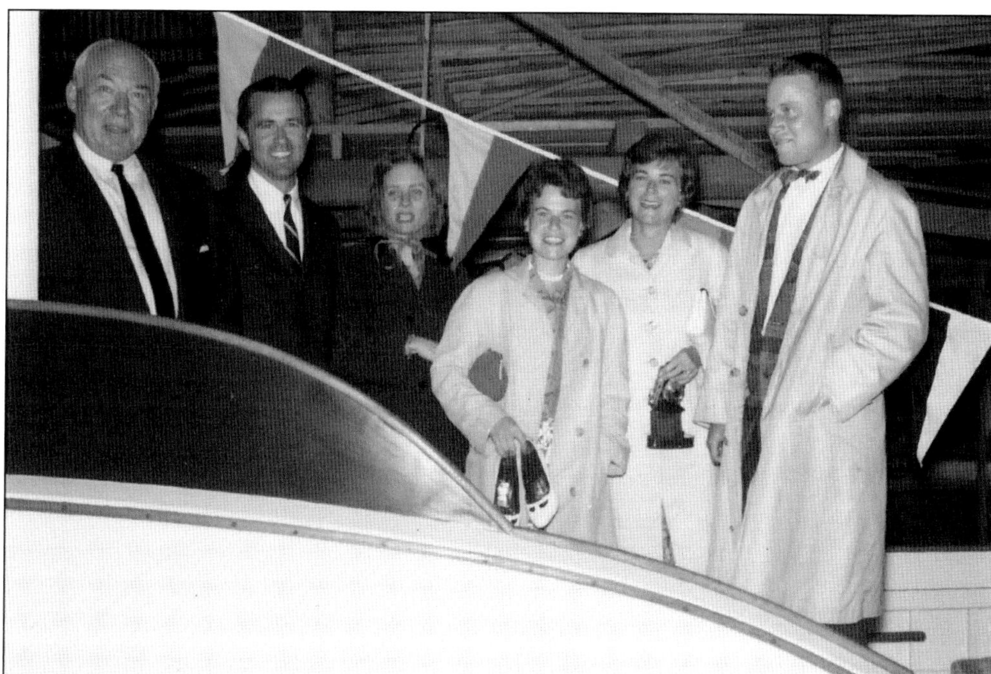

The group who launched the *Windless* was photographed as they waited for the time to come for the launching. The group consisted of the owner, Andrew Winslow, and his family.

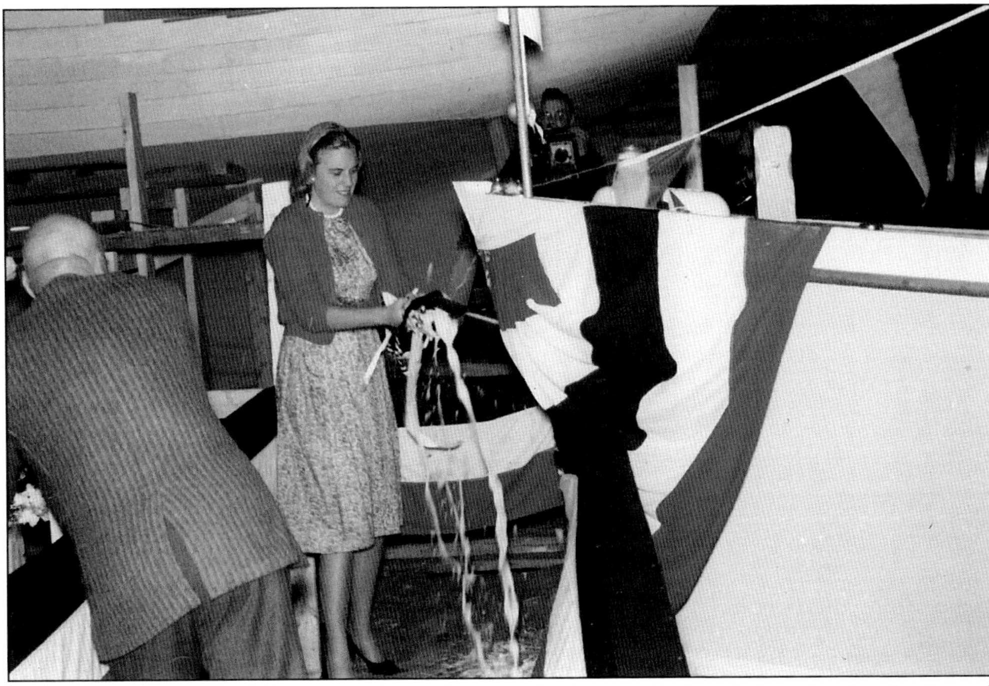

Miss Judith Winslow of Boston is shown hitting the bow with the christening bottle. It took three tries before the bottle broke. Champagne, from the launching bottle, can be seen on the floor of the launching platform.

Christening Party for the Launching of the

Yacht, WINDLESS

Mr. and Mrs. Andrew N. Winslow, Jr.

Designed by
Geerd N. Hendel, N. A.

Built by
CAMDEN SHIPBUILDING CO.

Sponsored by
Miss Judith Winslow of Boston, Mass.

Saturday, June 24, 1961
at
Marion Village

Menu

Hors d'Oeuvres — Canapes

Roast Sirloin of Beef
Lobster Newburg
Roast Cold Ham
Lobster Salad
Roast Cold Turkey
Smoked Salmon

Cherry Jubilee

Coffee

This invitation shows that a nice luncheon was served at one of Camden's finer restaurants, called Marion Village.

This 40-foot ketch was designed for an around-the-world cruise. Mr. Philip Merriman contracted to have the vessel built. Mrs. Merriman asked me to christen *The Frances USA*. It was exciting, but I did not know just how exciting until the day arrived. It was rather cold on December 27, 1961, and so was the launching grease in the seawater. She started rather hesitantly down the ways, and upon reaching the high-water mark she stopped and refused to move. Two lobster boats tried to coax her off the ways. As the owners were launched aboard, they were stuck there surrounded by water. As the ketch had quite a keel, they were high but not dry. It took a fair amount of maneuvering to get them off and into small boats. *The Frances USA* remained there until a higher tide the next day, when a large sardine carrier managed to pull her into the water.

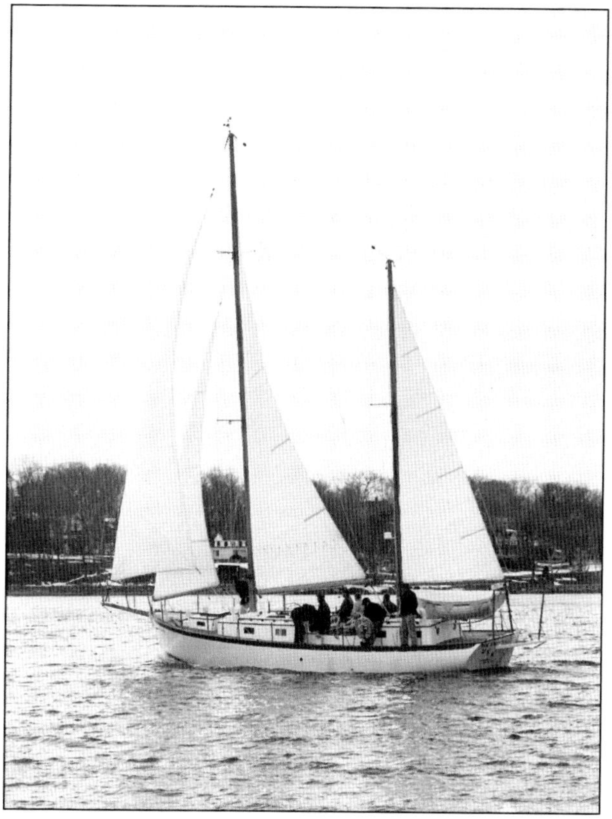

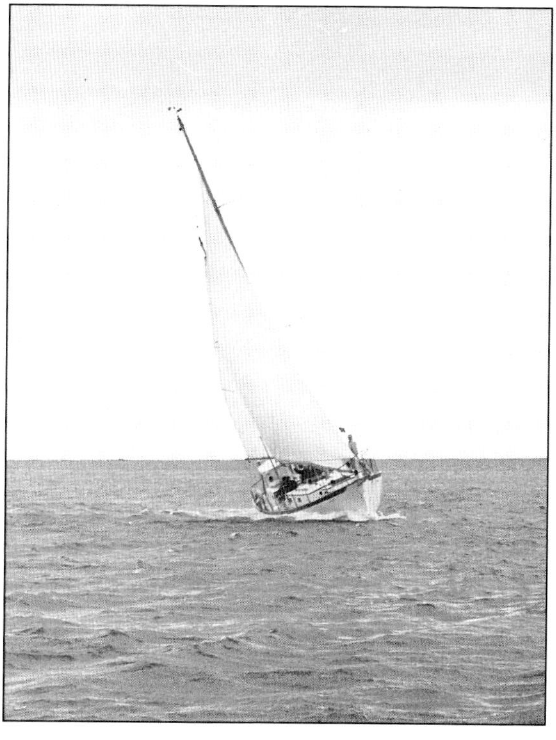

The ketch is shown here sailing in Penobscot Bay, but she was very well equipped for transatlantic cruising. She featured an Apelco Automatic pilot, a depth sounder, and a radio transmitter and receiver, among other things. She was designed to accommodate the owner's party of four and a crew of two.

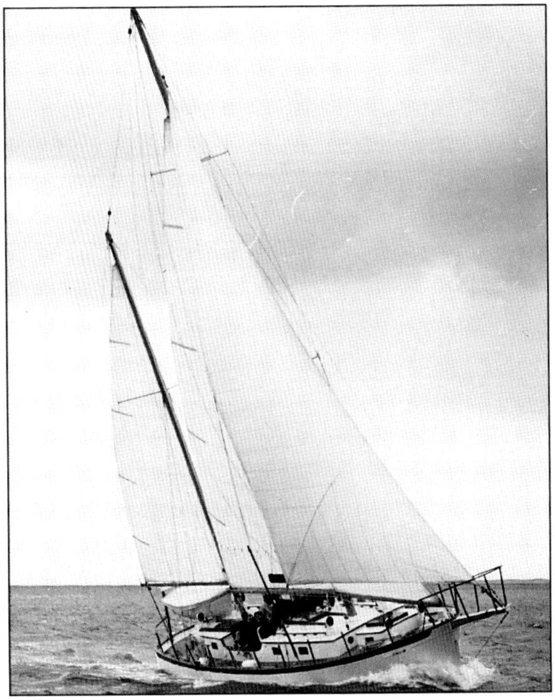

The cabins of *The Frances USA* were furnished in exotic woods. She was built of mahogany over oak frames, with the deck, hatches, and trim of teak. After trials, she was delivered to Mobile, Alabama, where her owners began their dream cruise. From there they planned on sailing to Panama and up the west coast of Mexico to Acapulco. We never heard if they made the trip, but we do know that Mr. Merriman died in 1969. His wife sent us medals showing the date of his birth and death on one side, and *The Frances USA* on the other side.

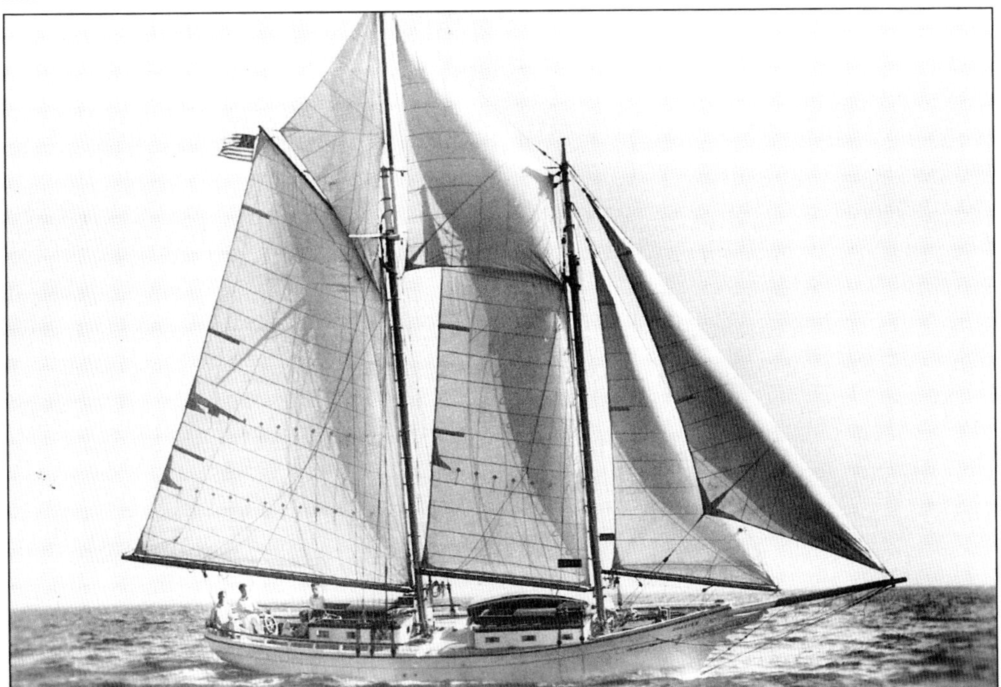

The last two yachts built by Camden Shipbuilding were coastal schooners, designed by Murray G. Peterson. Mr. Silas Foot, owner of a leather business in Red Wing, Minnesota, signed a contract to have the *North Star* built. She was 36 feet in length, with 796 feet of sail, and had a Mercedes Benz engine for auxiliary power. Mrs. Foot christened the vessel on June 23, 1962. She had beautiful detail and accommodations for four.

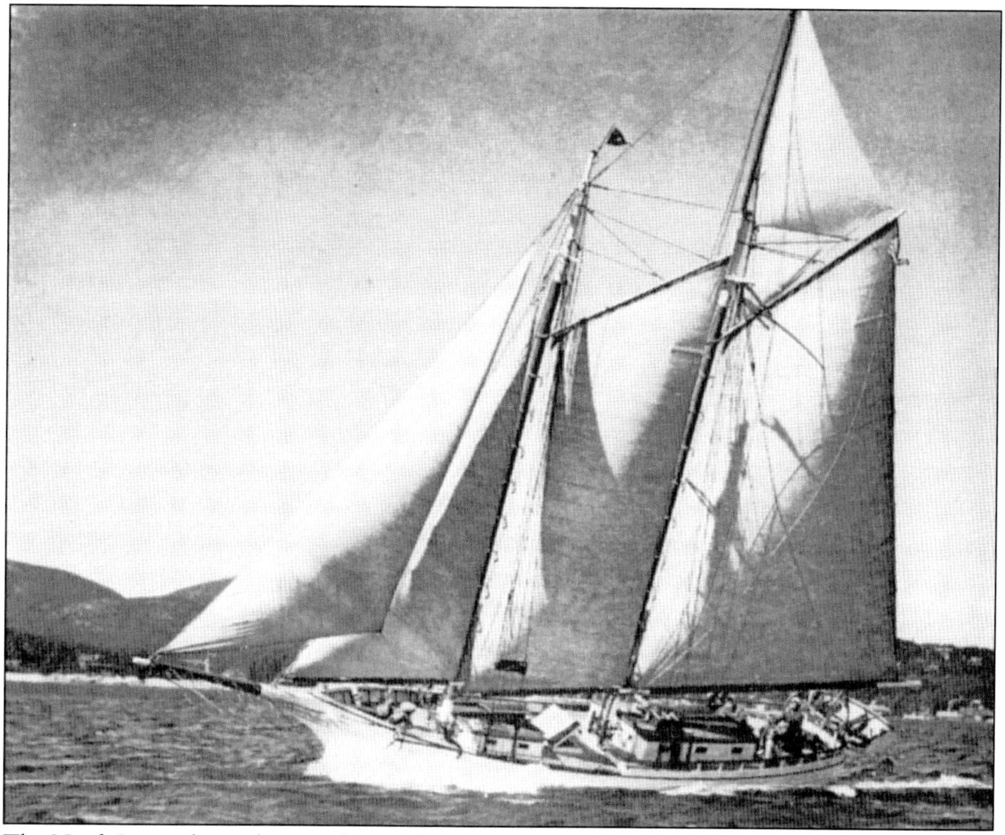

The *North Star* is shown here under sail. Her frame was oak, with Philippine mahogany planking and a deck of teak.

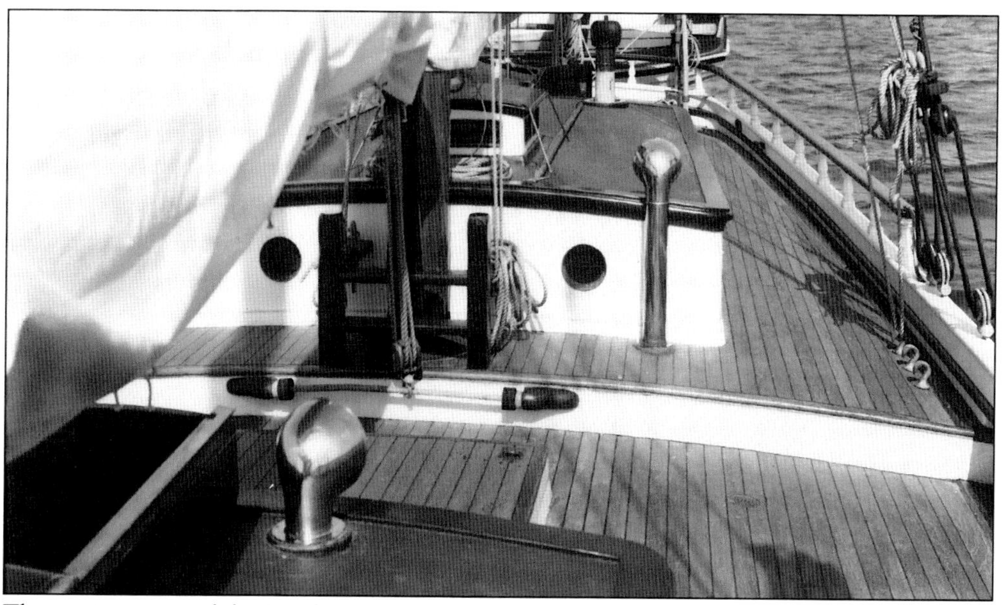

The engine room of the *North Star* was between the two cabins, fore and aft. The vessel used quite a bit of sail and rigging.

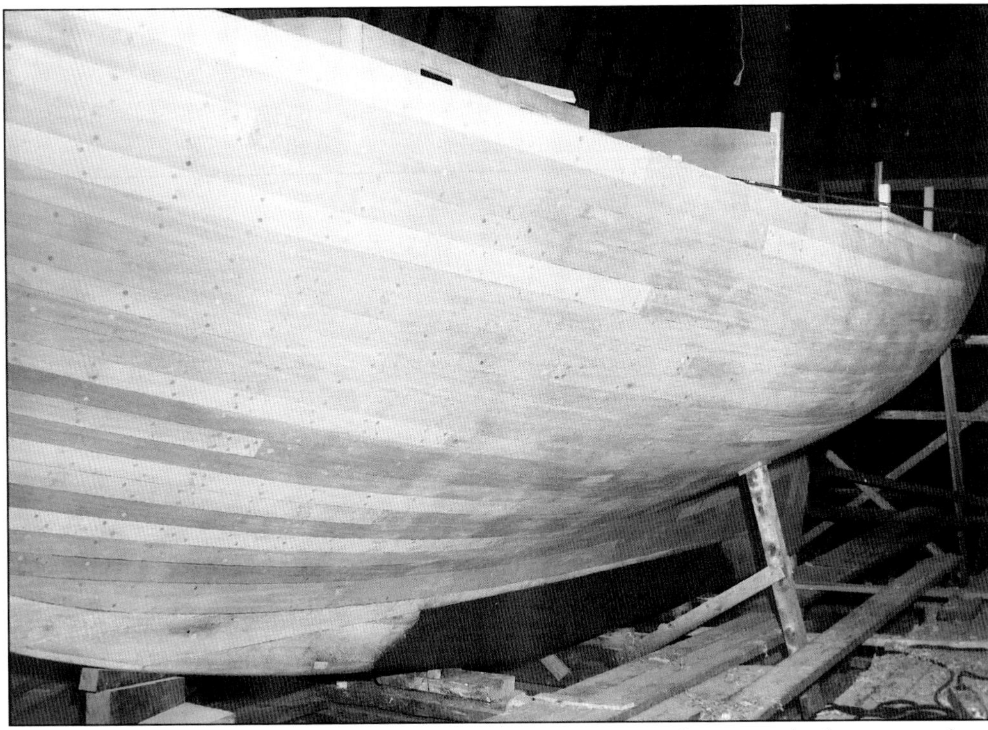

The last vessel built here was named *Silver Heels*. She was a 42-foot coastal schooner, and was built for Mr. Howland Jones of Short Hills, New Jersey. Mr. Jones, at that time, owned a yacht designed by Murray Peterson in 1931.

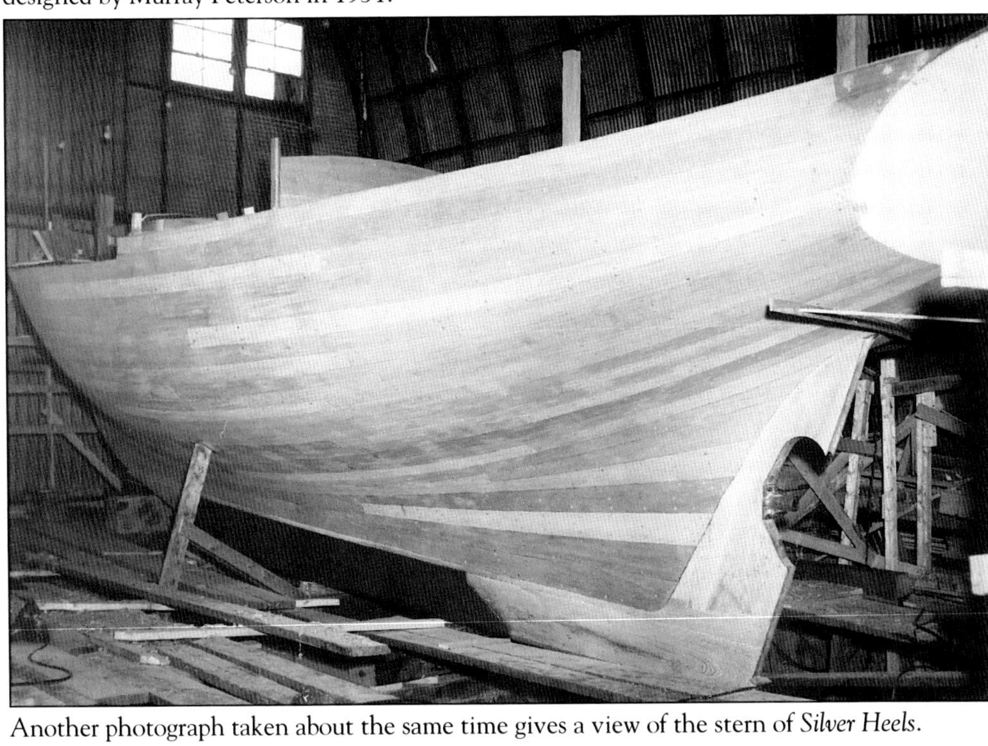

Another photograph taken about the same time gives a view of the stern of *Silver Heels*.

The same coastal schooner is shown here on trials.

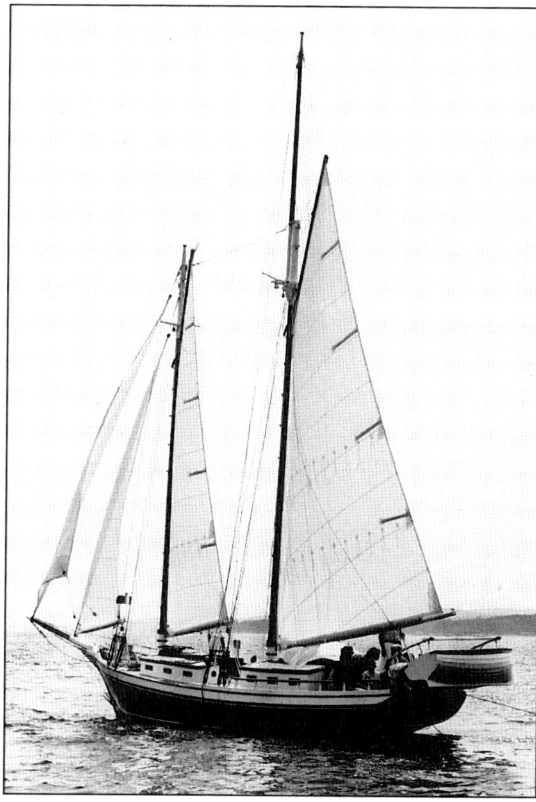

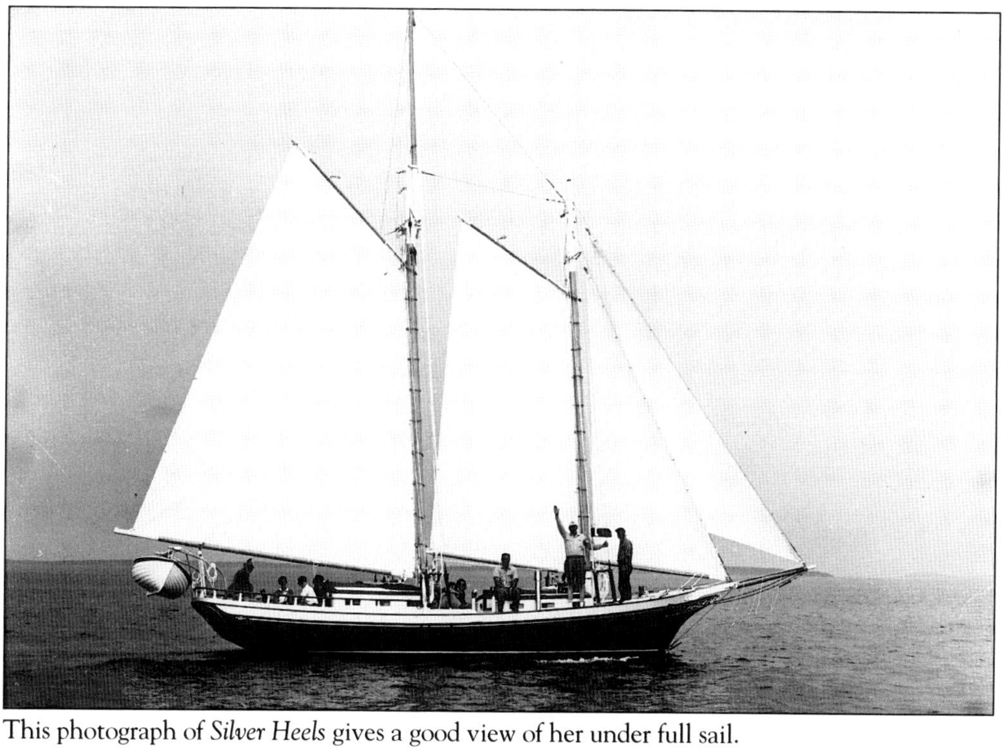

This photograph of *Silver Heels* gives a good view of her under full sail.

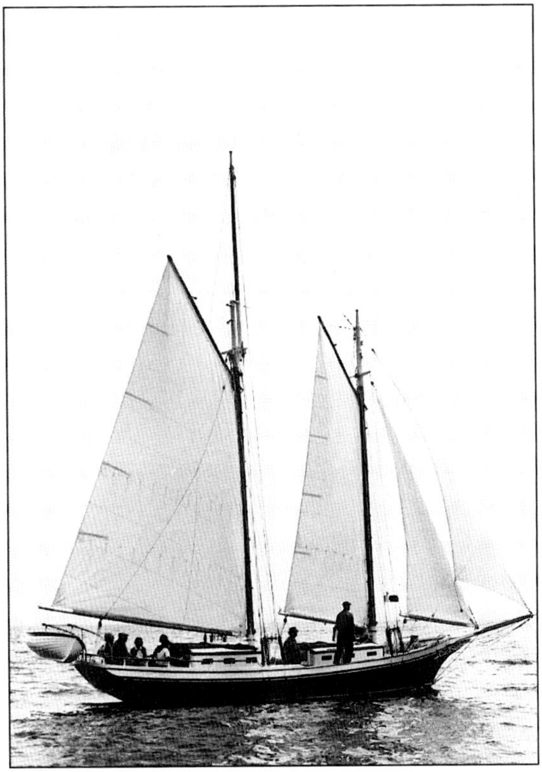

Although *Silver Heels* was on her way, Camden Shipbuilding was in financial difficulties. The vessel was scheduled for delivery in the spring, but due to a combination of circumstances, the Camden Shipbuilding Company had to declare bankruptcy. It was a sad day for the 34 workers, many of whom had been employed there for years.

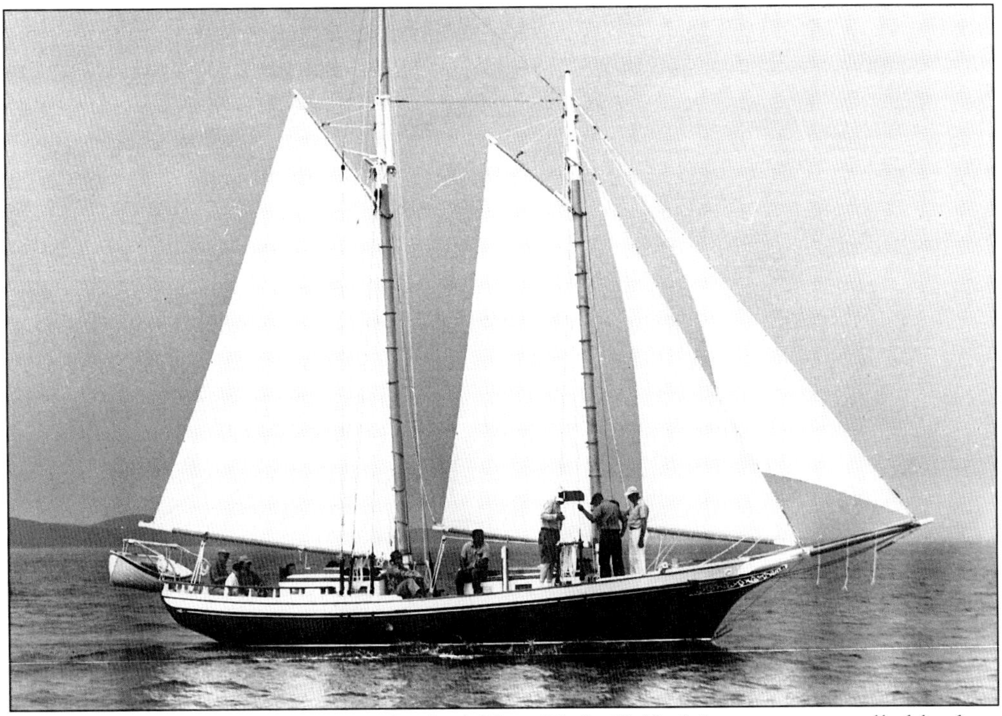

Malcolm Brewer and his own crew finished *Silver Heels*. Half of the men were called back to prepare the boats that were in storage, and the building of vessels was suspended.

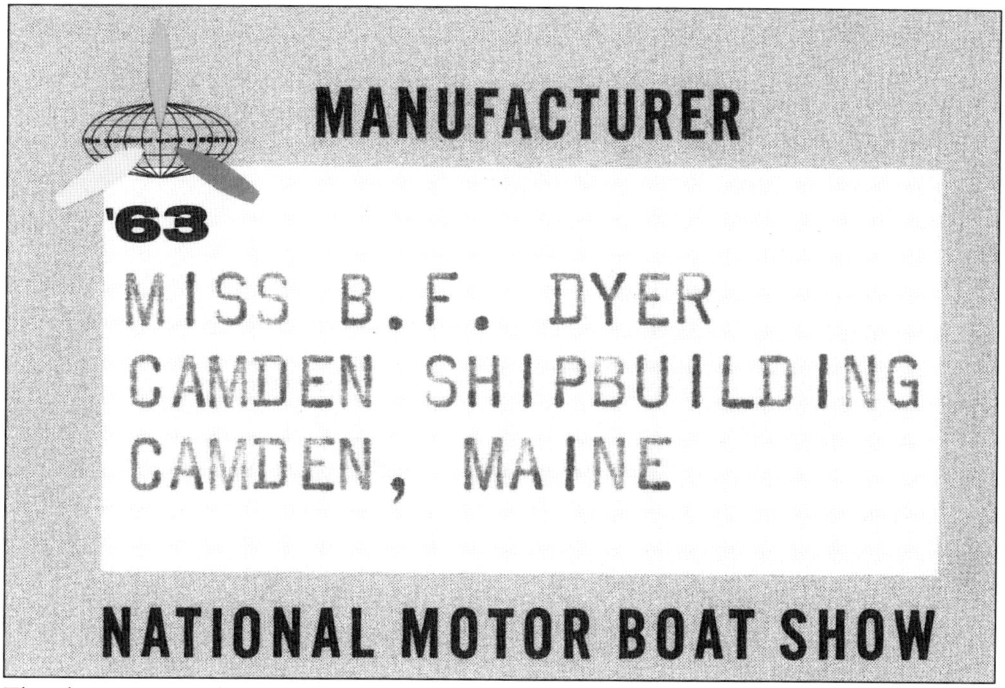

The above picture shows a ticket to the last National Motor Boat Show attended by people from the Camden Shipbuilding Company.

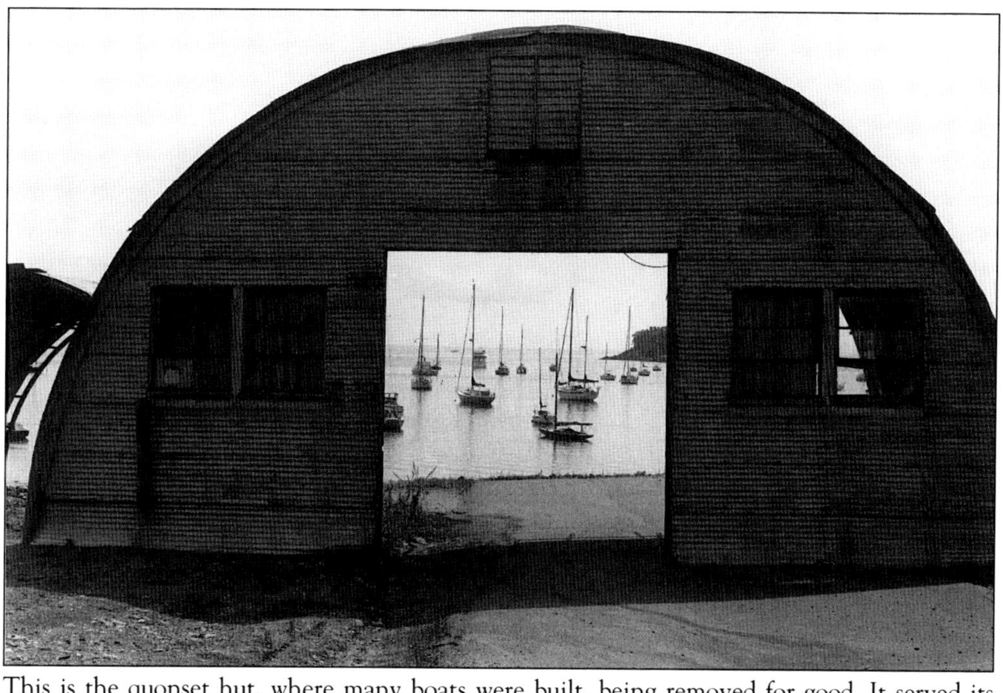

This is the quonset hut, where many boats were built, being removed for good. It served its purpose for 40 years. Wayfarer Marine placed an offer for the Camden Shipbuilding Company for $88,000 and it was approved by the court in September 1963. The construction of wooden vessels stopped and it became a storage, service, and repair yard.

List Of Custom-Built Yachts 1945-1963

Date	Yacht	Owner	Hull #	LOA/Type of Yacht
1946	ANDREA B	Earl Boardman	Y-1	40' sport fisherman
1946	MARBARU	Clinton Lunt	Y-2	40' sport fisherman
1947	ALBERT & VANCE	Harold Bunker	F-1	36' lobster boat
1947	NORTHERN CROSS	Cary Bok	Y-5	55' cruiser
1947	MADELYN E	Bradbury Young	F-4	36' lobster boat
1947	GONE AWAY	Morris Cheston	Y-6	42' sloop
1948	SANDY J			18' lobster boat
1948	LYDIA & DICK	Harold Ames		32' lobster boat
1948	ALPHARD	Judge Curtis Bok	Y-7	42' sloop
1948	KINNERETH	Saul Brodsky	Y-8	50' sport fisherman
1949	FANTASY	Donald Parsons	Y-9	55' cruiser
1949	MIRAGE	Russell Spangee	WB-2	45' tow boat
1949	CHAUSSER	Mr. Gardiner	Y-10	22' bass boat
1950	ANAHITA	Alfred Epstein	Y-11	70' cruiser
1950	SNAPPER	Sen. L. Saltonstall	Y-12	35' power boat
1951	WILD GOOSE	Ferdinand Eberstadt	Y-123	42' sport fisherman
1952	JOSEPH H. STUART	William Brown	Y-14	40' lumber tug
1952	PORPOISE	Allison Laytham	F-10	60' sword fisherman
1952	NIGHT OWLER	Donald Owler	F-11	22' bass boat
1952	SEA COOT	Winslow Hall	F-12	22' bass boat
1953	WARDEN'S WORRY	Anthony Bok	F-8	18' lobster boat
1954	SOONER	E. Julian Davis	Y-15	68' house boat
1956	ADMIRAL BLAKE	John Blair	Y-16	73' house boat
1957	PEARL NECKLACE	Marine Development	V-1	71' express cruiser
1958	PROJECT	William Brown	Y-18	33' sport cruiser
1960	SABINA	Dr. Paul Jones	Y-17	33' sport cruiser
1960	WILD DUCK	Gordon D. Bok	Y-19	26' deluxe ketch
1961	WINDLASS	Andrew Winslow	Y-21	40' twin cruiser
1962	THE FRANCES	Philip Merriman	Y-22	40' ketch
1962	NORTH STAR	Silas Foot	Y-23	36' coastal schooner
1962	SILVER HEELS	Howland Jones, Jr.	Y-24	42' coastal schooner
1963	SERENITY	Dr. E. P. Richardson, Jr.	Y-25	coastal schooner

Six

The Workmen

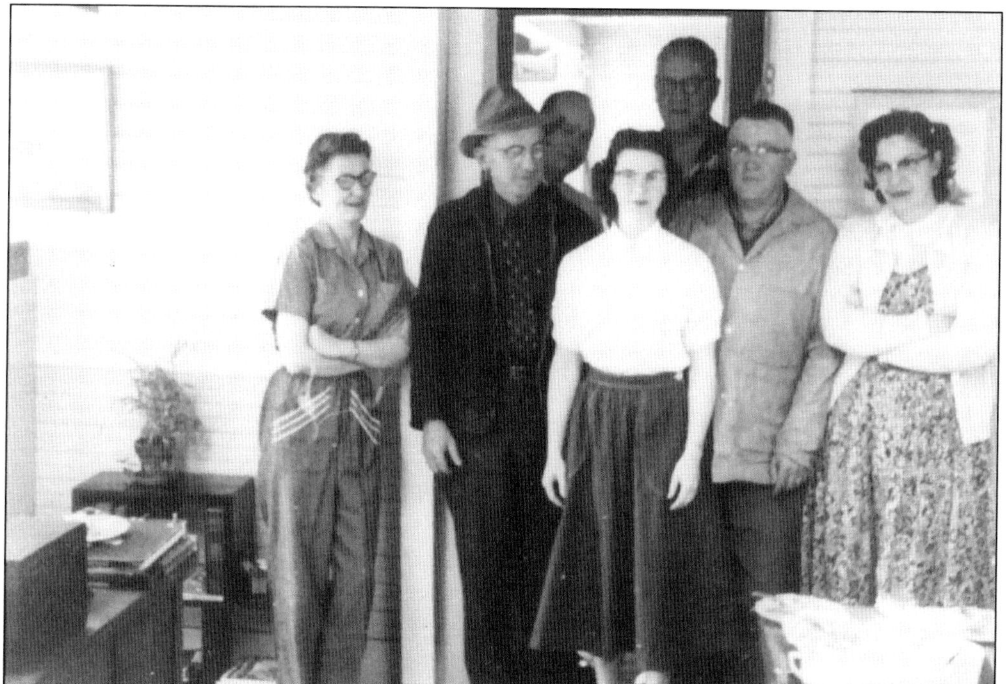

Shown here is a happy group, who made sure that the Camden Shipbuilding Company ran. From left to right are Grace Peterson, Malcolm Brewer, Geerd Hendel, Barbara Dyer, Cary Bok, Hale Handley, and Martha Winslow.

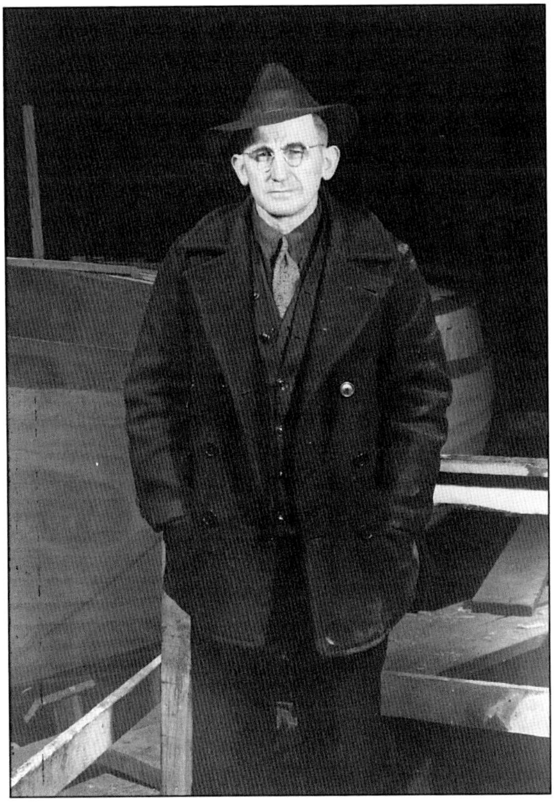

Malcolm H. Brewer was a master builder.

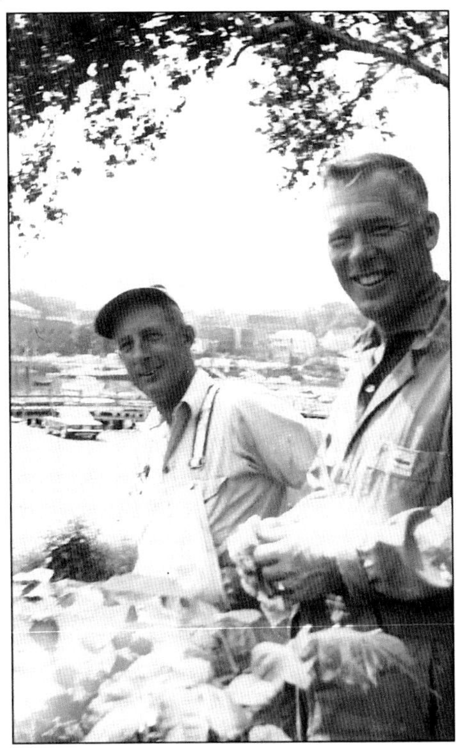

Dana Stone and David Sivewright were both painters.

Tom Knight was a carpenter.

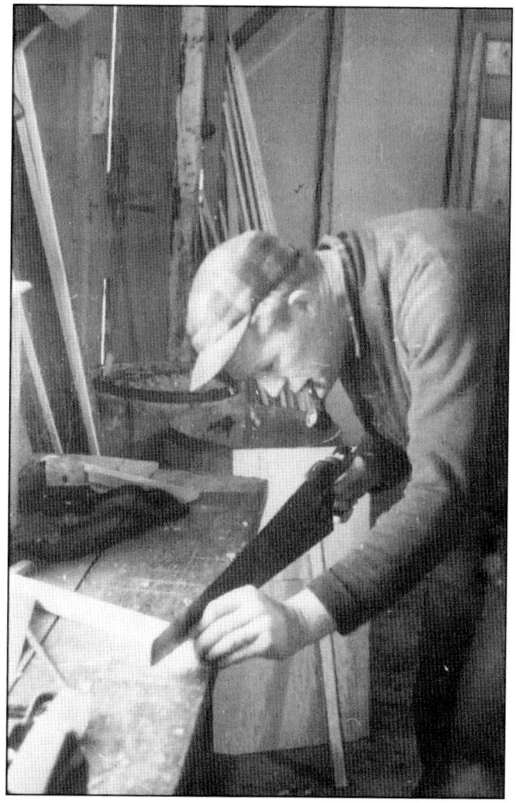

Shown here, from left to right, are Tom Knight, carpenter; William Hastey, carpenter; Hale Handley, stockman; John Peers, mechanic; Richard Burgess, rigger; Freeman Brewer, yard foreman; and Lloyd H. Thomas, joiner.

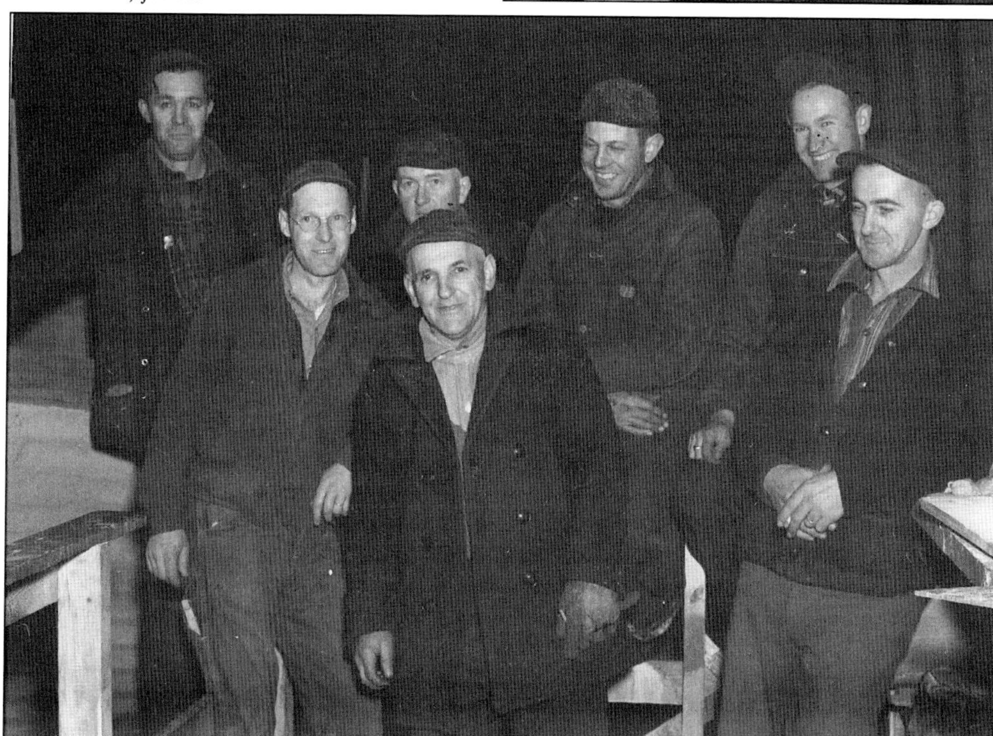

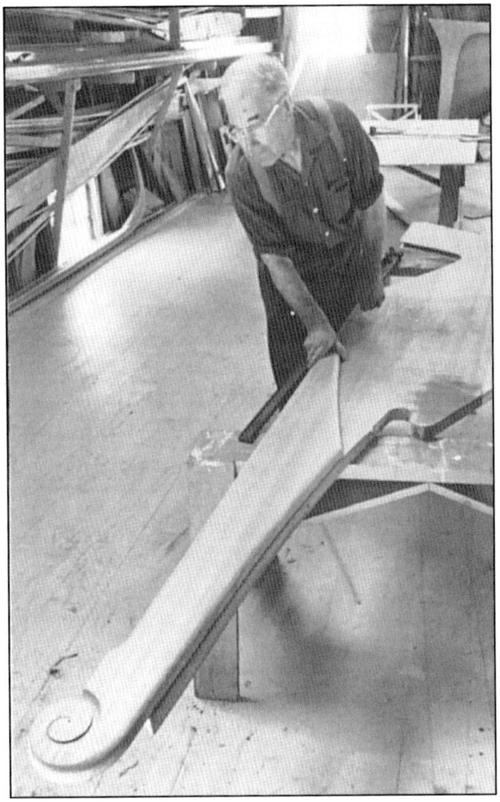

Manson Littlefield was a carpenter.

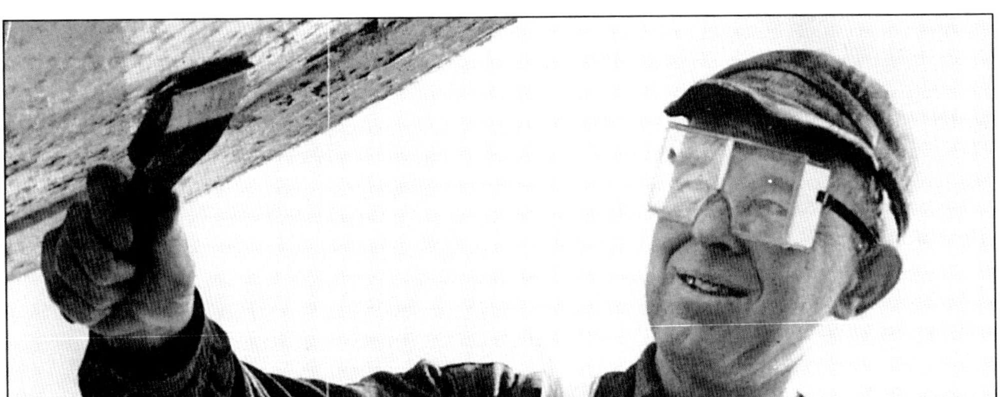

Les Gray was a painter.

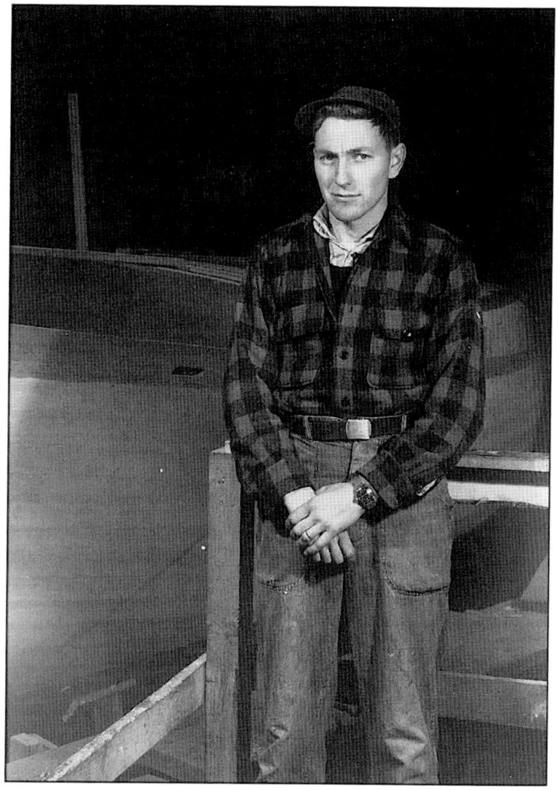

Franklin Kennedy (right) and Chris Windvand were carpenters.

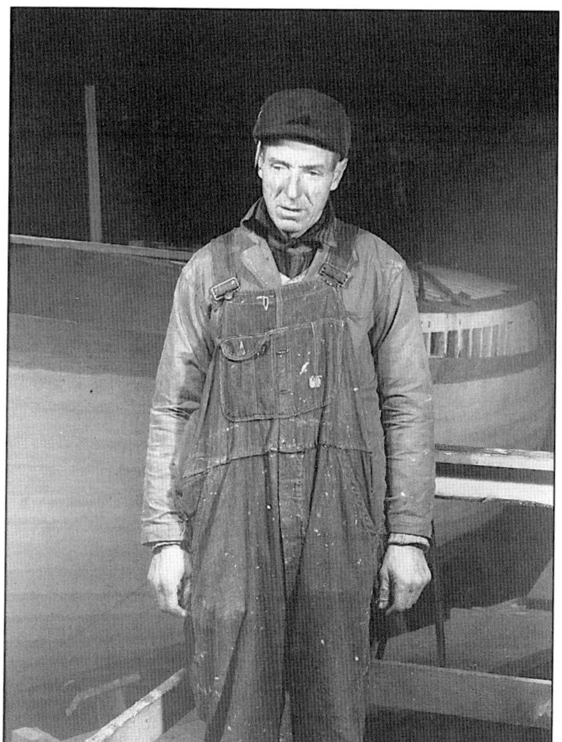

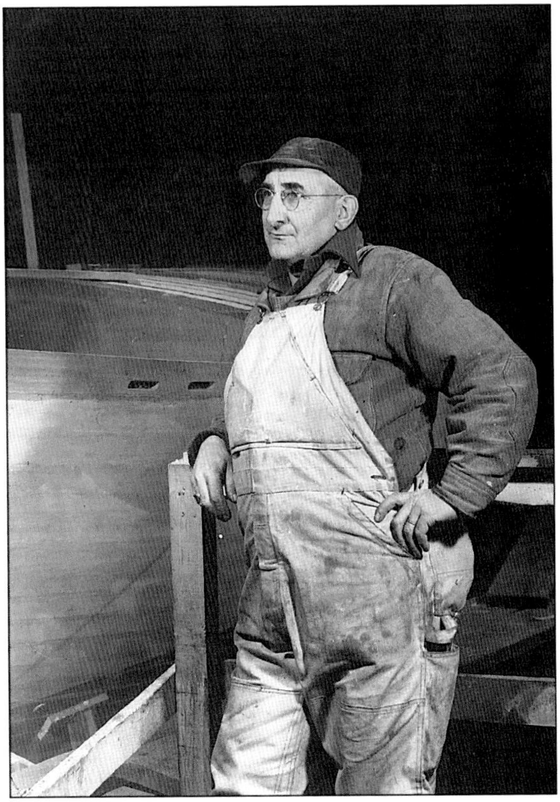

Bill Morse (left) and Orvil Young Sr. were carpenters.

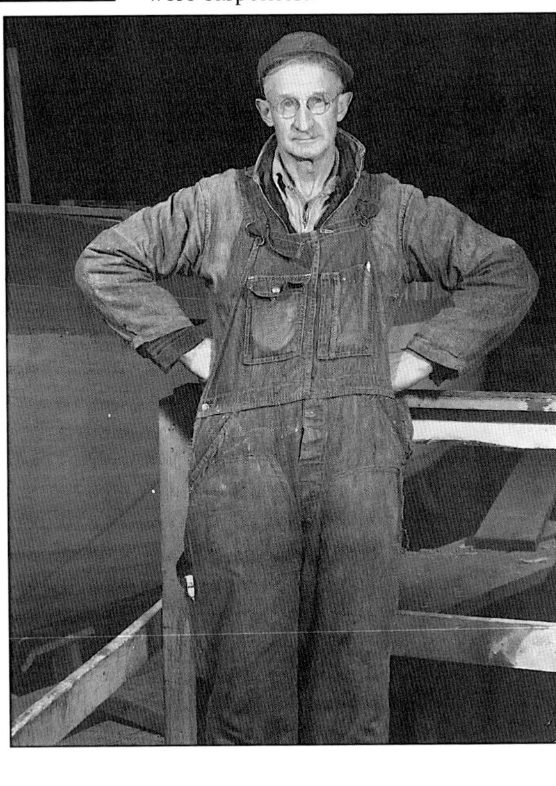

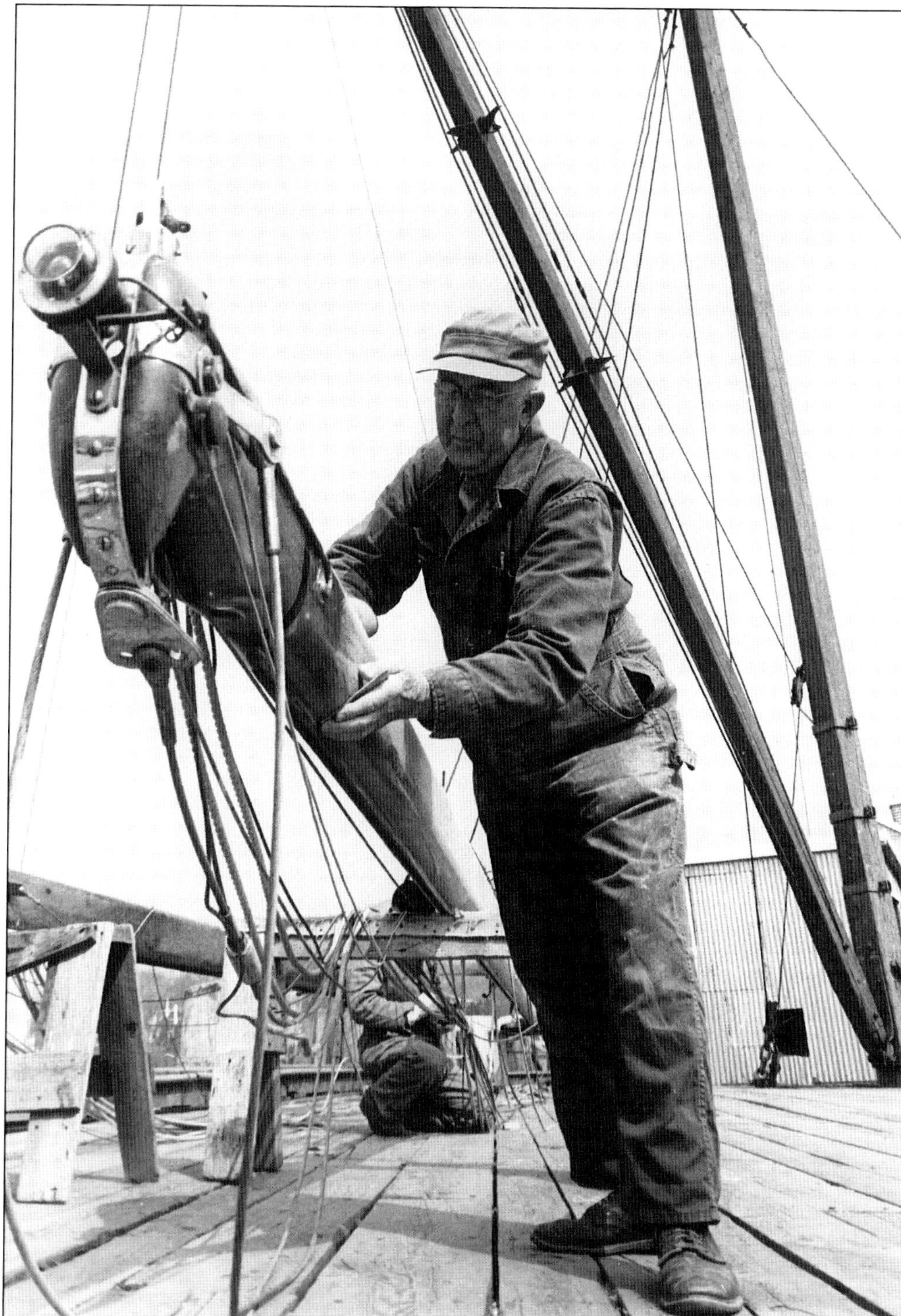

William Murray Smith is the painter in foreground and David J. Sivewright is the painter shown kneeling.

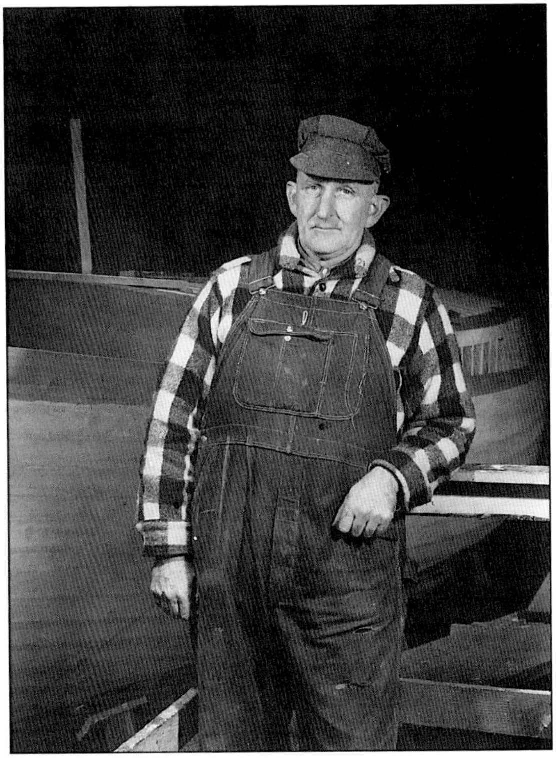

William Hemenway Sr. was a mechanic.

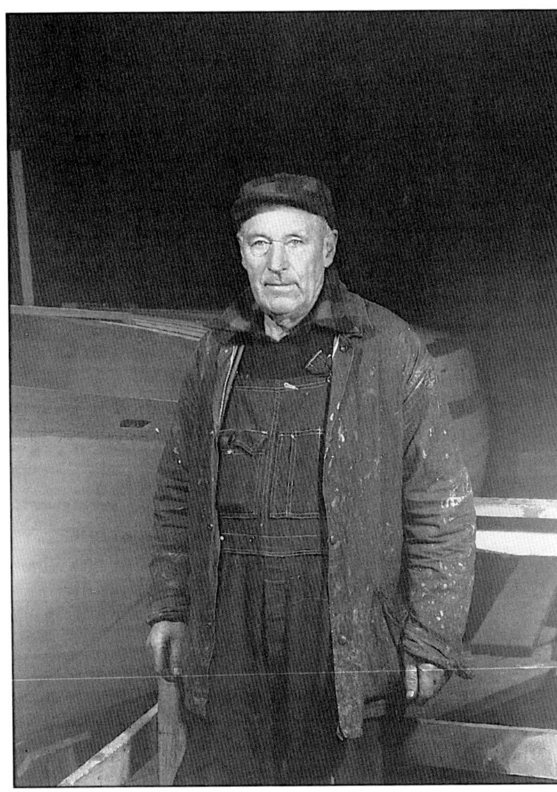

Freemont Arey was a caulker.

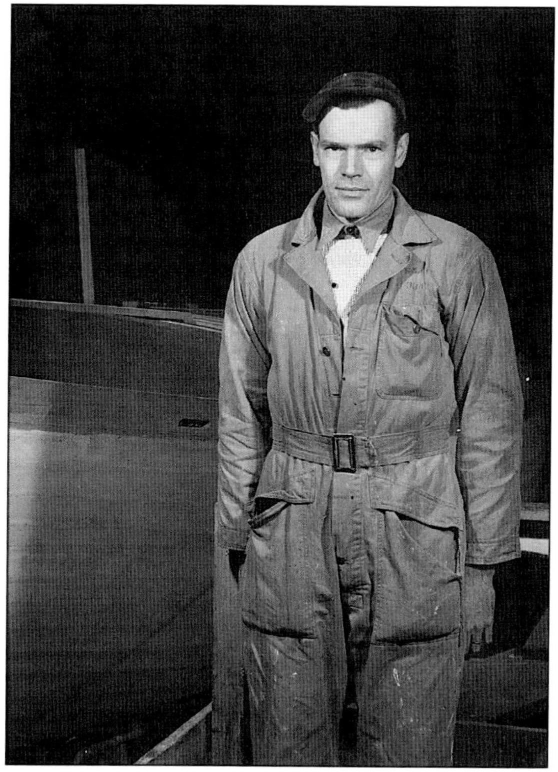

Orren Smart (right) and Joseph Wheeler were carpenters.

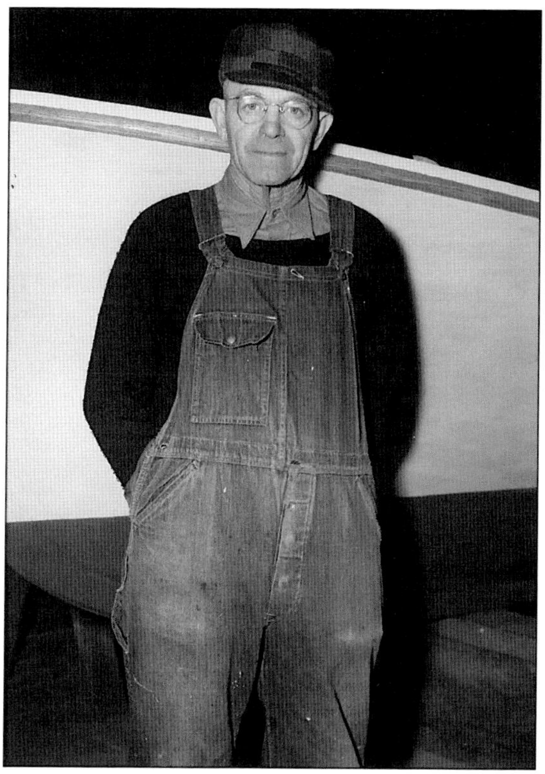

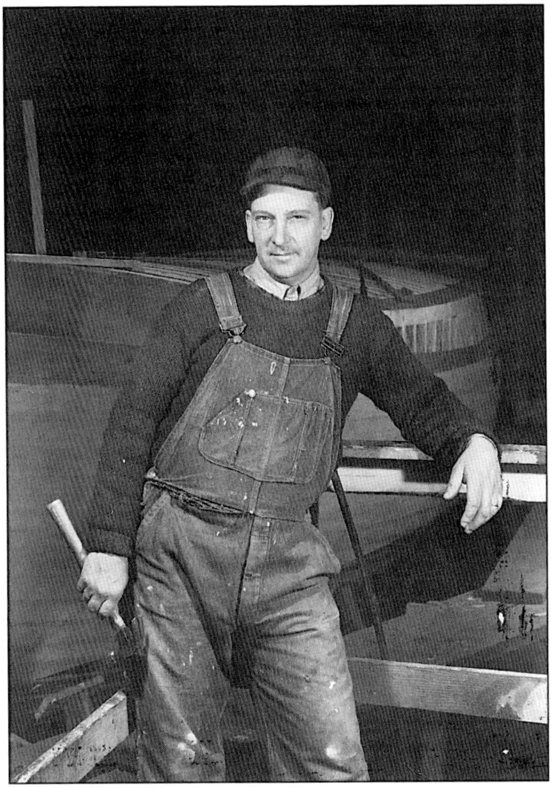

Chester Pooley (left) and Oscar Grinnell were carpenters.

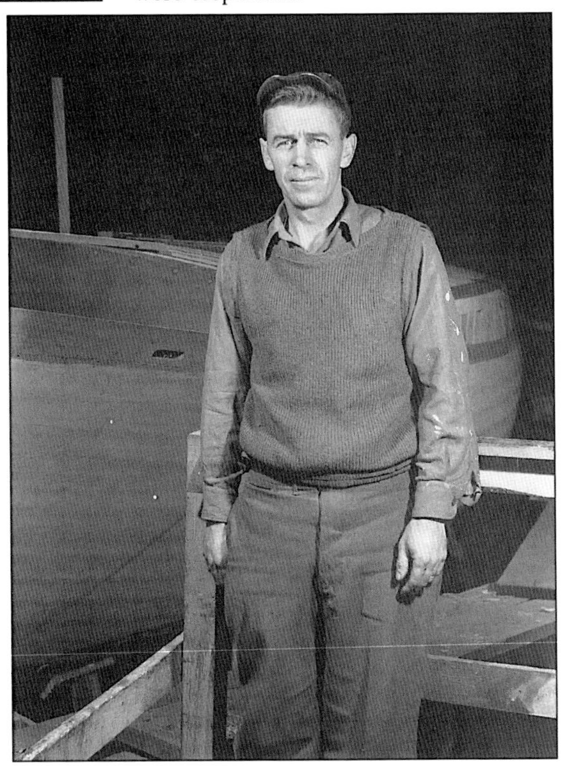

Lloyd H. Thomas and Tom Knight were both carpenters.

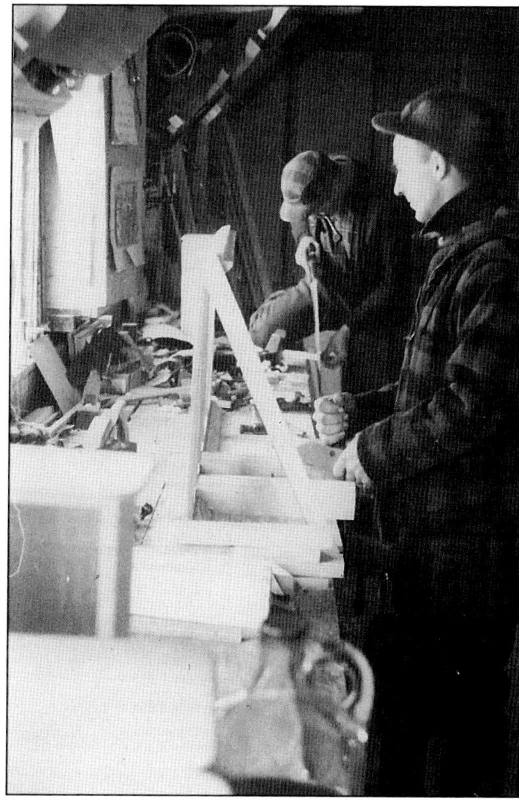

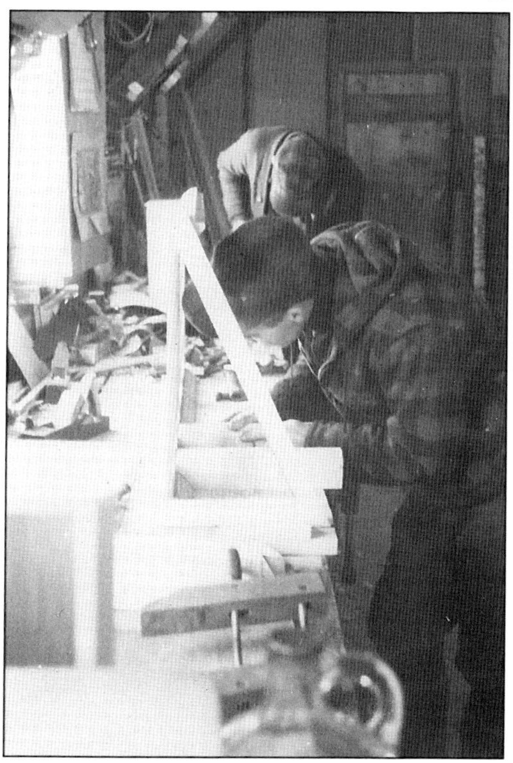

Lloyd H. Thomas and Tom Knight are shown again working at the same job.

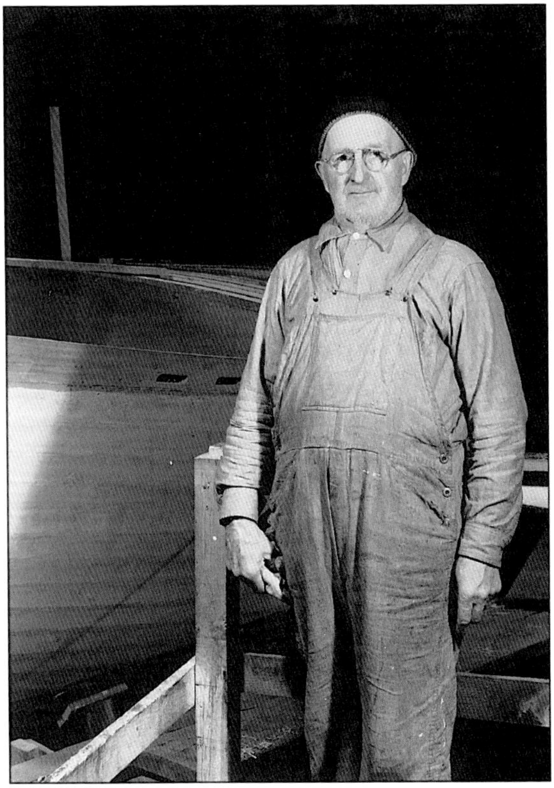

Mattie Molander was a carpenter.

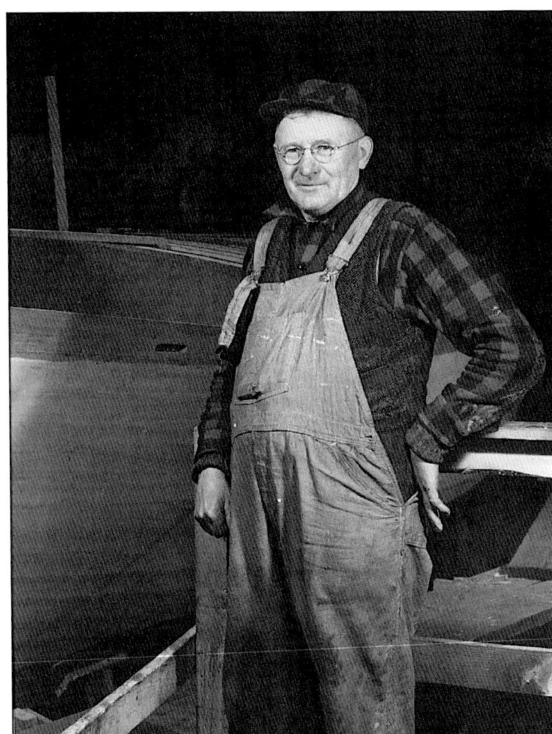

Frans Silonen was a carpenter.

Seven

THE "BOSTON BOATS"

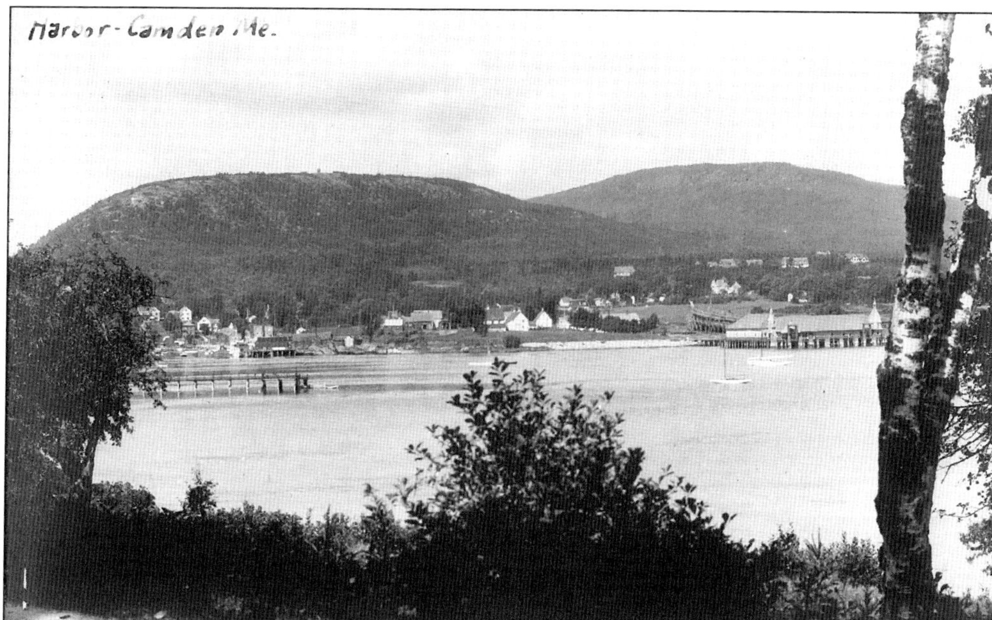

This view of Camden harbor shows the Eastern Steamship Wharf to the right. A vessel under construction can be seen behind the wharf.

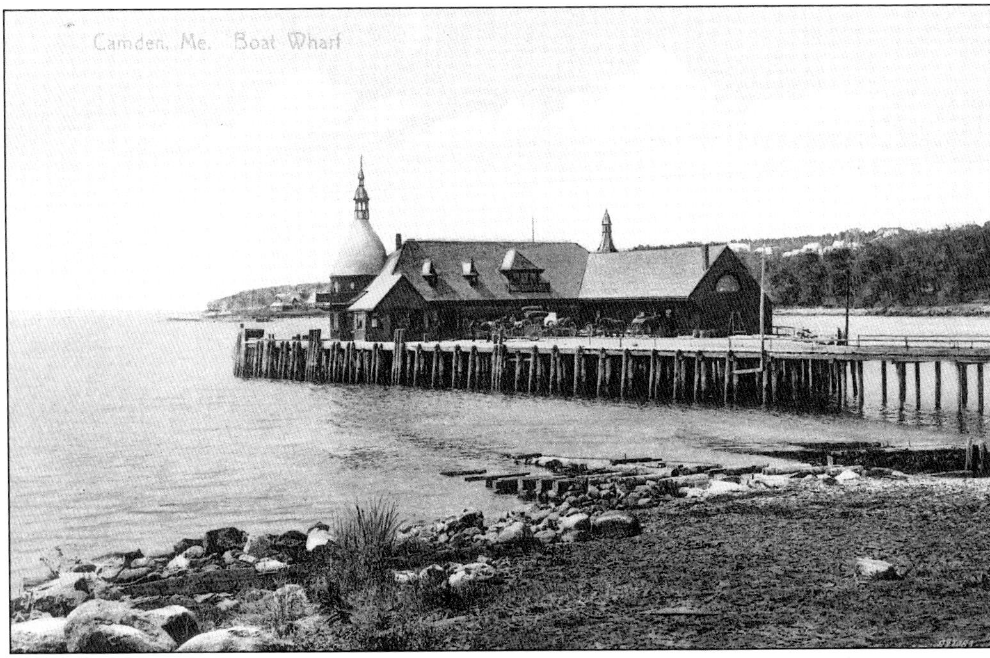

This was the Eastern Steamship Wharf; all vessels were launched to its left. The picture was taken before 1924, because that was when the first wharf burned. A new one was built the same year.

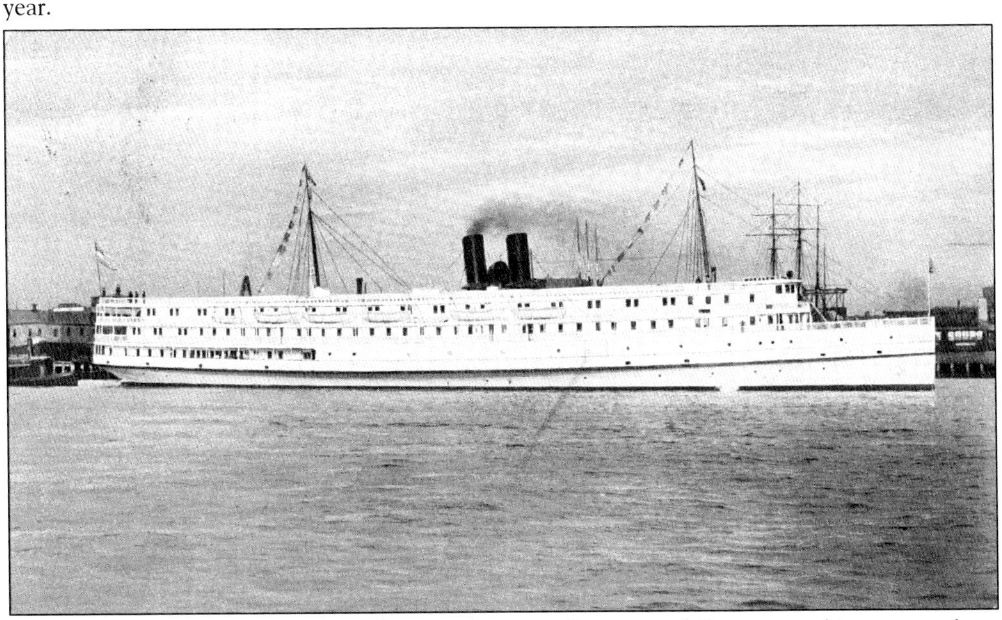

The wharf served the steamships that ran between Boston and Bangor, making stops along the way. It was a delightful way to travel on the "Boston Boat." The first steamboat entered Camden harbor in 1823, and people were afraid it would frighten away all the fish. The Boston-Bangor service was discontinued in 1937. The S.S. *Camden* (pictured above) was 320.6 feet long and was built in Bath, Maine, in 1907. During World War II, the vessel was rebuilt as a transport. In 1948 she was stripped and towed from Honolulu to Shanghai—no more was heard about Camden's treasure.

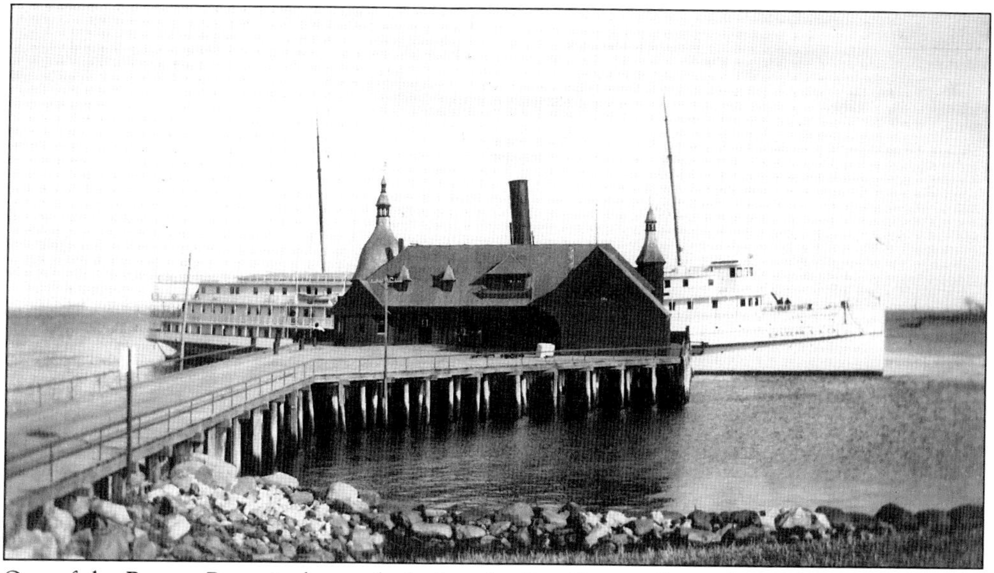

One of the Boston Boats is shown docked at the first Eastern Steamship Wharf, allowing the relative size of the two to be compared. Many Camden folk hurried to the wharf when they knew the boat was coming in to watch people get on or off the steamer. The crew would roll out a red carpet and polished brass spittoons lined it.

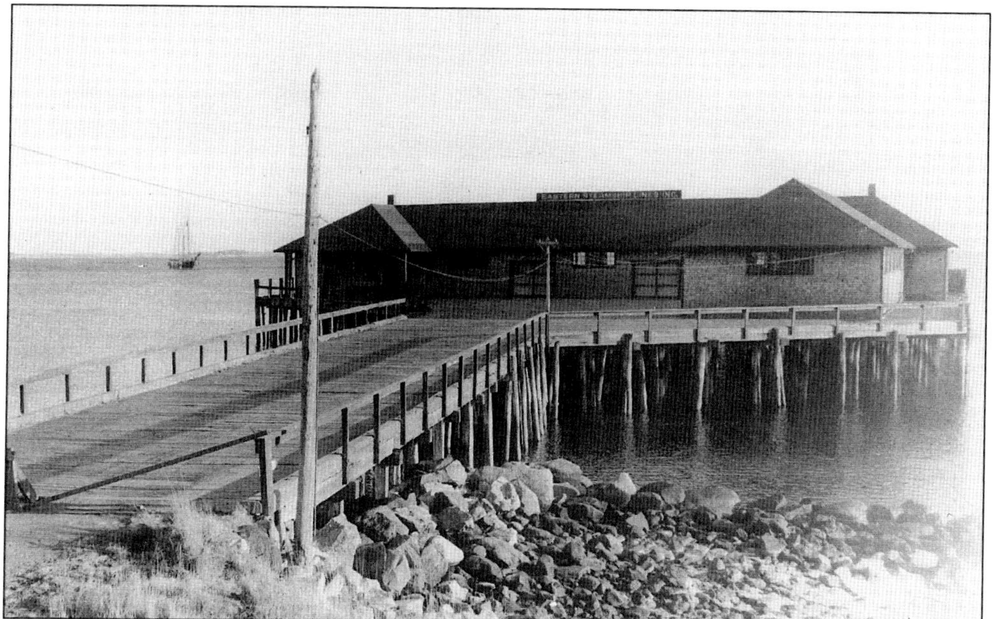

The second steamship wharf built, after the fire, was not quite as fancy as the first. When the Eastern Steamship Company went out of business, the wharf was bought by George H. Thomas and Adin Hopkins. In 1941, it was sold to the Camden Shipbuilding and Marine Railway Co., and used for a mold loft. It was sold again in 1951 to the Helioffs for a lobster holding and packing plant. Three years later, the center section gave way and 18,000 pounds of lobsters went back to their natural habitat. The piling began to give way and on May 11, 1959, the town of Camden voted to remove it. They soaked ropes in oil and ignited it. The wharf hated to "give up the ghost" and burned for three days.

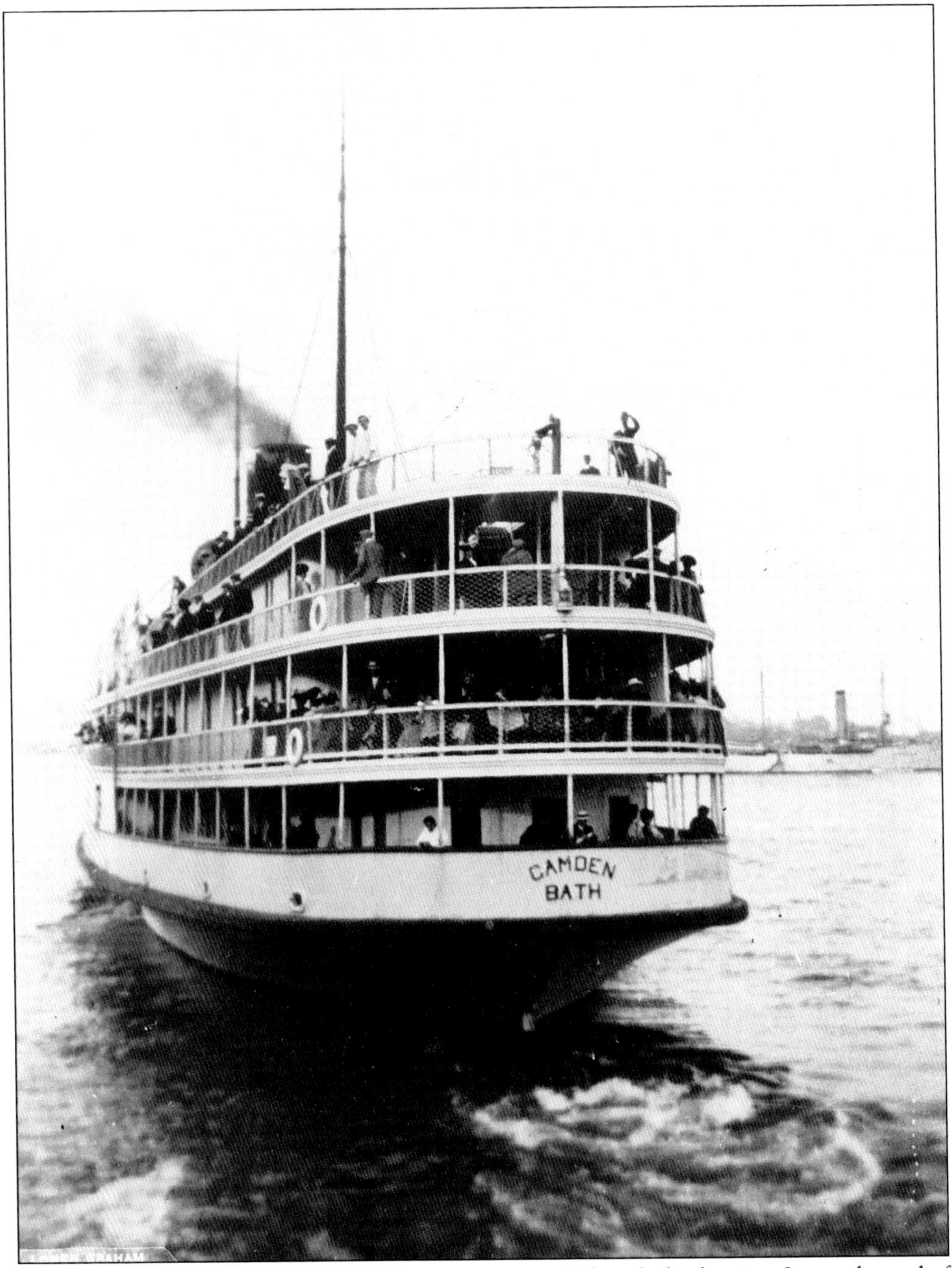

The final picture shows a steamer, with passengers on all four decks, leaving. It was the end of an era.